Collaborative Financial Infrastructure Protection

Roberto Baldoni · Gregory Chockler

Editors

Collaborative Financial Infrastructure Protection

Tools, Abstractions, and Middleware

 Springer

Editors
Roberto Baldoni
Dipartimento di Ingegneria Informatica,
Automatica e Gestionale Antonio Ruberti
Università degali Studi di Roma
"La Sapienza"
Roma
Italy

Gregory Chockler
IBM Research – Haifa
Haifa University Campus, Mount Carmel
Haifa
Israel

ISBN 978-3-642-20419-7   e-ISBN 978-3-642-20420-3
DOI 10.1007/978-3-642-20420-3
Springer Heidelberg Dordrecht London New York

Library of Congress Control Number: 2011946180

ACM Computing Classification (1998): C.2, J.1, K.6, H.4, D.4

Printed on acid-free paper

Springer is part of Springer Science+Business Media (www.springer.com)

Security is, I would say, our top priority, because for all the exciting things you will be able to do with computers—organizing your lives, staying in touch with people, being creative—if we don't solve these security problems, then people will hold back.

Bill Gates

To Dora, Edoardo, Camilla, and Luca

To Hana, Naomi, Michael, and Daniel.

Foreword

Societies have grown such a dependence on informatics, that a large part of their assets relies on the availability and correct operation of interconnected computer services. Of the several critical information infrastructures (CIIs) supporting the above-mentioned societal services, the financial infrastructure is an extremely important example. At the date of publishing of this book, the world is experiencing intense turmoil caused by instability in the financial sectors. Furthermore, their interdependence is such that countries' crises contaminate each other, and local problems quickly become global.

Two things become obvious: (i) the financial infrastructure (FI) is a crucial asset whose balance is easily disturbed by "natural" causes; (ii) this organisational vulnerability is amplified by FI stakeholders traditionally operating in isolation, as well as by technical vulnerabilities in the supporting computer systems and networks. Given this scenario, the FI is a natural target for cyber attack, with ample margin for damage. This is confirmed by recent public statistics of actual intrusions and, still, given the traditionally discreet posture of the sector, we may be just looking at the tip of the iceberg.

The ComMiFin EU project had the great merit of tackling this problem with the adequate valences, through a balanced mix of state and financial sector stakeholders on one side, and technology suppliers and researchers on the other.

Based on the argument that FI components are more vulnerable if they operate alone, the project took what seems to be the right approach, and, following the motto *unity makes strength*, it studies the problem of Collaborative Financial Infrastructure Protection, from its roots to concrete solutions, and presents it in two parts. Groups of authors from the project deal with several relevant subjects, in a flow made easy by the contribution of editors Roberto Baldoni and Gregory Chockler.

In the first part, the several groups of authors from the project start by characterising the sector and the risks and vulnerabilities it is subject to, and then detailing a selection of real attack scenarios and common protection strategies. One of the pillars of the proposed solution is *collaboration*, a sensitive issue for financial sector operators. In consequence, the book introduces a model of interacting banks and guides the reader through the risks and benefits of an information sharing process, motivating potential followers for the approach. The second part deals with a concrete proposal to implement such a collaborative information sharing and protection infrastructure, in the form of middleware components guaranteeing trust and enforcing privacy. In a set of very practical chapters, the several components and their merits are presented.

The result is a very interesting and timely work which, by its completeness and coverage of the problems of the information infrastructures of the financial sector, should be a must read for any stakeholder of the sector.

Lisbon, Portugal   Paulo Esteves Verssimo

Preface

The recent virus attacks on the control center of the Iranian nuclear plants[1] as well as those targeting the telecommunication and power grid infrastructures of Estonia[2] and Georgia[3] show how cyber attacks against the critical infrastructure (CI) are becoming increasingly prevalent and disruptive. In many respects, this results from growing exposure of the CI IT to the Internet, which is in turn motivated by the desire to cut operational costs by switching to open networking technologies and off-the-shelf computing equipment.

The Critical Infrastructure Protection (CIP) Survey, recently released by McAfee,[4] found that 53% of the interviewed CI IT security experts have experienced at least ten cyber attacks in the last five years, and 90% expect that the number of cyber attacks will grow in the short to medium term. In addition, the survey indicated that today, one out of five attacks is accompanied by an extortion, and financial institutions are often subject to some of the most sophisticated and large-scale cyber attacks and frauds. For example, an extensive financial fraud that hit the world-wide credit card system in 2008 involved clones of hundreds of credit cards, which were created in 49 countries, and subsequently used at ATMs to withdraw a total of 9 million US dollars. This fraud was carried out within a few minutes and was only discovered at a later stage by analyzing and correlating all the information of the transactions involved. By far, the most prevalent cyber attack against financial institutions is the distributed denial of service against their web-based services, which render them unavailable for legitimate users for prolonged periods of time. Such attacks have been shown to incur serious tangible costs, which, according to some estimates, could exceed 6 million US dollars per day. This is in addition to numerous intangible costs associated among others with damage to reputation and degraded user experience.

---

[1] IW32.Stuxnet Dossier, Symantec Security Response, 2011.

[2] 2007 Cyberattacks on Estonia, wikipedia.org.

[3] Cyberattacks during the 2008 South Ossetia war, wikipedia.org.

[4] In the Crossfire—Critical Infrastructure in the Age of Cyber War, McAfee, 2010.

The global scope and massive scales of today's attacks necessitate global situational awareness, which cannot be achieved by the isolated local protection systems residing within the IT boundaries of individual financial institutions. There is a growing realization in the financial community of the necessity of information sharing, which however, at this point, is mostly done through rudimentary means (such as daily phone consultations among the security experts). The obstacles hampering adoption of more advanced communication means range from cultural to governance ones, such as incompatible privacy protection legislations.

The goal of this book is to study autonomous computing platforms as the means to enable cross-organizational information and resource sharing within the financial sector without compromising the individual institutions' security, privacy, and other constraints. We analyze the structure of a financial infrastructure, its vulnerabilities to cyber attacks, and the current countermeasures, and then we show the advantages of sharing information among financial players to detect and react more quickly to cyber attacks. We also investigate obstacles from organizational, cultural, and legislative viewpoints. We demonstrate the viability of an information sharing approach from an ITC perspective by exploring how massive amounts of information being made available through a sharing mechanism can be leveraged to create defense systems capable of protecting against globally scoped cyber attacks and frauds in a timely fashion.

In particular, the book introduces the Semantic Room (SR) abstraction, through which interested parties can form trusted contractually regulated federations for the sake of secure information sharing and processing. SRs are capable of supporting diverse types of input data, ranging from security events detected in real time to historical information about past attacks. They can be deployed on top of an IP network and (depending on the needs of the individual participants) can be configured to operate in either peer-to-peer or cloud-centric fashion. Each SR has a specific strategic objective to meet (e.g., detection of botnets, stealthy scan, and man-in-the-middle attacks) and has an associated contract specifying the set of rights and obligations for governing the SR membership and the software infrastructure for data sharing and processing. Individual SRs can communicate with each other in a producer-consumer fashion resulting in a modular service-oriented architecture.

The material is organized into the following two parts.

- Part I explores general issues associated with information sharing in the financial sector. Chapter 1 provides background information on the financial sector, with the focus on its IT organization, vulnerabilities to cyber attacks, and state-of-the-art protection strategies. Additionally, it explores the value of information sharing for facilitating global cooperation and protection. Chapter 2 proposes a model of interacting banks, and explores risks, costs, and benefits associated with participation in the information sharing process. Finally, Chap. 3 presents an overview of possible attack scenarios. It provides detailed descriptions of some cyber attacks as well as IT protection systems employed by financial institutions to guard themselves against those threats.
- Part II presents the CoMiFin middleware for collaborative protection of the financial infrastructure developed as a part of the EU project by the same name

(www.comifin.edu) funded by the Seventh Framework Programme (FP7). Chapter 4 describes the CoMiFin architecture and introduces the Semantic Room abstraction. We discuss various aspects of enforcing trust and privacy within each SR (Chap. 6) and compliance monitoring (Chap. 5). Finally, Chaps. 7, 8, and 9 present concrete implementations of the SR based on three different event processing technologies.

Part I presents a survey of various types of CIs along with their vulnerability analysis, which, to the best of our knowledge, has not yet appeared in textbookstyle publications. It is self-contained and might be of independent interest. The design, implementation, and case studies of the collaborative protection middleware, whose functionality is motivated by the analysis presented in Part I, appears in Part II.

The content of the book does not require specific prerequisites. Holding an undergraduate or a graduate degree in computer science (with some familiarity with cyber security) is sufficient to follow the material. The content of the book is particularly well suited to CI protection practitioners, people working at national and European Working Groups establishing information sharing processes among independent organizations (not necessarily restricted to protection from cyber attacks or to the financial setting) at both the military and civil levels, professionals of event processing and security, and the academic audience.

The editors want to thank primarily all the authors who have contributed to this book. A special thank goes to Giorgia Lodi, who helped us in fixing many details of the book and who is also one of the main pillars of CoMiFin. The editors are also indebted to all the persons who have been involved in the CoMiFin project during its lifetime, including Luca Nicoletti and Andrea Baghini (Italian Ministry of Economics and Finance), András Pataricza (Budapest University of Technology and Economics), Massimo Santelli (SelexElsag), and Jim Clarke (Waterford Institute of Technology). Special thanks go to Angelo Marino and Mario Scillia from the European Commission for having closely followed CoMiFin activities, providing appropriate suggestions for the technical and project management side. Members of the CoMiFin Financial Advisory Board were also instrumental in focusing on issues relevant for the financial players. The following have served as Board members: Thomas Kolher (Chair—Group Information Security at UBS), Finn Otto Hansen (SWIFT Board), Henning H. Arendt (@bc), Guido Pagani (Bank of Italy), Ferenc Alfldi (Capital Budapest Bank), Bernhard M. Hammerli (University of Lucerne), Matteo Lucchetti (ABI, currently Poste Italiane), and Ferenc Fazekas (Groupama). The editors also want to acknowledge Wikipedia, from which the definitions of many of the glossary terms have been taken.

Rome, Italy   Roberto Baldoni
Haifa, Israel   Gregory Chockler

Contents

Contributors

Enrico Angori Elsag Datamat, Rome, Italy; SelexElsag, Roma, Italy

Leonardo Aniello Dipartimento di Ingegneria Informatica, Automatica e Gestionale Antonio Ruberti, Università degli Studi di Roma "La Sapienza", Roma, Italy

Roberto Baldoni Dipartimento di Ingegneria Informatica, Automatica e Gestionale Antonio Ruberti, Università degli Studi di Roma "La Sapienza", Roma, Italy

Walter Beyeler Sandia National Laboratories, New Mexico, Albuquerque, NM, USA

Vita Bortnikov IBM, Research Division, Haifa, Israel

Dmitri Botvich Waterford Institute of Technology, Waterford, Ireland

Gregory Chockler IBM, Research Division, Haifa, Israel

Michele Colajanni University of Modena and Reggio Emilia, Modena, Italy

György Csertán OptXware Research and Development Ltd., Budapest, Hungary

Eliezer Dekel IBM, Research Division, Haifa, Israel

Giuseppe Antonio Di Luna Dipartimento di Ingegneria Informatica, Automatica e Gestionale Antonio Ruberti, Università degli Studi di Roma "La Sapienza", Roma, Italy

Atle Dingsor Kredit Tilsynet, Oslo, Norway

Hisain Elshaafi Waterford Institute of Technology, Waterford, Ireland

László Gönczy OptXware Research and Development Ltd., Budapest, Hungary

Hamza Ghani Technical University of Darmstadt, Darmstadt, Germany

Robert Glass Sandia National Laboratories, New Mexico, Albuquerque, NM, USA

Abdelmajid Khelil Technical University of Darmstadt, Darmstadt, Germany

Davide Lamanna Dipartimento di Ingegneria Informatica, Automatica e Gestionale Antonio Ruberti, Università degli Studi di Roma "La Sapienza", Roma, Italy

Gennady Laventman IBM, Research Division, Haifa, Israel

Giorgia Lodi Consorzio Interuniversitario Nazionale Informatica (CINI), Roma, Italy

Matteo Lucchetti Poste Italiane, Roma, Italy

Mirco Marchetti University of Modena and Reggio Emilia, Modena, Italy

Jimmy McGibney Waterford Institute of Technology, Waterford, Ireland

Michele Messori University of Modena and Reggio Emilia, Modena, Italy

Luca Montanari Dipartimento di Ingegneria Informatica, Automatica e Gestionale Antonio Ruberti, Università degli Studi di Roma "La Sapienza", Roma, Italy

Barry P. Mulcahy Waterford Institute of Technology, Waterford, Ireland

Hani Qusa Dipartimento di Ingegneria Informatica, Automatica e Gestionale Antonio Ruberti, Università degli Studi di Roma "La Sapienza", Roma, Italy

Neeraj Suri Technical University of Darmstadt, Darmstadt, Germany

Gábor Urbanics OptXware Research and Development Ltd., Budapest, Hungary

Ymir Vigfusson School of Computer Science, Reykjavík University, Reykjavík, Iceland

Acronyms

ABI	Italian Banking Association
ADSL	Asymmetric digital subscriber line
AN	Agilis node
AS	Agilis site
ATM	Automated teller machine
CA	Central Authority
CAPTCHA	Completely Automated Public Turing test to tell Computers and Humans Apart
CASoS	Complex Adaptive System of Systems
CEP	Complex event processing
CERT	Computer Emergency Response Team
CI	Critical infrastructure
CII	Critical information infrastructure
CINS	Critical Infrastructure Notification System
CIP	Critical infrastructure protection
COBIT	Control Objectives for Information and related Technology
CP	Closed port
CPS	Collaborative processing system
CPU	Central processing unit
CSS	Cascading Style Sheets
CVE	Common Vulnerabilities and Exposures
C&C	Command and control
CoMiFin	Communication Middleware for Monitoring Financial Critical Infrastructure
DDoS	Distributed denial of service
DHT	Distributed hash table
DMZ	Demilitarized zone
DNS	Domain Name System
DPI	Deep packet inspection
DR	Detection rate
DoS	Denial of service

EDP	Electronic data processing
EECTF	European Electronic Crime Task Force
ENISA	European Network and Information Security Agency
EPC	European Payments Council
EPL	Event Processing Language
FC	Failed connection
FI	Financial infrastructure
FI-ISAC	Financial Institutions Information Sharing and Analysis Center
FN	False negative
FP	False positive
FPR	False positive rate
FS/ISAC	Financial Services Information Sharing and Analysis Center
FSM	Finite state machine
FTP	File Transfer Protocol
GB	Gigabyte
GHz	Gigahertz
GQM	Goal question metric
GSM	Global System for Mobile communications
Gbit	Gigabit
HDFS	Hadoop Distributed File System
HIDS	Host-based intrusion detection system
HOC	Half-open connection
HTTP	Hypertext Transfer Protocol
HTTPS	HTTP Secure
ICMP	Internet Control Message Protocol
ICT	Information and communication technologies
IDS	Intrusion detection system
IP	Internet Protocol
IPS	Intrusion prevention system
IPSec	IP Security
IRC	Internet Relay Chat
ISAC	Information Sharing and Analysis Center
ISM	Information security management
ISP	Internet service provider
ISSG/CISEG	Information Security Support Group/Cybercrime Information Sharing Expert Group
ITSG	IT Security Group
JMS	Java Message Service
JT	Job Tracker
KPI	Key performance indicator
LAN	Local area network
LCG	Linear congruential generator
LEA	Law enforcement agency
LSE	London Stock Exchange
MAC	Media Access Control

MB	Megabyte
MDA	Model-driven architecture
MEP	Mediated event processing
MOM	Message-oriented middleware
Mbit	Megabit
MitB	Man in the Browser
MitM	Man in the Middle
NCB	National Central Bank
NIDS	Network-based intrusion detection system
NIPS	Network-based intrusion prevention system
NIST	National Institute of Standards and Technology
NRPE	Nagios Remote Plugin Executor
NSCA	Nagios Service Check Acceptor
NSM	National Security Authority
OS	Operating system
OTP	One-time password
PC	Personal computer
PCI DSS	Payment Card Industry Data Security Standard
PDD	Presidential Decision Directive
PGP	Pretty Good Privacy
PIN	Personal identification number
POJO	Plain Old Java Object
POS	Point of sale
PRNG	Pseudo-random number generator
QoS	Quality of service
RAM	Random access memory
RDBMS	Relational database management system
RFC	Request for Comments
RMI	Remote Method Invocation
ROI	Return on investment
RSA	Rivest, Shamir, and Adleman
SDT	Security, dependability, and trust
SEP	Simple event processing
SEPA	Single Euro Payments Area
SIEM	Security information and event management
SLA	Service level agreement
SLS	Service level specification
SME	Small or medium enterprise
SMS	Short Message Service
SOAP	Simple Object Access Protocol
SOC	Secure Operations Center
SP	Stream processing
SQL	Simple query language
SR	Semantic Room
SSL	Secure Sockets Layer

SWIFT	Society for Worldwide Interbank Financial Telecommunication
SoD	Segregation of duties
TCO	Total cost of ownership
TCP	Transmission Control Protocol
TFTP	Trivial File Transfer Protocol
TLS	Transport Layer Security
TM	Trust management
TN	True negative
TP	True positive
TT	Task tracker
UDP	User Datagram Protocol
UML	Unified Modeling Language
URL	Uniform Resource Locator
VM	Virtual machine
VPN	Virtual private network
WAN	Wide area network
WSLA	Web service level agreement
WXS	IBM WebSphere eXtreme Scale
XML	Extensible Markup Language
XOR	Exclusive OR

Part I
The Financial Infrastructure

Let us not look back in anger or forward in fear, but around in awareness.
James Thurber

Chapter 1
The Financial Critical Infrastructure and the Value of Information Sharing

Enrico Angori, Roberto Baldoni, Eliezer Dekel, Atle Dingsor, and Matteo Lucchetti

Abstract The financial system is quintessential to the functioning of a modern nation's economy. Therefore this system can be definitely considered as a critical infrastructure of our society and, due to the continuously increasing penetration of the Internet world inside this infrastructure, it has to be protected from cyber attacks. This chapter introduces the main actors forming the financial system and their relationships and analyzes the system's vulnerabilities to cyber attacks. Along this direction, the chapter investigates the financial ICT infrastructure of Norway as a case study and shows the current protection strategies adopted by financial players. The importance of information sharing at the level of a sector-specific market, such as the financial one, has been pointed out in eight added values, and examples of how poor information sharing results in sector-specific vulnerabilities are discussed. Finally some examples of information sharing methodologies are analyzed.

E. Angori
SelexElsag, Via Laurentina, Roma, Italy
e-mail: enrico.angori@elsagdatamat.com

R. Baldoni (✉)
Dipartimento di Ingegneria Informatica, Automatica e Gestionale Antonio Ruberti, Università degli Studi di Roma "La Sapienza", Via Ariosto 25, Roma, Italy
e-mail: baldoni@dis.uniroma1.it

E. Dekel
IBM, Research Division, Haifa University Campus, Mount Carmel, Haifa 31905, Israel
e-mail: eliezer.dekel@ibm.com

A. Dingsor
Kredit Tilsynet, Oslo, Norway
e-mail: Atle.Dingsor@kredittilsynet.no

M. Lucchetti
Poste Italiane, Roma, Italy
e-mail: lucch102@posteitaliane.it

R. Baldoni, G. Chockler (eds.), *Collaborative Financial Infrastructure Protection*,
DOI 10.1007/978-3-642-20420-3_1, © Springer-Verlag Berlin Heidelberg 2012

1.1 Introduction

The financial system comprises many entities that interact with each other to provide financial services that are the lifeline of the world economy. It is a complex landscape of actors, including stakeholders, regulatory agencies, financial service providers, and the communication networks linking them. The economic role of financial intermediates and regulators in financial markets is that of increasing welfare in the economy through efficient capital allocation and risk sharing. For example, commercial banks are basically intermediates between individuals (who deposit their funds in the bank and don't need the capital at the moment) and firms (for which the banks issue loans, as they need the capital for their operation). They serve as a pooling device in the financial markets. Clearing houses facilitate trading by mediating two traders entering a future contract. Central banks have a regulatory role; for example, the central bank requires commercial banks to hold a certain percentage of their assets as capital (capital requirement). In this chapter we review this financial system, its stakeholders, and their interrelations. We identify and classify the vulnerabilities of interconnected financial infrastructures. Specifically, the chapter includes the current state of the art of financial communications, describing its actors, its high-level needs, and the existing structures that support financial communications.

Communications form a key basis for the financial world and necessitate a high level of security and privacy. Today these requirements are fulfilled by private network and proprietary communication protocols, which guarantee the high level of security needed in financial transactions. Driven by the growing popularity of mobile commerce, the interconnections across financial institutions are growing worldwide. The need exists to consider the use of open networks as well as private and public clouds to drive this level of pervasive access while maintaining the needed security and responsiveness levels and reducing the total cost of ownership (TCO). Nowadays the new IT technologies can guarantee a high level of security and dependability; however, they are not widely used due to the actors' reluctance to use public communication networks.

The financial information and communication technologies (ICT), the interrelationships and interconnection between financial actors and regulators, are high on the agenda today, as banks played an important role in the current financial crisis. Regulations or the lack thereof were part of the problem. Banks used asset-backed securities to evade capital requirements, and when housing prices went sour, banks did not have enough capital to operate, and lending activity came to a halt. Government intervention was needed to make the banks operational again, lending to firms and other players. Research in financial infrastructure (FI) falls somewhere between the fields of finance/economics and information systems. Finance/economics needs to define the roles of financial players and the nature of the connectivity required among them. Information systems should then address how such relationships are best implemented by technological infrastructure.

In order to satisfy the requirements of the financial ecosystem, there are a number of market-specific technical requirements for responsiveness, data integrity, security, and privacy. The financial market indeed stipulates its own specific needs;

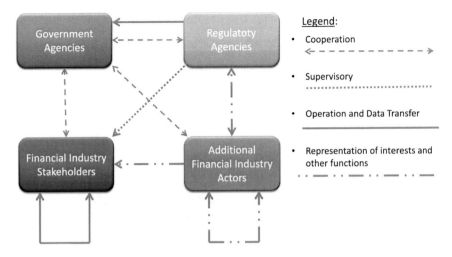

Fig. 1.1 Simplified logical connections between the players of the financial industry

therefore, software and service providers have, over time, implemented domain-specific solutions to meet them. Section 1.2 provides an overview of the financial infrastructure: the business actors, regulatory agencies, and the associated ICT and its requirements; in Sect. 1.2 we survey the main stakeholders. We then review, in Sect. 1.3, the financial system as a critical infrastructure. An overview of the ICT in use today in financial operations with examples from the Scandinavian landscape is provided in Sect. 1.4. Following this overview we discuss, in Sect. 1.5, the vulnerability of this interconnected system to cyber attacks. In Sect. 1.6, we review cyber security measures, and in Sect. 1.7, we discuss the state of the art in bank cyber security. The last part of this chapter (Sect. 1.8) discusses the value of cooperation between the financial actors for achieving cyber security.

1.2 Main Stakeholders and Players

Though each country has its own specific model for managing financial business, there exists a general model that is shared across the different European countries that are trying to converge toward a common European model. A simplified structure of the financial system is depicted in Fig. 1.1. The main groups of stakeholders are government agencies, regulatory agencies, financial industry stakeholders, and additional financial industry actors. Government agencies take part in the money transfer processes; for instance, the national central banks (NCBs) are involved in the clearing tasks, and the Bureau of Public Debt participates in the operation of the stock exchange market. Some players provide financial services, e.g., the State Treasury keeps the accounts of the state institutes (for example, the mandatory pension funds).

These functionalities require the cooperation of related stakeholders such as the NCB and the clearing house, or the State Treasury and the mandatory pension funds. In some cases there is close cooperation between participants, e.g., between the NCB and the supervisory agency, to help improve the financial culture and the awareness of the people.

Regulatory agencies have regulatory and supervisory functionalities to ensure reliable, continuous, and transparent operation of the financial markets. For instance, banks are liable for reporting created bank accounts to a supervisory authority.

The regulatory agencies are connected with different kinds of associations that are members of the additional FI actors group. The main missions of the associations are the representation, transmission, and reconciliation of interests of the institutes they stand for and communication with similar domestic and foreign institutes and agencies. For instance, supervisory agencies and banking and insurance associations can work in connection with each other; these associations usually coordinate the operation of their institutes. The other members of this group can take part in the settlement processes such as the stock exchange.

The last set is the group of FI stakeholders. This group covers the main stakeholders, except for the supervisory authorities. These stakeholders are directly involved in the operation of the settlement, clearing, and other financial services. This group is in connection with all other groups, and the participants of this group are in connection with each other as well. For example, banks connect with each other through the clearing and settlement systems, which involve data transfer between the institutes. In some cases, the bank, the insurance company, and the pension fund is operated by the same organization, thus involving close interconnection between these entities.

Figure 1.2 summarizes the main stakeholders of the financial system stemming from this general model. They can be divided into four main parts according to the scope of their activities: money markets, capital markets, funds, and insurance companies. The money markets group includes the banks and other credit institutions. The money market is where short-term obligations such as Treasury bills, commercial paper, and bankers' acceptances are bought and sold. The capital markets group consists of investment firms and fund managers. The capital market is the market for securities, where companies and governments can raise long-term funds. The funds group contains the different kinds of pension funds and the health and income replacement funds. Funds are related to handling people's savings. The last group consists of the different kinds of insurance companies and the related actors, such as brokers and consultants. Insurance brokers sell different kinds of insurances; they are in connection with several companies.

1.3 Financial Institutions as Critical Infrastructures

The importance of protecting infrastructures has greatly increased in recent years. In particular, governments and international agencies and organizations are focusing on critical infrastructures, i.e., those assets, systems, and functions vital to the

Main Groups of Stakeholders	Members	
Regulatory Agencies	Financial supervisory authorities Tax and financial control office	
Government Agencies	National Central Banks State treasuries	
FI Stakeholders	Money Markets	Banks
		Specialized Credit Institutions
		Co-operative Credit Institutions
		Savings Co-operatives
		Credit Co-operatives
		Financial Enterprises
	Capital Markets	Investment Firms
		Investment Fund Managers
		Other Institutions
	Funds	Private Pension Funds
		Voluntary Pension Funds
		Health and Income-Replacement Funds
	Insurance Companies	Proprietary Insurance Companies
		Mutual Insurance Companies
		Insurance brokers
		Insurance consultants

Fig. 1.2 Main stakeholders of the financial industry

smooth, safe, and peaceful operation of a society. Critical infrastructures (CIs) include those physical resources, services, and information technology facilities, networks, and infrastructure assets which, if disrupted or destroyed, would have a serious impact on the health, safety, security, or economic well-being of citizens or the effective functioning of governments and/or economies [4]. These categories comprise utility infrastructure (water, gas, fuel, electricity, transportation, communication), banking and financial services, and food supply, etc. With the advent of the digital age and the Internet of Things (where everything is connected), these CIs become interrelated, interconnected, and even more accessible, both for legitimate users and for adversaries. Protecting the digital access for these CIs now has a special focus: cyber security.

The financial system described in Sect. 1.2 is a CI, as it is essential to the functioning economy of modern nations. Financial institutions, in fact, play the role of intermediaries, accepting funds from various sources and making them available as loans or investments to those who need them. Their operational effectiveness is rated in terms of how efficiently the financial system as a whole allocates resources among suppliers and users of funds to produce real goods and services [5].

During the last two decades, the infrastructure supporting the global economy has changed. In order to manage their internal processes and provide their services, CIs, and in particular financial institutions, increasingly rely on ICT systems and networks, and many of them are also connected to the public Internet. The dependency on information systems and technological infrastructures allows financial institutions to provide innovative and high-quality services, thus preserving efficiency and cost-effectiveness. However, whereas the benefits have been enormous for both public and private organizations, the CIs' increasing reliance on networked systems also poses significant risks to the critical operations and infrastructures they support. The result is a new form of CIs, generally referred to as critical information infrastructures (CIIs), that totally or partially rely on one or more information infrastructures for their monitoring, control, and management and are therefore vulnerable to new forms of cyber threats and attacks, in addition to traditional physical threats. Such technological information infrastructures must be dependable; i.e., they must guarantee availability, reliability, correctness, safety, and security, under normal working conditions and in case of an emergency, that is, when critical events occur. It is therefore crucial to protect those infrastructures and adopt strategies to guarantee that the different infrastructures are able to correctly and continuously supply their services in spite of any event [6].

Some industries and types of businesses are more susceptible to cyber-related crimes and attacks, and the risk level is particularly high for the banking industry and financial institutions. Moreover, this sector is also extremely vulnerable to public perception: an impression of weakness could easily result in a damaging cascading effect. Business continuity is therefore necessary to maintain public confidence.

Attacks targeted to financial institutions [7] are typically performed in order to:

- gain unauthorized access to sensitive or confidential information
- disrupt normal business
- create costly distractions
- steal funds
- reduce confidence

Potential damage and possible consequences that may occur when systems supporting critical financial operations are threatened include:

- services and benefits interruption
- sensitive data disclosure
- data integrity corruption
- money and information theft
- commercial structures and financial systems bankruptcy
- international business transactions failure

- markets destabilization
- unauthorized access and/or modification of personal information
- loss of confidence and reputation

It is important to adopt protection strategies and measures in order to reduce vulnerability to cyber threats, prevent cyber attacks against CIs, and minimize damage and recovery time from attacks that do occur. Taking preventive measures and improving early detection and reaction capabilities allows financial institutions to limit the effects and impact of disruptions and attacks on governments and society, and to ensure business continuity, guaranteeing that affected systems are always able to provide a minimum service level or that they can be restored within the shortest possible time.

1.4 Standard Solutions for Securing the Financial Infrastructure

Financial IT infrastructures are used to process, store, and exchange critical and sensitive information; hence they are characterized by strict security requirements. Systems, networks, data, and exchanged information should be protected against any type of malicious activity (such as interception, insertion of fake information, update, delete). The relevance of security requirements in the financial context is highlighted by the Basel II accord [8]. Damages caused by security breaches within the financial IT infrastructure fall within the operational risk category, as defined in the Basel II first pillar [9] and Annex 9 [10]. In particular, system security issues (such as hacking activities and data theft) are considered as examples of the external fraud event type, defined (among others) within the operational risks. System and network issues also represent the main focus of the standards with which financial institutions and their customers can voluntarily comply in order to obtain widely recognized international certifications, such as the Payment Card Industry Data Security Standard (PCI DSS) [11].

The financial IT infrastructure is a key critical infrastructure (CI) for financial operators and consequently must be dependable or trustworthy. The attributes of dependability/trustworthiness [12] refer to the degree of (quantifiable) user certainty that the system will operate as expected and that the system will not fail in normal use. Basically, the IT financial infrastructure must satisfy the following dependability and security requirements and properties:

- Availability: the capacity to access systems, networks, and critical data for the infrastructure survival anytime, even if the infrastructure is operating under extreme conditions.
- Reliability: the capacity to ensure that a system or network will perform its intended functions without failures when operated under specific conditions for a specified time interval.
- Authentication: the capacity to identify a user that is appropriate to the specific information and service type.

- Access control: the capacity to ensure that only authorized users can access system and network resources.
- Data and message confidentiality: the capacity to ensure that only authorized users can access protected data and messages.
- Data and message integrity: the capacity to ensure that data managed by systems and messages transmitted over the network are not altered by unauthorized users or non-guaranteed software or hardware.
- Reliable message delivery: the capacity to avoid message loss and replication and guarantee ordered delivery, along with the ability to provide verifiable proof of delivery to both the endpoints of a communication.
- Non-repudiation: the capacity to provide verifiable proof of message delivery to both the endpoints of a communication, in order to ensure that the sender of a message cannot deny having sent the message and that the recipient cannot deny having received the message.

In addition to dependability and security requirements, the financial infrastructure has to meet performance and quality of service (QoS) requirements, characterized by specific low-level technical metrics for interconnection networks (such as packet drop, network latency round trip time, jitter, out-of-order delivery, and transmission errors) as well as higher level business-level metrics (such as number of transmitted transactions, percentage of rejected transactions, and number of incorrect transactions).

The most challenging aspect in financial CII is the new model that is becoming established for financial transactions. Up to twenty years ago a financial transaction was originated by a financial stakeholder (such as a bank) and was received through a complex communication network and few intermediate nodes by another financial stakeholder (such as another bank elsewhere). Communication networks at that time were quite controlled and secure. Nowadays the new model foresees online and real-time transactions that are generated by a non-financial stakeholder (usually a business customer), flow through financial stakeholders and intermediate nodes, and sometimes arrive to another non-financial stakeholder (for example, an enterprise or an SME). In this new model the communication network includes many different network types and often includes Internet as well. In such a case the communication network cannot be considered as intrinsically controlled and secure.

Communications among financial players are carried out through quite different technological solutions providing different performance, reliability, and security levels: communications among financial institutions usually leverage dedicated leased lines; central bank offices are connected to local agencies through other dedicated lines or through secure virtual private networks (VPNs) over Internet links.

Financial organizations are nowadays interconnected through extensive proprietary networks to provide their financial customers with advanced services and to exchange financial messages securely for business purposes (e.g., cash management, fund transfers, credit advices, and alerts). These networks are for financial transactions only, and complex requirements related to security and privacy lead to proprietary and closed networks. Usually, financial networks are hierarchically interconnected according to a tree structure. In this interconnection model, each network can be considered as a tree node at a well-defined level. Therefore, two networks standing at the same level can communicate by sending their messages to the network at the upper level, which guarantees a secure and reliable exchange of information.

Leased lines interconnecting financial institutions are specifically designed for high availability. Fault tolerance is provided by means of multiple redundancy. High dependability is also achieved through isolation of these dedicated communication lines with respect to the Internet traffic. This choice protects financial communications from availability issues. Dedicated communication lines used for information exchange among financial players can provide a tightly monitored and controlled environment, in which it is possible to enforce performance-oriented policies. In this context, the possibility of performance guarantees is a direct consequence of the isolation of the dedicated communication lines with respect to the shared Internet. In isolated networks, it is rather simple to design and provide a communication infrastructure where the performance cannot be jeopardized by uncontrollable Internet phenomena and/or attack that could result in the degradation of the communication channel performance. Moreover, the complete isolation of financial networks from other networks ensures a high level of security against intrusions or malfunctions from outside. However, it is often difficult to separate financial networks from external ones because they have the need or the convenience to interconnect to other networks to exchange essential data for financial purposes. Hence it is important to ensure maximum network interconnection security under these conditions, using suitable protection policies and technical solutions that guarantee full access and data exchange security. Financial CIIs include connections among financial institutions and their customers. While high security guarantees can be achieved through dedicated channels, communications between a financial player and their customers are carried out through the Internet. Nevertheless, it is possible to guarantee authentication, non-repudiation, privacy, and integrity by leveraging state-of-the-art encryption and key distribution algorithms. Virtual private networks (VPNs) can be established to enable secure communication between a known and authenticated user and (virtually) any host belonging to the internal network of a financial organization. This solution can be effectively used to enable secure (but not dependable) communication channels for customers or employees of a financial institution that is connected through the Internet. Transaction security is implemented at the platform and application levels, and performances usually cannot be guaranteed. Processes for establishing and securing the communication link and for managing transactions are defined by the financial institutions and then carefully implemented by the customers (such as the use of one-time passwords (OTPs) to confirm transaction).

Communications that use the Internet as a backbone cannot be characterized by performance guarantees. It is possible to stipulate service level agreements (SLAs) when there is one provider among the financial institutions or when the traffic is confined in one autonomous system. In the more general case, however, it is impossible (or very difficult) to guarantee SLA contracts when multiple autonomous systems are involved between the communication endpoints. In fact, Internet traffic can be arbitrarily delayed or dropped by intermediate autonomous systems that are based on a best effort routing service.

The Society for Worldwide Interbank Financial Telecommunication (SWIFT) is the most important worldwide financial communication infrastructure that enables the exchange of messages between banks and other financial institutions. It was founded in 1973 as a cooperative society owned by member banks. SWIFT does not generate transactions, but it is responsible for providing a fast, secure, available, and accurate means of transferring a variety of financial instructions on behalf of its international members. It is a private network which provides the platform, products, and services to connect and exchange financial information among financial organizations all over the world. Therefore, SWIFT can be considered as one of the nodes on the top of the tree model representing the interconnection structure of the European financial networks. National financial networks are lower level nodes that can be connected to SWIFT by specific backbone access points that act as communication gateways, and they can provide different services. An example of secure communication infrastructure among financial players is represented by SWIFTNet, which is a secure IP-based network to which financial players can gain direct access.

SWIFT security mechanisms helped to create a large step forward in the safe and reliable transfer of financial messages. SWIFT has numerous security advantages; thus financial institutions opted for the SWIFT network, rather than the traditional (and much less secure) Telex instruction, as a preferred method of transfer. Currently SWIFT has changed to its IP network infrastructure, known as SWIFTNet, totally replacing the previous X.25 infrastructure.

Basically, SWIFT provides a centralized store-and-forward mechanism including transaction management. Bank A, which needs to send a message to bank B with an authorization of institution C, formats the message according to a well-defined standard and securely sends it to SWIFTNet. SWIFT guarantees secure and reliable delivery of the message to bank B after the appropriate action of institution C.

1.5 Financial ICT Infrastructure in Norway: Tradition of Cooperation and Associated Risks

Norway FIs and customers are heavily dependent on the Internet. As of January 2011, there were close to 5 million signed agreements for the use of Internet banking. Norway has a population of approximately 5 million. The number of invoices paid through Internet banking increased by 5.6 percent last year (2010). More than 90% of all invoices being paid in Norway are paid using Internet banking.

There were 70 million ATM withdrawals in Norway in 2010, down by 25 percent over the last five years. An increasing number of Norwegians use mobile banking services, such as mobile banking, bank applications (apps) for iPhone and other smartphones, as well as Short Message Service (SMS).

Norwegian banks traditionally have pooled resources and jointly developed systems in key areas. There is a bank-wide debit card system. Each bank issues debit cards under its own brand. Merchants are customers of a bank of their choosing. A card issued by one bank may be used interchangeably at any point of sale (POS) terminal. The debit card may also be used at any ATM, regardless of which bank owns the ATM. There is a common scheme for checking PINs and a common scheme for checking an account balance and making reservations against the balance. The banks have common procedures for dealing with offline situations.

There is a bank-wide e-invoice system in Norway. The payment information is held in one bank-wide database, which also contains information about which Internet bank(s) the customer uses. Any e-invoice is sent to the Internet bank(s) of the customer. The customer may pay the e-invoice through any of her Internet banks. Any other Internet banks that the customer may use are automatically updated to reflect that payment has taken place; i.e., the e-invoice is no longer shown as pending.

Likewise, the banks have worked together to develop a system for standing orders. The beneficiary enters into an agreement with her bank to the effect that the beneficiary will offer the payer the option of paying by a standing order. Information that the beneficiary offers regarding the standing order payment is made available to all banks. Hence, on entering payment details of the beneficiary the first time, the payer is informed by her Internet bank that she may enter into a standing order agreement. The payer sets a maximum amount per invoice applicable under the agreement, and may cancel it at her discretion. The infrastructure for this transaction is developed jointly by the banks.

The banks have also jointly developed an authentication system for the Internet, called BankID. Each bank is a separate certificate-issuing authority. User private keys are stored centrally on hardware and premises shared among the banks. The user enters a user ID, an OTP, and a fixed password, which is consumed by a signed applet and communicated to the central security server for access to the private key. The user may authenticate to a number of web sites using her BankID. Given the increasing number of web sites asking for BankID authentication, there is a risk that the user may be less critical with respect to whom to submit authentication credentials, which would increase the risk of phishing and other attacks against the ID. Securities trading is increasingly done over the Internet, through Internet banks or stand-alone brokers. These examples illustrate that there is a strong tradition for cooperation and information sharing and for joint systems development among Norwegian banks.

A comparison among members of the IT Security Group (ITSG) reveals that Norwegian banks are heavily outsourced. Within Norway, a few "hubs" supply the bulk of banks with IT services. One bank has its corporate IT operation in Sweden, supplied by IBM. Two other bank groups are outsourced to Denmark; IBM is the main IT supplier.

As a consequence of being heavily outsourced, IT skill in the FIs is probably deteriorating. It is difficult to uphold procurement skill in FIs, when the FI is not involved day to day in the IT operation. It is particularly disturbing that IT risk probably also would be less understood and acknowledged under these circumstances. As the specialist, the supplier's view carries a lot of weight and the supplier's arguments often override arguments internally within the FI itself. However, the supplier might have a different perspective than the FI. Based on years of observation, we would like to point out the following. Firstly, IT suppliers tend to have a shorter term perspective than the FIs when it comes to the company's bottom line. The suppliers may not have the right incentives to invest long term in security up front. Secondly, IT suppliers may not fully understand and acknowledge that IT security is of prime concern and should permeate all IT development and operation. Thirdly, the supplier may not be fully aware of the concentration risk to national critical infrastructure that arises from serving several FIs on the same system. Recently, supervisors noticed that a microcode error reported on one CPU with a key supplier in Norway seemed to coincide with irregular service reported by the majority of banks in Norway. The seriousness and symptoms varied among the banks. The supplier indicated that not all banks were served by the CPU in question; rather banks were spread across CPUs. On further investigation it turned out that the banks were indeed in some way or other dependent on the malfunctioning CPU. Hence a serious concentration risk was discovered.

In 2010 a key supplier had aggressive plans for outsourcing IT operations to Ukraine and to India. Apparently this made for a good business case, and the banks were about to accept the arguments from the supplier more or less at face value. The supervisors questioned some aspects related to control, governance, integrity, and availability of information processed and stored off-shore. Ukraine scores high on Transparency International's corruption index. The supervisors felt that the prospect of the outsourced financial institution having to resort to nontraditional payment methods in order to renew the lease on the data premises or to get more bandwidth from the local telecom supplier was somehow not to be desired. The supervisory authority issued a statement to this effect, and the statement contained other warnings as well. After further study, the FIs seem to have withdrawn their plans for off-shoring.

The arguments above indicate that there is an inherent risk that FIs are gradually leaving more decisions in the hands of the IT suppliers. Also, the market for supplier services is very thin; in key areas there will be only one or a few suppliers. Because there are few practices to compare, it is hard for the FIs to establish what is "best practice", which poses the danger of the FIs becoming less critical than they should be.

Being outsourced for a number of years, the FIs are heavily embedded in the supplier software and hardware. Running time-critical systems around the clock, the idea of changing suppliers seems like a daunting one. It is to be expected that FIs feel uncomfortably locked in under these circumstances, and that suppliers drive the FIs, rather than the other way around.

1.6 Vulnerabilities to Cyber Attacks

FI services are becoming more automated. Several suppliers, systems, protocols, and carriers (mobile, IP, voice) are involved. The experience of the supervisory authority tells us that the interfaces between suppliers are particularly risky areas. The interface may involve protocol conversion, format conversion, decryption and re-encryption, scheduling, etc. An example would be mobile banking. Transactions are carried over GSM and IP networks on their way from the handset to the bank. This calls for decryption of the GSM payload once it hits the mobile server, and then re-encryption to facilitate further IP transmission to the bank. At this conversion point, the traffic is exposed. This calls for some sort of end-to-end encryption on a higher (application) level, which in turn may be hard to realize given the plethora of different handsets. Key management may be hard to administer.

The risk is amplified as the transactions chains become longer, bringing together different technologies. Recently banks have introduced online loan application and processing. At the other end of the transaction chain, encrypted personal online storage facilities are being offered, like an electronic security deposit box. Let's say you apply electronically for a loan, maybe using your handset. The loan is being processed electronically, involving communication with various non-bank authorities, e.g., notaries, real-estate registrars, credit information agencies, tax authorities, and marital registers. The loan is granted and discounted. All pertinent documents and information are stored in the electronic storage of the customer and the bank. At various steps along the way digital authentication and signing takes place, probably involving different authentication mechanisms and different suppliers. Given the complexity of the chain of events, there is a substantial risk of something going wrong. Upholding confidentiality requirements is one of the challenges. The last year has seen several incidents of unwanted exposure of confidential information.

Eventually, the customers themselves are part of the cyber security problem. Viruses, Trojans, and any other type of malware may infect an unprotected endpoint, stealing information required to complete a financial transaction. The whole process that was agreed on and established to secure financial transactions (such as connection to an https site, use of credentials to identify and authenticate the customer, personal information for further user identification) is implemented by the customer and may be compromised by wrong customer behavior. Phishing and other similar techniques are examples of these types of threats that impact cyber security.

Vulnerability analyses over the whole service chain are complex tasks. Where are the weak points?

1.7 Security Systems and Technologies

A secure FI includes several software solutions providing tools to prevent, recognize, resist, tolerate, and recover from events that intentionally or accidentally threaten the dependability of the infrastructure. In order to secure IT systems and networks and protect FIs from cyber attacks and other threats, a wide range of security technologies is used. These include access control technologies, system integrity technologies, audit and monitoring tools, and configuration management technologies. Security solutions have three main objectives, which are all critical for properly protecting financial infrastructures:

1. *Prevention*: Preventive activities aim at stopping a fault from occurring or an attack from succeeding. Preventing security breaches is possible only for well-known vulnerabilities.
2. *Detection*: Despite preventive activities, new attacks can occur because of newly found vulnerabilities or attack techniques. Detection activities aim at identifying that a security breach has occurred. In order to properly react, detection should be achieved in real time.
3. *Reaction*: Once a security breach has been detected, reaction activities aim at stopping the attack, mitigating the effects, and reducing the damage it has caused. Reaction activities may include the collection of detailed information in order to prevent and detect attacks in the future.

The following paragraphs provide an overview of the main security technologies and solutions. A detailed analysis on how the specific technologies work can be found in [13].

Identity and access management: tools that provide a secure, automated, and policy-based user management platform supporting user access control, authentication, and authorization. In order to protect internal systems, networks, and data, access control technologies ensure that only authorized users can access protected information and resources. In particular, authentication technologies associate a user with a specific identity. Users can be authenticated by different methods, including shared secret systems, digital certificates, token-based systems, and biometrics. Authorization technologies manage user rights and privileges in order to grant or deny access to a protected resource (a network, a system, an individual computer, a program, a file, etc.). Operating systems and sensitive or mission-critical applications incorporate appropriate access controls that restrict which application functions are available to users.

Transaction control: tools that implement a structured process to control transactions, for example, by using off-band communication. These tools may be used to reinforce transaction input by using two separate communication channels (for example, Internet connection and mobile device). In this way a transaction is started using one channel (for example, a web-based windows operating over the Internet) and is then confirmed using the other channel (an SMS message to a customer mobile number). This process is based on the idea that compromising two separate channels is much more complex than compromising one.

Network access control: tools that protect the logical or physical boundary of a network, in order to prevent access to the network by external unauthorized users. Network access control technologies include firewalls and network-based intrusion prevention systems (NIPSs). Basically, firewalls block or allow network traffic based on static or dynamic rules configured by the network administrator. A NIPS allows or disallows access based on an analysis of packet headers and packet payloads. The NIPS can detect security events and, after detection of malicious activities, may take specific actions, such as blocking traffic flows. A NIPS not only can detect an intrusive activity, it also can attempt to stop it.

Application monitoring: tools that monitor performance and availability of the applications and services running on the servers. In particular, they perform monitoring of hardware (CPU utilization, memory, disk space, etc.) and software components and monitoring of operating systems status. Collected data may be used for historical reporting, performance analysis, trend prediction, and other data mining activities. Application monitoring tools typically provide web-based interfaces and alerting mechanisms for notifying administrators about potential issues.

Network management and monitoring: tools that are able to automatically discover devices and hosts on a network, build a routing map to reflect network logical organization, and display network topology. They provide support for fault management (i.e., identification of network failures), configuration management (i.e., monitoring of network configuration information), and performance management. Network management and monitoring tools typically provide a centralized management console for event visualization and network diagnostics.

Data and storage management: tools that provide a platform for managing complex storage in distributed heterogeneous environments. They are able to protect and manage a broad range of data, from workstations to corporate server environments. Provided functionalities include centralized administration of data and storage management, fully automated data protection, efficient management of information, and automated high-speed server recovery. In addition, data and storage management tools protect an organization's data against hardware failures and other errors by storing backup copies of data in an offline repository.

Activity monitoring: tools that perform host and network data gathering and analysis in order to identify security-related events and anomalous behavior that may indicate an intrusion or an ongoing attack. Activity monitoring tools include network-based intrusion detection systems (NIDSs), deep packet inspection (DPI), honeypots, and host-based intrusion detection systems (HIDSs). NIDSs and HIDSs are able to identify potential attacks and intrusions using predefined signature or anomaly detection techniques, and may take predefined response actions. A honeypot is a network device that an institution uses to attract attackers to a harmless and monitored area of the network. DPI is a form of computer network packet filtering that examines packets as they pass an inspection point, searching for protocol noncompliance, viruses, spam, intrusions, or predefined criteria. Once the DPI detects a suspicious behavior, it can generate an event to an analytics tool or it can decide not to allow the packet to pass.

Configuration management and assurance: technologies that support security administrators to view and change the security settings on hosts and networks, verify the correctness of the security settings, and maintain continuity of operations and services. Configuration management and assurance technologies include policy enforcement tools, continuity of operations tools, and patch management. Policy enforcement technologies allow system administrators to perform centralized monitoring of compliance with the institution's security policies. These tools examine desktop and server configurations that define authorized access to specified devices, compare these settings against a baseline policy, and provide multilevel reports on computer configurations. Continuity of operations tools, which adopt clustering, load balancing, and replication techniques, provide a complete backup infrastructure that increases fault tolerance to keep the institution's services online and available at multiple locations in case of an emergency or planned maintenance. Patch management tools automate the otherwise manual process of acquiring, testing, and applying patches to multiple computer systems.

System integrity: tools used to ensure that a system and its data are not illicitly modified or corrupted by malicious code. System integrity tools include antivirus software and integrity checkers. Antivirus software, using specific scanners, provides protection against viruses and malicious code, such as worms and Trojan horses, by detecting and removing the malicious code and by preventing unwanted effects and repairing damage that may have resulted. File integrity checkers are software programs that monitor alterations to files that are considered critical to either the organization or the operation of a computer, by comparing the state of a file system against a trusted state, or a baseline, built using one-way hash functions.

Virtual private networks (VPNs): use cryptography to establish a secure communication link across unprotected networks (e.g., the Internet), allowing connection between two or more remote physical locations. Data privacy is maintained through security procedures and protocols, such as tunneling, IPSec, and Secure Sockets Layer (SSL), that encrypt communications between two endpoints.

Online and offline analytics: tools for identifying and recognizing anomalous behavior patterns. In order to detect attacks, malware, potentially dangerous misconfigurations, and internal misuse, a security team must analyze a huge amount of event data coming from the different components of the security infrastructure (e.g., intrusion detection systems, firewalls, VPNs, and antivirus applications). Since analyzing logs and or events produced by a single device is insufficient to gain a full understanding of all system activity, sophisticated attacks and intrusion techniques may be detectable only by correlating events and logs produced by several security systems and devices. Unfortunately, the huge volume of data and the number of machines in a typical network can make manual analysis of security data impossible. Therefore, it is important to automate the process of aggregating events from disparate devices and systems into one logical central location, where the data can be correlated in order to simplify incident response and reporting. In order to automate the process of aggregating and correlating events, financial institutions typically deploy security information and event management (SIEM) systems within their domains.

1.8 Financial Systems Protection Strategies

1.8.1 Online Protection

This section covers protection strategies that aim at preventing attacks from having any effect. The strategies typically are twofold. The first strategy is to accept that a particular service is indeed vulnerable, and counter this vulnerability by making the potential rewards from an attack as small as possible. Another strategy is to reduce the vulnerability to near zero. Both strategies would make it unattractive to attack the service, and one could expect that attacks would not occur. In the next section, on the other hand, we explore protection strategies that are targeted to specific ongoing attacks, i.e., protection strategies that aim to isolate, contain, mitigate, and stop an attack.

The use of standing orders is increasing. A standing order is an agreement between a bank and its customer that the bank shall automatically effect payments, i.e., debit the customer's account and send a corresponding credit instruction to the creditor bank. There is one agreement for each debtor/creditor pair. The agreement often sets a limit as to the value of each payment. The agreement is running; i.e., one and the same agreement applies to repeat payments until the agreement is canceled by the customer. The creditor must also enter into an agreement with her bank. A perpetrator would have to be accepted as a legitimate creditor for standing order payments as a first step in defrauding customers. The payments are effected automatically based on information stored centrally with the banks. The customer does not have to be logged on for the payment to take place. Hence there is limited scope for a Trojan, Man in the Middle (MitM), or Man in the Browser (MitB) when it comes to modifying transaction information. Increasing use of standing orders would limit the playing ground for fraudsters.

The use of e-invoicing is slowly increasing in Europe. With e-invoicing, all payment instruction information is made available to the customer through the Internet bank. In other words, the customer does not enter payment information such as amounts or credit account number. The customer either accepts the e-invoice or declines it. The creditor and debtor must enter into agreements with their respective banks in order to set up e-invoicing.

With both standing orders and e-invoicing the payer does not enter payment information, and there is very little scope for a perpetrator to modify payment information. Some countries, such as Singapore, have taken this even further by mandating each customer to predefine a list of creditor accounts to which payments may be effected. Additional security applies if the list needs to be updated, typically using out-of-band mechanisms like SMS. Needless to say, the prospect of transferring funds to an account on a list determined by the account holder would seem unappealing to most perpetrators. There is little scope for an MitM, MitB or a Trojan to do much harm.

Several banks now use a one-time password (OTP) in connection with customer log-in to the Internet bank. The primary idea is that once the customer is logged in, no impostor who has phished or otherwise obtained access to the code may log in using the same code. However, by using somewhat advanced phishing schemes, impostors have been able to get access to the code before it reaches the bank. One instance of a scheme took this close to full automation, in that attackers presented banking customers with an automated front-end to the banking application, through which the log-in occurred, giving the attackers full access to the customer account. In order to combat this kind of attack, some banks have introduced transaction authentication; i.e., the customer must enter a separate OTP upon submitting each transaction, after and in addition to the OTP submitted in connection with log-in to the Internet bank. However, many OTP tokens (the devices that produce OTPs) are time synchronized with the machine that hosts the Internet bank. Because clocks tend to differ slightly, and to allow for time to transmit and process the code, there is a time window within which an OTP is valid. This time window allows attackers to phish two codes that subsequently prove to be valid; one for log-in and one for authenticating a (fraudulent) transaction. One could also foresee a more advanced attack, where the fraudsters have made a copy of the entire payment sequence which is played up to the customer, while the fraudster simultaneously has an ongoing session with the Internet bank, using the codes that the customer submits to the false pages. However, OTPs are good for one thing; they are a deterrent to a pent-up, massive attack. It would not be possible for an attacker to harvest OTPs and store them for a later run on the bank accounts; the OTPs would not be valid.

Several banks now offer free antivirus software for customers to download and run on their computers. The offering has a prominent position on the home page of the banks, and customers are strongly encouraged to download it. Antivirus vendors are engaged in an arms race against malware producers, and they are up against a well-organized and resourceful adversary. Lately we have seen the merger of two malware producers (SpyEye and Zeus). Advanced malware, e.g., polymorphous variants, change their signature dynamically and escape antivirus software. Hence the effectiveness and efficiency of antivirus software is being questioned. In the aftermath of an attack against Norwegian online banking customers, security analysts reported that more than half of the investigated systems infected were running fully updated application and OS versions. To a certain extent it is possible from the server side of Internet banking to harness the browser session, i.e., to harden the browser session against attacks. Before any log-in or other transactions take place, all unnecessary browser functions are turned off. Exits from the browser to external programs are disabled, handles are disabled, and so forth. The idea is that banking customers are protected against Trojan attacks even when using an infected PC and even when the actual Trojan is configured to behave in a new and unexpected way, like polymorphous viruses. Several security vendors offer solutions in this area.

In order to become aware of and stop unauthorized transactions, banks perform back-end transaction analyses, both "on the fly" and retrospectively. In a recent wave of attacks against banks in Norway, back-end analyses are known to have prevented losses. Transactions were compared against black lists of accounts. The footprint of the Trojan was identified, and transactions that matched the footprint were stopped. Some companies are proficient in collecting traces and indications that authentication credentials have been compromised. The companies post these traces to drop sites which contain profiles of compromised users. Several banks scan these drop sites regularly for traces of compromised customers. In November 2010 one prominent UK bank came across traces indicating that customers of a Norwegian bank might have been compromised. The UK bank alerted the Norwegian bank and, thanks to this early warning, the Norwegian bank was able to limit the detrimental consequences of the attack. Also, upon further investigation the Norwegian bank found reason to believe that other Norwegian banks suffered compromised customers as well, and duly warned the banks. This is a vivid example of vigilance exercised by banks, and also illustrates the positive proactive attitude of cooperation among banks when it comes to security.

Several banks subscribe to a Computer Emergency Response Team (CERT). In several countries CERTs are government bodies. CERTs are manned with highly qualified technicians who analyze traffic and traffic patterns, looking for possible attacks. In a recent attack in Norway, the Norwegian national CERT played a prominent role in analyzing the Trojan and also in using its power to convince the ISPs to close down IP addresses of the command and control center of the Trojan.

The Banks try to educate customers. In a prominent place on their web sites, the Banks inform the customers on how to avoid becoming victims of attacks. This seems to have some effect. Norwegian banks recently experienced a massive e-mail phishing attack. Approximately 100,000 customers of one Norwegian bank received an e-mail containing a link to a phishing web site asking the customer to enter her log-in credentials, allegedly so that the credential could be verified. Many customers reported to the bank that they had been subject to a phishing attack, and very few had submitted their log-in credentials to the phishing site. The bank itself attributes this partly to the public being aware and alert, and partly to the fact that the wording in the e-mail did not fully comply with idiomatic Norwegian.

1.8.2 On-demand Protection Measures

In certain countries Internet banks use solutions for authenticating customers that are also used to authenticate the customers in other web sites [16]; that is, there is one authentication server serving all sites. The solution often employs OTP codes as part of the authentication. This implies that any OTP code would be valid for any one of the web sites, including the Internet bank. As the authentication solution gains ground, more and more web sites ask customers for their credentials. Previously the authentication credentials were submitted in the context of the Internet bank only. Now, people are being prompted for log-in credentials in different contexts, e.g., for various online shops, for log-in to public services, etc. Under these new circumstances, it is harder for the public to exercise vigilance and ask, "Who is behind this web site asking for my credentials?" Because they cannot exercise control, people will tend to become less critical regarding to whom they submit log-in credentials. This provides a case for phishing. An attacker could purport to be an online shop and phish log-in credentials and then use the credentials to log into the Internet bank. Or a web site which is authorized to accept credentials for authentication could use the credentials for unauthorized purposes, defrauding the customer. In order to combat this threat, the organization behind the authentication solution has come up with the idea of a context-sensitive OTP. This means that the OTP will be issued per web site; i.e., a phished OTP would be valid only in the context of one particular web site. An OTP obtained in connection with online shopping could not be used to log on to an online bank. This would remove the prime motivation for the phisher.

Many online banking authentication solutions are roaming; i.e., the customer may gain access to her Internet bank from PCs anywhere using the same authentication mechanism. This provides a case for phishing, inasmuch as the phished authentication credentials may be instantly used by the attacker from his PC. To counter this portability aspect of authentication, banks are known to build a table with Media Access Control (MAC) addresses and matching log-on IDs; they build this table by recording the MACs that the user regularly uses. If there is an attack, by looking up in this table, for any one customer the bank would check the MAC address and allow access only from this address or a limited number of other machines that the customer has been using.

1.9 Information Sharing for Infrastructure Protection

The need to protect CIs from all hazards (including both natural and man-made disasters and terrorism, as well as cyber-related threat or large-scale physical attacks) has been widely recognized in the US, especially after 9/11. The American Presidential Decision Directive 63 (PDD-63) of May 1998, updated in 2003 by the Homeland Security Presidential Directive 7, set up a national program of critical infrastructure protection (CIP) [2], and the federal government asked each CI sector to establish sector-specific information sharing organizations to share information, within each sector, about threats and vulnerabilities to that sector. In response, many sectors established Information Sharing and Analysis Centers (ISACs) to meet this need.

An ISAC [3] is defined as a trusted, sector-specific entity which performs the following functions:

- provides to its constituency a 24/7 secure operating capability that establishes specific information sharing/intelligence requirements for incidents, threats, and vulnerabilities
- collects, analyzes, and disseminates alerts and incident reports to its membership based on its sector focused subject matter analytical expertise
- helps the government understand impacts for its sector
- provides an electronic, trusted capability for its membership to exchange and share information on cyber, physical, and all other threats in order to defend the critical infrastructure
- shares and provides analytical support to government and other ISACs regarding technical sector details and mutual information sharing and assistance during actual or potential sector disruptions caused by intentional, accidental, or natural events

Today there are fourteen ISACs for CI including the Financial Services, Electric, Energy, and Surface Transportation sectors. When considered collectively, the individual private/public sector ISACs cover approximately 85% of the US CI.

There are ample real-world cases of cyber attacks against financial institutions with potentially grave consequences for the institutions as such and society at large.

The London Stock Exchange (LSE) is reporting (http://www.v3.co.uk/v3-uk/news/2031245/london-stock-exchange-cyber-attack) that the LSE and an unspecified US stock exchange were targeted by attackers intending to disrupt the markets. The LSE is investigating an attack at its headquarters last year; the US exchange has attributed an attack on its system to Russia. A May 6, 2010 flash crash (a large, short-lived decline in prices) saw the Dow Jones Industrial Average plummet 1000 points in one day. A similar event occurred at the LSE in August 2010. It has been claimed that the LSE systems are not Internet based, but such claims often are misleading. As was pointed out earlier, financial systems are interconnected. For example, a system is often being maintained remotely by means of devices that are connected to the Internet.

The Financial Services Information Sharing and Analysis Center (FS/ISAC) was established in 1999 by the Financial Services sector in response to the PDD-63 to enhance that sector's ability to prepare for and respond to cyber and physical threats, vulnerabilities, and incidents, and to serve as the primary communications channel for the sector [1]. There are six levels of service, ranging from Basic Participants to Platinum Founding Members. The FS/ISAC is owned by its members. The FS/ISAC Board of Directors, elected by the membership, determines member eligibility, enforces member eligibility verification through trusted third parties, and oversees the operation of the FS/ISAC.

The mission of the FS/ISAC is to facilitate sharing of information pertaining to physical and cyber threats, vulnerabilities, incidents, and potential protective measures and practices, and to disseminate trusted and timely information intended to increase sector-wide knowledge about physical and cyber security operational risks faced by the Financial Services sector.

All incoming information is sent to analysts for reviewing and scoring. Collected data is analyzed in the ISAC's Secure Operations Center (SOC) by financial services sector experts to determine technical validity, indications of a broader problem, trends, etc. A team of analysts and security professionals within the FS/ISAC assess each submission regarding the seriousness of the vulnerability or attack to identify patterns. Once a vulnerability or incident is analyzed, it can be categorized as Normal, Urgent, or Crisis, depending on the risk to the Financial Services sector. After the analysis, alerts are delivered to participants. Participants will receive Crisis and Urgent alert notifications within 15 minutes after receipt by the SOC. Alerts typically contain not only the details of the threat but also information about how to mitigate the threat.

Alert dissemination to participants is supported by the Critical Infrastructure Notification System (CINS), which allows critical alerts to be sent to multiple recipients near simultaneously, as well as to provide user authentication and confirmed delivery. The system uses multiple mediums including landline telephone, cellular telephone, pager, e-mail, and Short Message Service (SMS) messaging. Participants receiving Crisis or Urgent alert notifications must access the FS/ISAC web site for specific information relating to these notifications using their access credentials to log on and authenticate themselves. Each member is associated with a user profile that allows for filtering of notifications in order to receive advisement only when a relevant issue arises, and ensure that only meaningful alerts are delivered.

FS/ISAC members may regularly search and retrieve information from the FS/ISAC database. Information in the database is available via secure, encrypted web-based connections only to authorized members at the appropriate service level. Information available through the web site includes new threats and vulnerabilities, geographic distribution of attack sources, real-time news feeds, and other relevant data.

In order to deliver the FS/ISAC services to the members, FS/ISAC has established a business relationship with a service provider, represented by VeriSign. The FS/ISAC and the service provider have a formal SLA for the various services. The status of the IT infrastructure that supports FS/ISAC services and hosts the web portal is continuously and actively monitored, and on at least an annual basis a formal, documented penetration test of the web portal is performed by a third party.

The value of the information sharing for facilitating early intrusion and fraud detection cannot be overstated. Modern cyber security relies on analytics (see Sect. 1.7), and the identification of suspicious patterns is expedited combining information from multiple sources. Below we elaborate on how banks and society at large may derive value from cooperating and exchanging data.

1.9.1 Value n.1: Based on a Real-World Example Illustrating Potential Benefits

In late 2010 one bank was alerted that items on a drop list indicated that attackers were targeting the bank's customers. Figure 1.3 shows a log of some of the events and steps taken by the bank in order to combat the attack. Note that not all events are listed, as will be evident from the broken number sequence in column one.

With the risk of losing out on the subtleties of this attack, the brief list of events shown in Fig. 1.3 in itself gives rise to afterthoughts:

- The list of events shows that eight days go by and still the attack is not contained—on day eight newly compromised IDs are posted to the drop site.
- Bank 2 seems to be more mature and knowledgeable when it comes to handling malware. On its own initiative, Bank 2 alerts Bank 1 and makes its expertise available to Bank 1. The cyber police bring in expertise on how the malware works and consequently on how countermeasures should be designed. This leads one to think that if Bank 2 and the cyber police had coordinated their efforts early on, the lead time for developing effective countermeasures might have been shorter.
- The cooperation between the banks and between the banks and the cyber police seems informal and based more or less on good will. One cannot help thinking that a more formal cooperation and exchange of information might further benefit the parties involved. Countermeasures might then be ready at an earlier stage, reducing detrimental consequences of attacks and protecting society as a whole against attacks.

Event #	Day #	Time	Event
1	1	14:48	Bank1 is notified about infections
3	1	16:05	Logon attempt from UK IP
4	1	16:35	Bank2 sends Bank1 link to drop site
5	2	09:00	Bank 1 analyzes the information received from Bank 2
6	2	09:10	Bank 1 comes across login information of customers of Bank 3, and duly warns Bank 3.
16	3	13:04	Bank 1 analyzes the configuration file of the infection that Bank 1 has received from Bank 2.
17	3	18:45	Customer records are collected from drop site
20	3	20:56	Analysis of the configuration file reveals how the customer may recognize if the PC is infected.
26	4	09:10	The certificates of compromised customers are revoked.
29	4	09:16	The recent transaction history of compromised customers is analyzed.
37	4	12:38	The Financial Supervisory Authority of Norway is notified of the attack.
45	4	13:04	All certificates of compromised customers are revoked.
47	4	13:10	There is a successful logon from a PC in UK.
48	4	13:43	The infected PCs of compromised customers are collected.
53	4	14:10	There are telephone calls with the cyber police.
78	7	10:55	Bank1 receives samples of the Zeus virus from the cyber police.
81	7	12:02	Discussions with the cyber police about how the Zeus virus works.
104	8	09:21	New "stolen" login credentials are posted to drop site.
...	...	...	...

Fig. 1.3 Anatomy of an attack

1.9.2 Value n.2: Knowledge Dissemination

Many times it is hard to determine what to look for (hard to find the attack signature). Cooperation may help determine the signature early on. Malware authors go to great lengths in programming the malware so that it is difficult to discover the malware, it is difficult to remove, and it is hard to unravel how it works, e.g., the IP of the command and control center. The configuration file is encrypted several times. In one recent attack with SpyEye malware, the configuration file was encrypted twice. After being decrypted, the cleartext revealed that the malware targeted nearly 90 different banks. Hence there is a case for cooperation when it comes to analyzing malware attacks in that all copies of the configuration file will disclose which banks are targeted.

1.9.3 Value n.3: Increase Likelihood of Discovery

Looking at aggregated data from several banks may increase the likelihood of discovering an attack as compared to looking at data from one bank only. Aggregated data may show that there are multiple attempts originating from one and the same IP address to break into different Internet banks. In order to discover this, you would have to have data from more than one bank.

Cards being issued by different issuers belonging to one person being used in two different parts of the world at around the same time would be an indication of card fraud. It would take data from several issuers to see this.

The list of examples may be extended; the point is that not only the volume of data itself would increase the likelihood of discovery. Some attacks you simply cannot unravel looking at one bank in isolation, whereas looking at data from several banks would make the attack stand out.

1.9.4 Value n.4: Illicit Transactions That Span Banks

Money laundering is the act of passing illicit money through the payment system in an attempt to "wash off stains" from illegal actions of the money. One way to do this is to pass the money through a long chain of transferals and obfuscate the source of the money on the way so that in the end the illegal origin is no longer visible. Hence the money is being transferred between accounts, banks, and even countries. To trace this long chain of transferals banks will have to cooperate. Pooling data from several banks and analyzing the data could well reveal transfer patterns that seem to have no other purpose than to obfuscate the origin.

1.9.5 Value n.5: Shared Platform for Systems Development (Extended Applications)

Banks may find it beneficial to pool resources and develop applications together. For a number of years banks in Norway have developed applications together in several areas. Recently the banks developed a common system for authentication to be used by web sites, Internet banks being example sites. In this system there is one national authentication server. The user experience is that one and the same user ID is used for all web sites. Banks in Norway have also developed a national debit card scheme; card issued by any bank is accepted at all ATM and POS terminals, regardless of which bank is responsible for the terminal. There have been a number of similar joint development projects; examples are:

- e-invoicing business to business [15]
- debit cards
- clearing systems
- systems for standing orders

1.9.6 Value n.6: Economies of Scale

Substantial resources are being spent daily by FIs on security. It seems to be a common position among FIs that security is not a competition issue. In many areas, such as Internet banking, FIs face basically identical threats. Hence there is a case for cooperation in this area; potentially there are huge economies of scale to be had.

In the example of the recent attack against Norwegian banks, the banks claim unanimously that the coordination that took place was of great value to them. The first bank that was hit alerted the other banks, which raised their alert level. Once the encrypted configuration file was broken into, information about which banks were listed in the configuration file was swiftly distributed to the relevant banks. Transfers through the SWIFT system in all banks were monitored closely. Automated processing was switched off, and transactions were manually controlled before submitting them. One fraudulent transaction was sent over the SWIFT network to an account in a Portuguese bank. The Portuguese bank was alerted, and the transaction was reversed.

1.9.7 Value n.7: Aggregate Threat Picture

It takes time and resources to develop protection strategies against cyber threats. In order to be prepared, it is important that the FIs have detailed knowledge about the threat so that they may develop strategies to neutralize it. In the absence of co-ordination, each FI would monitor report and treat threats and attacks in its own individual way. We find that the different forms, formats, descriptions, and classi-fications that exist between FIs make it almost impossible to aggregate statistics to arrive at a composite threat picture for a region, country, or business type. Recogniz-ing this challenge, in Norway there has been an effort to harmonize the reporting of credit card losses, Internet banking losses, and undesirable events occurring within the EDP operation of the banks. The work so far has proven fruitful inasmuch as there is now a better understanding of the overall loss and incident situation in Nor-way. But there still is a long way to go. Needless to say, if low-level traffic data from all banks were subject to massive analysis, it would be much easier to arrive at a uniform, composite threat picture that would reflect on the situation within all participating banks. This could be used to furnish supervisors on a country level or EU level with a near-time, precise threat picture.

1.9.8 Value n.8: Uniform Reporting

Post the 2008 financial crash, the reporting burden has increased. Reports today come in disparate form, format, timeliness, and accuracy. Our recommendation is to pool resources, set up a development bed, and develop jointly uniform reporting systems. Then arrive at an aggregate report on a national/EU level.

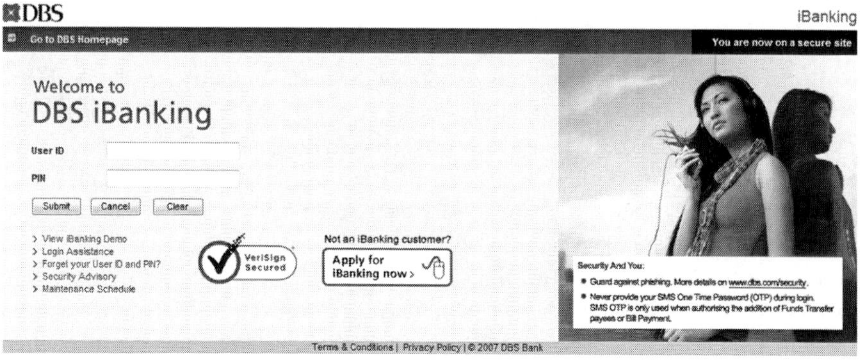

Fig. 1.4 Proper log-in page of DBS Bank

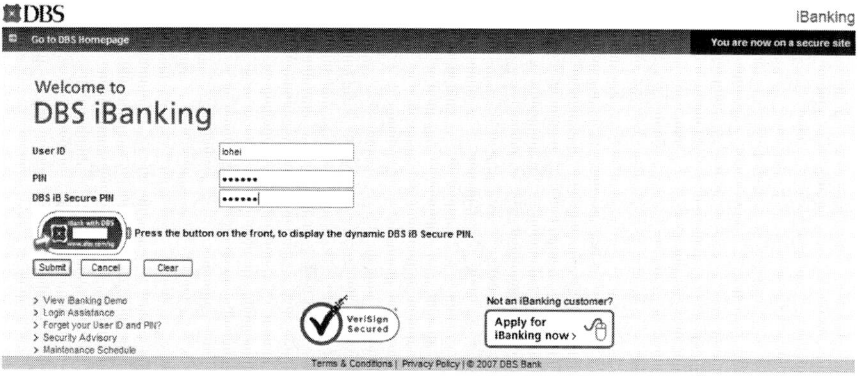

Fig. 1.5 Log-in page of DBS Bank produced by the malware

1.10 Collaboration and Information Sharing Between Banks: A Case Study

In February 2011 customers of several Norwegian banks were infected with SpyZeus, a powerful malware. SpyZeus is the result of a recent merger between SpyEye and ZeuS. SpyEye, which does much the same thing as ZeuS, came on strong in 2010 as a competitive rival to ZeuS. SpyEye is much more modular than ZeuS, and it makes the creation of additional plug-ins and extensions easier. There are many more plug-ins in SpyEye than in ZeuS to customize tasks, such as stealing credit card information. The extent of the infection, during week seven, was that about 2000 computers were infected.

Recognizing that this book is intended for an international audience, we have included an example of an infected log-in page stemming from an English-speaking bank rather than a Norwegian one. Figure 1.4 illustrates the proper log-in page, while the log-in page produced by the malware is shown in Fig. 1.5.

SpyZeus has configuration files for attacking specific countries and a user-friendly interface that is available in different languages. Still, the quality of the content of the configuration file does not seem to be fully developed. In the Norwegian version of the malware, there are a few eye-catching spelling mistakes and odd phrases. This weakness of the virus had been identified by many Norwegian customers who did not enter the fake site.

In the wake of a malware attack, we often see phishing attacks exploiting fear among the public that their IDs have been compromised. In the aftermath of the attack against the Norwegian banks, customers received e-mails purporting to be from their bank, in which the customer was asked to confirm log-in details, supposedly so that the bank would be able verify that the customer ID was not compromised. Of approximately one million recipients of phishing e-mails, only less than one hundred are reported to have submitted their authentication credentials. This fact is indicative of the vigilance and security awareness level of the public in Norway. The number of defrauded customers is very low, indicating that the public is highly security aware. This is an indication that the FIs have been successful in their attempt to educate their customers as to security risks that they face.

During log-in, the Trojan presents a false log-in page. When this happened, one bank had certain log entries posted to the bank's web-server log. The bank identified the signature of the log entry and developed an automated process that recognizes the signature, stops the log-in, and also automatically and instantly revokes the log-in credentials of the customer. Sharing this information allowed other banks to implement similar countermeasures. Analysis revealed that at the time of writing this, the Trojan is very context sensitive; i.e., a small change to the web of the Internet bank would fool the Trojan. This suggests that using random names for JavaScript functions and CSS class names would make the Trojan unable to recognize where to inject the malicious code and probably render the Trojan useless or less effective.

One important quality of a Trojan is its ability to hide itself. Encryption, hashing, and other techniques are being used for this. If the obfuscation techniques are elaborate, it takes resources and expertise to break them. Together the banks were able to "undress" the Trojan effectively. Once it was "undressed", the banks were able to devise effective countermeasures.

For more than 20 years, Norwegian banks have cooperated closely in the IT security area. Pooling resources, small and larger banks alike have developed resilient and uniform security systems enjoyed by all banks and their customers. Even though there are several different Internet banks being used, the system used for authenticating customers used by most Internet banks is jointly developed by the banks.

Banks exchange intelligence information related to IT security and together develop contingency solutions and emergency fixes. Once they were under attack, the banks swiftly convened under the auspices of a banking security organization; they were in day-to-day contact. In this way intelligence information was coordinated. Likewise, contact with other organizations, like the Norwegian National Security Authority (NSM), took place in a coordinated way.

This coordinated defense approach produced a number of countermeasures and other information that was shared between the banks.

An example of the coordinated defense approach is described here. The NSM discovered the attack. As the attack progressed, NSM sent regular updates containing more details on the progression and characteristics. It also notified banks and ISPs about which PCs had been infected. NSM did a comprehensive technical analysis of the specific malware (for example, a SpyEye-based attack) to be shared by all FIs. During this they discovered the IP of the command and control (C&C) center. By contacting the Norwegian ISPs, they were able to monitor the amount of traffic going from Norwegian customers to the C&C. In this way they got a picture of the severity of the attack, and also steps could be taken to close down the attack sites.

1.11 Information Sharing Against Cyber Crime in Italy

As far as cyber crime against the financial institutions is concerned, as we pointed out in the previous section, it is crucial to be able to quickly exchange updated information among the whole community of involved stakeholders. When a crime is committed against some financial target, the overall impact has to be analyzed on a chain of different players, ranging from service providers to mobile telecom operators, public institutions, law enforcement agencies (LEAs), payment systems, and end users, whose co-operation then becomes of paramount relevance to stop the consequent fraud, repress crime, and prevent its reappearance in the future. Two very good examples are represented nowadays by two initiatives realized in Italy, respectively led by the Italian Banking Association (ABI) and Poste Italiane.

1.11.1 Financial Institutions Information Sharing Working Group

The most important initiative specifically dedicated to creating a trusted community within the financial sector to exchange operative information about cyber crime, refers to a collaboration network promoted and run by the ABI, in the framework of its research and innovation center, ABI Lab. The network has been joined by more than 200 banks, Poste Italiane, the LEAs entitled to prevent and repress electronic crime (e.g., Polizia Postale e delle Comunicazioni), and the main telecommunications operators. Activities are steered by a Technical Committee consisting of the main ICT security teams in the Italian financial sector, coming from banks and service providers, who physically gather once every six weeks to monitor trends in cyber crime scenarios, share best practices, and plan initiatives to be implemented at the system level. The Technical Committee is chaired by ABI Lab, who leads the activities and is in charge of developing the community through specific tools and coordination of the offline communications among members. In this group framework, many actions have been realized so far, ranging from lobbying public institutions to raising customer awareness, from forming technical focus groups to defining guidelines for banks.

1.11.2 Presidio Internet

From an operative point of view, a sub-group has been created among the whole constituency regarding where to share information useful to counter cyber crime; it is called Presidio Internet. Presidio Internet is joined on a voluntary basis, and at the end of 2010 it was counting on more than 300 trusted peers, among banks, LEAs, centrally acknowledged by the Italian Banking Association through ABI Lab. Information is exchanged through a dedicated mailing list, where members define the confidentiality level to label the data they want to send and choose the security measures to eventually code the message. To this end, Pretty Good Privacy (PGP) keys are exchanged between members in case information needs to be encrypted. Governance of the information exchange is kept very simple, as unstructured data are also welcomed, and the ABI holds only a supervising role; it is not mandatorily asked to acknowledge if eventual messages are privately exchanged by two members. Still, the ABI plays the role of a third body, so it is possible to use it as a channel to anonymize information to be sent to the list. Each peer is asked to participate in the information exchange via a unique, highly recognizable interface, setting up a dedicated corporate e-mail address. Most importantly, members have agreed on the basic rule *"no obligation to share, nor to share everything"*, which means that each one of them is allowed to choose how deeply to contribute to the information exchange. A crucial role to make things work effectively is played by the availability of LEAs to be part of an informal exchange of information. This allows members to be covered in case sensitive information must be communicated, as it would appear as a complaint filed to law enforcement.

ABI Lab continuously feeds the network with information from partnered info-providers, ICT security companies, specific mailing lists, international research centers, free alerting services, online resources, and European groups active in the field.

Information is exchanged on three different levels of confidentiality and can be addressed to one single member of the network, to a restricted sub-group, or to the whole constituency, either anonymously (via ABI Lab intermediation) or directly, as summarized in Fig. 1.6.

Operative information shared on the list refers to current threats and possible actions required of members, including informal requests for assistance to LEAs. Specifically, information shared on the list nowadays includes:

- malicious URLs, also sent to a blocking network and LEAs (approximately 100/week)
- stolen credentials recovered on malware drop zones (approximately 30 Mb/week)
- IP addresses from which fraud has been committed
- mobile telephone accounts used to charge credit from frauded credentials
- information regarding money mules activity
- phishing kits
- malware information from configuration files

Further, a monthly report to sketch trends, new threats, and possible countermeasures is produced and distributed to the whole constituency.

WARNING	Description	1-to-1	1-to-many	1-to-all	encryption
System Warning	Public information put together to point out an alert on ongoing threats potentially targeting the whole system			✓	✓
General Warning	Public or private information which could have a direct impact on development of digital crimes throughout the system, with a low criticality	✓	✓	✓	✓
Specific Warning	Critical information on threats targeting one specific bank, coming from mostly private sources or LEAs, which require a real time reaction by that bank	✓			✓

Fig. 1.6 Information exchange in Presidio Internet

Last, with reference to contexts where information is collected, three initiatives worth mentioning have been started in Europe, with the aim of gathering expertise on the subject and proposing action plans to the relevant communitarian institutions:

- IT Fraud Working Group (European Banking Federation) is promoted by the European Banking Federation for sharing information on Internet fraud and discussing relevant initiatives activated by national banking associations.
- FI-ISAC Financial Institutions Information Sharing and Analysis Center (ENISA) is promoted by ENISA with the aim of focusing on all the issues related to electronic crimes, also through a dedicated mailing list. Constituency: banks, national banking associations, CERTs, and LEAs.
- ISSG/CISEG Cyber Crime Information Sharing Expert Group (European Payments Council) provides information sharing about cyber crime in the European community and defines formal documents supporting EPC initiatives in its definition of a roadmap to Single Euro Payments Area (SEPA).

1.11.3 Collaboration Between Banks and LEAs

Starting from the good experience and connections created in the framework of Presidio Internet activities, in 2010 a formal agreement was signed between the ABI and Polizia Postale e delle Comunicazioni, to make banks and LEAs share information on electronic crimes via a central database, owned and managed by the LEAs themselves. Technical interfaces have been jointly defined and each bank is allowed to upload data and/or information relevant to investigation and analysis purposes. A format has also been defined to collect information on frauds that have already been committed as well as on potentially suspect operations. Thus the information flow is more structured than the one on Presidio Internet, and it is not allowed for the banks to communicate with each other, but each bank receives feedback from the LEAs and is warned if it is involved in some suspect operation. The benefits of this cooperation system are twofold. From a police perspective, having more structured data can help speed up an investigation process and provide more useful information on where to implement automatic intelligence and semantic analyses. From a banking system perspective, besides benefiting from a faster investigation, it is also possible to monitor the state of processing of the events, and each bank is able to access some aggregation of data, which is also useful in defining internal security policies.

1.11.4 The European Electronic Crime Task Force

The European Electronic Crime Task Force (EECTF) was founded in 2009 on the basis of a formal agreement between Poste Italiane, the United States Secret Services, and the Italian LEAs called Polizia Postale e delle Comunicazioni, who shared the mission to support the analysis and development of best practices against cyber crime in European countries through the creation of a strategic alliance between law enforcement, academic, legal, and private sector entities.

A governance model has been set up by the founding members, according to which an invitation to participate has been extended thereafter to the main stakeholders playing a lead role in countering cyber crime. Nowadays the EECTF is run via monthly meetings of permanent members, quarterly open events extended to a wide community of selected experts, and continuous sharing of relevant information within the whole community, also through dedicated specific tools.

The constituency of the EECTF is made up of founding members, permanent members, and a community of experts. Founding members are entitled to steer activities and define strategy, define policies for information sharing within and outside the community, define partnerships and decide new memberships, define outputs and dissemination strategies, and maintain the knowledge base. Permanent members are asked to actively participate in the community, with specific reference to share information according to a non-disclosure agreement, attend monthly expert group meetings, speak at quarterly plenary meetings, contribute to the growth of the knowledge base, propose new members, review and contribute to research outputs, and interact with each other via the members portal. The community of experts is continuously selected by EECTF founding members among LEAs, public institutions, banks and financial intermediaries, ICT, and a consultancy, and also from proposals made by permanent members. The community today has more than 200 members, who are invited to attend quarterly plenary meetings, are evaluated as a basis for potential new members, and who receive briefs of research outputs.

With the aim of collecting all of the available information and sharing best practices at an international level, the EECTF has been establishing international collaborations with some of the most relevant organizations, such as the European Network and Information Security Agency (ENISA), the Anti-Phishing Working Group, and the Digital Crimes Consortium. From a national point of view, links have been established with the Ministry of Economics and Finance and the Ministry of Internal Affairs, as well as the Italian Banking Association and the Information Sharing Working Group mentioned in the previous paragraph.

In order to make the most out of the competencies of the whole community of the EECTF, an Expert Group has been set up, which gathers on a monthly basis and is restricted to only founding and permanent members, with the aim of sharing highly technical information about new threats and possible countermeasures.

In order to identify trends and depict current scenarios, the EECTF has been carrying out yearly surveys on cyber crime in Europe by gathering reports, information, and analyses made by the key players in the field, including businesses, LEAs, and security intelligence experts at the international level. Key findings of the 2011 survey [14] point out characteristics of the cyber crime scenario, from both an operational point of view, sketching attack schemes and relevant countermeasures, and an organizational one, underlining a basic discrepancy between real threats and perceived risks, stressing the consequent need for a closer cooperation among the whole community of stakeholders.

A possible evolution at a strategic level of the EECTF depicts main goals on the medium term, which can be summed up in two directions: growth of community and growth of capabilities. If it is true that community grows on new memberships, it must also be considered that it grows above all with the increase of trust among members and the use of community tools, making it deeper and more reliable. The capabilities of the EECTF will grow together with the possibility to count on a wider knowledge base and on a plethora of specific competencies made available by each member.

1.12 Compliance to EU Regulation on Data Privacy

Financial institutions have to comply with several requirements as mandated for IT management and for data security. These standards identify three main security parameters: confidentiality, integrity, and availability. In this section we describe those regulations that are most relevant to information sharing and their implications for the deployment and use of collaborative platforms like the one presented in Part II of the book.

Directive 95/46/EC of the European Parliament and of the Council of 24 October 1995 on the protection of individuals with regard to the processing of personal data and the free movement of such data, requires Member States to protect the rights and freedoms of natural persons with regard to the processing of personal data, and in particular their right to privacy, in order to ensure the free flow of personal data in the community. The directive defines personal data as any information relating to an identified or identifiable natural person. An identifiable person is one who can be identified, directly or indirectly, in particular by reference to an identification number or to one or more factors specific to his physical, physiological, mental, economic, cultural, or social identity.

Directive 2002/58/EC of the European Parliament and of the Council of 12 July 2002 concerning the processing personal data and the protection of privacy in the electronic communications sector (directive on privacy and electronic communications) translates the principles set out in Directive 95/46/EC into specific rules for the electronic communications sector.

Articles 5, 6, and 9 of Directive 2002/58/EC state the rules applicable to the processing by network and service providers of traffic and location data generated by using electronic communications services. Such data must be erased or made anonymous when no longer needed for the purpose of the transmission of communication, except for the data necessary for billing or interconnection payments. Subject to consent, certain data may be processed for marketing purposes and the provision of value added services.

Article 15(1) of Directive 2002/58/EC states the conditions under which Member States may restrict the scope of the rights and obligations provided for in Article 5, Article 6, Article 8(1), (2), (3), and (4), and Article 9 of that directive. Any such restrictions must be necessary, appropriate, and proportionate within a democratic society for specific public order purposes, i.e., to safeguard national security (i.e., state security), defense, public security, or the prevention, investigation, detection, and prosecution of criminal offenses or of unauthorized use of the electronic communications system.

Under Article 8 of the European Convention for Protection of Human Rights and Fundamental Freedoms (ECHR), everyone has the right to respect for his private life and his correspondence. Public authorities may interfere with the exercise of that right only in accordance with the law and where necessary in a democratic society, inter alia, in the interests of national security or public safety, for the prevention of disorder or crime, or for the protection of the rights and freedoms of others.

Article 15(1) of Directive 2002/58/EC applies to data, including data relating to unsuccessful call attempts, the retention of which is not specifically required under this directive and therefore falls outside the scope thereof, and to retention for purposes including judicial purposes, other than those covered by this directive.

Article 30(1)(c) of Directive 95/46/EC requires the consultation of the Working Party on the Protection of Individuals with regard to the processing of Personal Data established under Article 29 of that directive.

Council Framework Decision 2005/222/JHA of 24 February 2005 on attacks against information systems provides that the intentional illegal access to information systems, including the data retained therein, is to be made punishable as a criminal offense.

According to Article 23 of Directive 95/46/EC, any person who has suffered damage as a result of an unlawful processing operation or of any act incompatible with national provisions adopted pursuant to that directive is to receive compensation.

The 2001 Council of Europe Convention on Cybercrime and the 1981 Council of Europe Convention for the Protection of Individuals with Regard to Automatic Processing of Personal Data also applies.

Articles 7 and 8 of the Charter of Fundamental Rights of the European Union defines citizens' fundamental right to respect for private life and communications and to the protection of their personal data.

Directive 2006/24/EC of the European Parliament and of the Council of 15 March 2006 on the retention of data generated or processed in connection with the provision of publicly available electronic communications services or of public communications networks has been highly debated in many countries. Under much controversy and with a very slim margin, the directive was finally adopted by Norway on 4 March 2011.

Many EU countries have legislation on a national level covering data privacy. In Norway there is both a law and a regulation pertaining to protection of personal data. In line with the EU definition, personal data is defined as any data relating to one individual. Processing of personal data is defined as being any use of the information, e.g., collection, registration, compilation, storage and distribution or a combination of such. Personal data may be processed on the condition that the person has given her consent, or if the law paves the way for processing, or if operation on personal data is necessary in order to do the following:

1. to honor an agreement with the person, or to prepare for such an agreement,
2. for the operator to be able to fulfill a contractual obligation,
3. to defend the person's vital interests,
4. to perform a task of public interest,
5. to exercise public authority,
6. for the operator or a third party to whom the data is handed over, to maintain a valid interest, subject to the person's data privacy interests not being greater than said interest.

We conclude that the basic premise is that information relating to a person is to be kept private. Within the strict privacy rules of the current legislation, the question is then whether there is room for a collaborative system that collects, shares, correlates, distributes, and mixes and matches data. Under what conditions may such a system work?

Each person whose transaction data is to be received and processed by a collaborative platform would have to give her individual consent. Customer contracts would have to be amended to include provisions for data sharing, data protection, data processing, and data deletion. Any collaborative platform would have to guarantee that the data is maintained according to the provisions set out in the contract throughout the lifetime of the data.

The collaborative platform would have to maintain the data according to best practices when it comes to securing integrity, confidentiality, and availability. Data in transit would have to be end-to-end encrypted; i.e., the endpoints of the encryption tunnel would have to be either the data owner or a custodian approved by the data owner, the provider of the collaborative platform being one such custodian. Data at rest should be encrypted. Access to data should be granted on a need basis, which means that there should be a hierarchy of encryption keys; one key giving access to limited amounts of data, and other keys granting access to larger data sets.

1.13 Concluding Remarks: Offline Collaborative Systems for Information Sharing

This chapter introduced the financial critical information infrastructure (CII) concept and the different types of stakeholders that may operate upon this specific communication infrastructure. Financial institutions and the communication network they use shall be considered one more type of CII to be protected, as well as other CII types such as the utility infrastructure and food supply chain. Nevertheless, financial CIIs have specific features and suffer different types of attacks than the other critical infrastructure types. The Norwegian CII has been described to exemplify required communication infrastructure characteristics and existing risks. Over the last 20 years financial CIIs have evolved according to new business models. The new communication channels that have been included at the edge of financial CIIs do not provide the same performance and security guarantees offered by traditional channels, thus creating vulnerabilities to cyber attacks. Transaction security is based upon software products to be installed at endpoints (such as VPN and crypto tools) and a set of process steps to be implemented by customers (such as an OTC-based identification process). It has opened the door to new challenges and new types of attacks that change their behavior over time, in turn starting a never-ending loop of implementation of countermeasures to face attacks that evolve over time, and thus requiring newly evolved countermeasures. Short descriptions of standard implemented countermeasures are provided. In this battlefield the financial stakeholders have discovered that coordination and information sharing may be strong weapons that reinforce all implemented countermeasures and speed up their deployment. Another important countermeasure relies upon information sharing with customers who are informed on how to reinforce their endpoints and on how they should react to threats. Some real-world cases exemplify the importance of information sharing. The creation of team experts to analyze threats is another way to react to threats. This is of special importance for viruses and malware that may be injected at any level of the CII, including endpoints. The expert team may "undress" the Trojans and identify antidotes to infection and procedures to neutralize the attack. This information may then be circulated to financial stakeholders in order to set up countermeasures.

However, the circulation of information and the corresponding analysis is done on a periodic basis that is too long, mainly through reports on mailing lists and physical meetings (such as Presidio Internet). This low frequency does not help in setting adequate countermeasures to attacks that take a very short time to be carried out. One of the most known collaborative systems for information sharing at the networking level is Dshield [6]. DShield could be seen as a world-wide sensor network that collects data coming from the firewalls and the IDSs of volunteers. Currently, it covers 500,000 IP addresses over 50 countries. The data collected by the DShield system are sent to the Internet Storm Center, inserted in the central database, and analyzed offline by the staff of Internet Storm Center, called *handlers*, in order to detect spikes or malicious activities or evidence that an attack is taking place. This allows the creation of statistics about the most targeted ports, the top attackers, and the risk of worm outbreaks. A particular feature enabled for the active participants of Dshield is *fightback*, DShield forwards an authenticated mail to the ISPs of the identified attackers, which allows, in the case of massive attacks (such as DDoSs or Distributed Bruteforce), a quick response that can mitigate the attack. This system is based on a strong human component (the *handlers* of the Internet Storm Center). The team analyzes the records in the databases using aggregation tools, and if it finds evidence of a new attack it can alert the owners of the local sensors to ask for more data. If the attack is considered particularly dangerous, they can alert the core Internet backbone providers involved, and they may activate possible countermeasures. Apparently DShield does not enable sector-specific information sharing; it is focused on generic information sharing for networked ISPs.

To conclude, while the importance of information sharing is widely recognized, there is still no legal-technical framework that can manage sharing and correlation of events (possibly on the fly) among organizations that belong to the same market sector or that have specific market relationships (such as the financial sector). The implementation of such a framework could potentially reduce the time of threat detection and reaction by raising the level of awareness of any organization participating in the information sharing. Very often organizations from the same sector suffer very similar specialized attacks. Part II of this book is devoted to the description of one of these frameworks.

References

1. Financial Services Information Sharing and Analysis Center (FS-ISAC). Helping to protect the critical infrastructure of the United States. Available online at: http://www.fsisac. com/files/FS-ISAC_Overview_2007_04_10.pdf
2. US Presidential Decisional Directive (PDD-63). Available online at: http://www.fas.org/ irp/offdocs/pdd/pdd-63.htm
3. The Role of Information Sharing and Analysis Centers (ISACs) in Private/Public Sector Critical Infrastructure Protection. Available online at: www.isaccouncil.org/whitepapers/ files/ISAC_Role_in_CIP.pdf
4. Commission of the European Communities, On a European Programme for Critical Infrastructure Protection, Green Paper (2005)
5. Jackson, W.D.: Homeland security: banking and financial infrastructure continuity, CRS Report for Congress (2004)
6. Bologna, S., Setola, R.: The need to improve local self-awareness in CIP/CIIP. In: Proceedings of the First IEEE International Workshop on Critical Infrastructure Protection (IWCIP05) (2005)
7. Guard, M.B., Guard, L.M.: Physical and digital threats to financial institutions in the wake of the terrorist attacks. Available online at: http://www.bankersonline.com/security/ cyberthreats.html

8. Basel II: Accord. Available online at: http://www.bis.org/bcbs/bcbscp3.htm
9. Basel II: Pillar One. Available online at: http://www.bis.org/bcbs/cp3part2.pdf
10. Basel II: Annex 9. Available online at: http://www.bis.org/bcbs/cp3annex.pdf
11. PCI Security Standard Council, Payment Card Industries (PCI): Data Security Standard Requirements and security assessment procedures. Available online at: https://www.pcisecuritystandards.org/security_standards/download.html?id=pci_dss_v1-2.pdf
12. Sommerville, I.: Software Engineering. Addison-Wesley, Reading (2001)
13. Federal Financial Institutions Examination Council (FFIEC): Information Security Booklet, Information Technology Examination Handbook (2006)
14. EECTF cyber cryme Survey (2011). http://www.poste.it/salastampa/CYBER_CRIME.pdf
15. www.elektroniskfaktura.com (2011)
16. Baldoni R.: Federated Identity Management systems in e-government: the case of Italy. Electron. Govern. Int. J. **1**, 64–84 (2012)

Chapter 2
Modeling and Risk Analysis of Information Sharing in the Financial Infrastructure

Walter Beyeler, Robert Glass, and Giorgia Lodi

Abstract This chapter defines the community of banks as a Complex Adaptive System of Systems (CASoS) and analyzes the value of information sharing as a general policy to protect the community against cyber attacks. We develop a model of interacting banks that have networks of business relations with a possible overlay network of shared information for cyber security. If a bank suffers a cyber attack, it incurs losses, and there is some probability that its infection will spread through the business network, imposing costs on its neighbors. Losses arising from financial system compromise continue until the problem is detected and remediated. The information sharing system allows detection events to be broadcast and also increases the probability of detecting the experimental probes that might precede the actual attack. Shared information is a public good: one institution's agreeing to share information speeds responses at other institutions, reducing their probability of initial compromise. Information sharing participation carries with it costs which must be balanced by direct expected gain or subsidized in order for a critical number of banks to agree to share information and to discourage free riding. The analysis described in this chapter examines the incentives that motivate banks to participate in information sharing, the benefits to the financial system that arise from their participation, and the ways in which banks' incentives might be shaped by policy to achieve a beneficial outcome for the system as a whole.

W. Beyeler (✉) · R. Glass
Sandia National Laboratories, New Mexico, Albuquerque, NM 87185, USA
e-mail: webeyel@sandia.gov

R. Glass
e-mail: rjglass@sandia.gov

G. Lodi
Consorzio Interuniversitario Nazionale Informatica (CINI), via Ariosto 25, Roma, Italy
e-mail: lodi@dis.uniroma1.it

R. Baldoni, G. Chockler (eds.), *Collaborative Financial Infrastructure Protection*,
DOI 10.1007/978-3-642-20420-3_2, © Springer-Verlag Berlin Heidelberg 2012

2.1 Introduction

The community of banks is a quintessential Complex Adaptive System of Systems, or CASoS. Each institutional bank is composed of a number of components (e.g., branches, ATM machines) and acts as a system, composed of technology, policy, and protocol, and manned by people who both make and implement decisions. In this way, adaptation occurs at multiple scales driven by the ability to provide for the customers. Banks are linked together into a community through the movement of funds from one to another (e.g., a payment system) and customers who can choose to move from bank to bank based on their view of the security of their funds and the cost of services. As such, the community of banks constitutes an adaptive system of systems. While this adaptive system of systems is indeed complicated, more importantly, it is complex. It is composed of a number of similarly behaving components that are linked together in similar ways, many of which implement binary decisions. For instance, do I keep my funds with this bank or move to another? These binary decisions are often influenced by a limited assessment of security and, frequently, reaction on the part of customers who may mimic the behavior of others. As such, emergent behavior ensues that is very difficult to predict except in stylized form and through statistical analysis.

Designing solutions within a CASoS, or CASoS Engineering, is a new and growing discipline [3, 5, 9]. Because many CASoS are high-consequence systems that contain people, CASoS Engineering requires that we first recognize the system for what it is and develop a model which reflects that system in a way that allows us to test design alternatives. Examples of the application of CASoS Engineering include financial payment system operation and cascading [1, 7, 8], the design of mitigation strategies for pandemic influenza [2, 6], and analysis of the global energy system to foster multi-scale security [4], to name a few. In this chapter, we begin our process at a very high level and consider the value of information sharing to the individual and the community of banks in the context of cyber attacks.

The rest of this chapter is organized as follows. The next section discusses the advantages and the current obstacles in adopting information sharing systems. Section 2.3 presents the problem of information sharing as a dynamic multi-player game. Section 2.4 introduces the model, representing how cyber attacks can impose costs on the financial system and the benefits that financial institutions can gain from information sharing. Specifically, the goals, limitations, and elements of the model are described as well as the possible evolution and the output metrics. Section 2.5 concludes the chapter.

2.2 Cyber Security as a Common Good: Balancing the Risks and Rewards of Sharing Information

System designs, such as the one presented in Part II of this book, counter the increasing threats that financial institutions face from cyber attacks. The perpetrators of these attacks, whether motivated by the prospect of financial gain or because they see such attacks as a means of garnering publicity or otherwise pursuing a political cause, benefit from sharing technology and other information among themselves. Banks can also use information sharing to help speed their detection of, and response to, such attacks. The benefits of having a robust, secure information sharing platform are clear, both for the system as a whole and for the individual financial institutions composing the system.

While we can stipulate that a financial system in which all participants share information related to cyber security will be more secure, with increased likelihood of attack detection, it is less clear that there is an incremental path from the current situation, in which no institutions share information or do so informally, to the more secure condition, in which all institutions share information. The path to complete participation may be blocked by the particular incentives to join that each institution faces.

Agreeing to share information entails some cost to the participating institution: these include the costs of acquiring and maintaining equipment, training the staff to use it, and integrating it into existing business practices. Although these expenses may be small in relation to existing operating costs, non-monetary costs might also have some influence on the decision to participate.

Incorporating any innovation into a functioning operation may be resisted on principle by inherently conservative institutions. This resistance would be especially important during the initial stages of adoption, when the favorable experience of peers is unavailable. Sharing information of any kind with competitors may be seen as a cost in that it might be exploited in some way for competitive advantage. System designs incorporate protection mechanisms (e.g., see Chap. 7) against this prospect, but anxiety on this account might still be a deterrent to adoption.

The benefits of information sharing include a decreased probability that a particular attack will be successful, and an increased rate of detection and recovery should an attack succeed. A large part of this benefit is naturally seen by the institutions in the system; however, there may be important positive externalities as well. If an attack on a particular bank is successful, it may create problems for other banks in the system. If the attack introduces propagating malware, for example, it might be spread to other institutions through business or social communications. Operational disruptions at one institution might impose costs on other banks by preventing clearing and settlement of interbank or customer transactions. There are also possible reputation costs to the system as a whole arising from a successful attack on a single institution. Such externalities create an incentive for each institution in the system to see other banks join in an information sharing arrangement. Conversely, some of the benefits created by a joining institution are experienced by other institutions in the system, whether or not they themselves participate.

The information sharing benefit to the system as a whole will depend on the number of institutions choosing to participate. We might see large benefits from a small fraction, or it may be that nearly all banks must join before substantial collective returns are achieved.

2.3 Information Sharing Problem as a Dynamic Multi-player Game

The interaction between a bank's decision to participate in information sharing and the subsequent costs and benefits confronted by other banks as a consequence of this decision suggests that game theory [10] would provide an effective lens on the problem of fostering beneficial systemic outcomes. The problem can be posed as a multi-player game in which the benefits to each bank of joining the information sharing system are a function of the decisions of all other banks in the system. This provides a good conceptual picture of the problem, but it is not a realistic way of solving it. First, the number of players and variety of interplayer interactions make it impractical to calculate the benefits to each player for each possible pattern of participation. Second, the astronomical complexity of this payoff matrix means that banks would not use it as a basis for making their decisions. Instead, we treat the problem as an iterated game, in which banks repeatedly update their information about their environment, and assess their decision using this updated information.

At each step institutions evaluate the anticipated costs and benefits of joining, and move accordingly. These moves change the cost/reward structure for the other banks in the system, which then revisit *their* decisions on the next iteration. The game concludes when no bank has an incentive to change its decision. In some situations the game may not have an equilibrium endpoint of this kind: oscillatory solutions are possible, particularly if the calculation of costs and benefits involves lagged observations of the performance of the system.

2.4 Model Formulation

2.4.1 Purpose and Scope

The model is intended to provide an understanding of how the various factors that influence adoption of information sharing by individual banks can interact to influence the overall level of participation. This also allows us to identify any obstacles to achieving a degree of participation leading to a globally beneficial condition, and to assess the effectiveness of policies designed to overcome those obstacles by shaping the incentives confronted by the participants in the financial system.

The model represents the way in which cyber attacks impose costs on the system, and on how a successful information sharing system can reduce those costs by increasing the chance that they will be detected and effectively blocked or mitigated. The particular nature of the attack and of the mitigation are not specified, but we assume the probability that an attack will be detected by the information sharing system is a function of the number of banks that participate in the system and that are targeted by the attack. This dependence reflects the essential benefit conferred by information sharing.

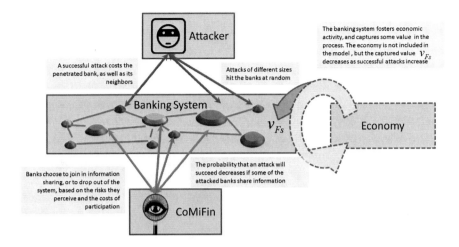

Fig. 2.1 Schematic of model components and processes

2.4.2 Limitations

The model is a highly stylized representation of the complex processes and relationships that compose a modern banking system. It is designed to focus on the most critical factors and processes controlling adoption of a protective technology having substantial externalities within a system that has both cooperative and competitive interrelationships among its components. It might be refined in many details; for example, attacks might be differentiated based on their expected cost and the efficacy of information sharing in detecting them, or the social networks interconnecting bank customers might be considered in modeling the evolution of customers' risk perceptions. However, not all refinements are likely to produce new insights regarding the question of concern: How can adoption be fostered by policy?

The model does not include adaptive moves by the adversary, which might be very important. Adoption of the information sharing platform might cause adversaries to adjust their mode of attack in order to evade its detection algorithms. The platform itself might become a target of attack, either with the direct goal of causing operational problems at a number of banks, or as a preliminary step in a campaign directed at financial institutions themselves. Conversely, the presence of an integrated system for information sharing might make defensive responses more adaptable, in that defenses against novel attack strategies can be implemented for all participants at once.

2.4.3 Model Elements and Governing Equations

Figure 2.1 illustrates the components of the system that we model and the basic processes we consider.

The banking system contains N interacting financial institutions b_i. Each bank has an overall size parameter s_i that influences its role in the system as described below. These institutions provide financial services in some economic environment, which is not represented directly in the model; however, the economic value captured by the banking system as a whole is represented as a net flow of v_{Fs} (see Eq. (2.1)) from the economy to the banks. This flow is relevant to the present problem because it may depend on the perceived risk, arising from successful cyber attacks, that economic actors impute to the banking system as a whole. We model this dependency as a logistical function of the current probability of successful attack at any institution $\hat{p}_a$:

$$v_{Fs} = \frac{v_{\max}}{1 + e^{(\hat{p}_a - p_c)s_a}} \tag{2.1}$$

The logistical function reflects the assumption that there is some critical level of attack probability p_c at which users begin to regard the system as risky, and to impose risk premiums in some way that degrades the economic value available to the financial system. At high levels of attack probability, the economic value is driven toward zero. The sensitivity of value to attack probability around the critical point is determined by s_a.

Banks compete for shares of the total value v_{Fs}, and the probability that a particular institution will be attacked is assumed to play some role in its success in the competition for market share. Successful attacks on the system will change risk perceptions, tending to shift business away from banks seen as riskier and toward those seen as less risky.

We model this process through a network of business interactions among banks. The links in this network represent the extent of interactions between pairs of banks. These interactions include relationships between the banks themselves as well as business transactions between the sets of customers served by the banks. Strong business ties among financial institutions, represented by these links, have several implications in the model.

First, linked financial institutions are assumed to be potential competitors for each other's customers, with some part of the relative attractiveness of a bank related to the relative risk of attack. In part, links between banks reflect business relationships among their customers, and these relationships allow customers of different banks to compare information about the services and performance of their banks. Differences in risk across links are assumed to drive business from the more risky to the less risky bank to some extent. A link in the network between banks b_i and b_j represents business connections with a strength s_{ij}. The proportion of this business assigned to bank b_i is:

$$w_{ij} = \frac{1}{1 + \hat{p}_i/\hat{p}_j} \tag{2.2}$$

where $\hat{p}_i$ is the current estimate of the probability of successful attack on bank b_i. These probability estimates, and the estimated probability of attack at any bank $\hat{p}_a$, are based on the history of successful attacks that the overall system experiences.

These estimates are formed over a period τ_m which represents a memory time over which banks and their customers base their expectations about performance:

$$\hat{p}_i(t_{n+1}) = \hat{p}_i(t_n) + \frac{\Delta t}{\tau_m}\left(Ia_i - \hat{p}_i(t_n)\right) \tag{2.3}$$

where Ia_i is an indicator of successful attack against bank b_i during the period $t_n \rightarrow t_{n+1}$.

Attacks on the system are modeled as a random process that occurs at some specified frequency f_a. A particular attack is directed at some number n_a of the banks in the system. Some number of these banks, n_{sa}, will be participants in the information sharing system at the time of the attack. The probability that an attack will be detected by the information sharing system is assumed to increase as the number of attacked banks that share information increases, and to have a maximum detection probability of p_{max} that is achieved when all banks participate:

$$p_{det} = p_{max}\left(\frac{n_{sa} - 1}{n_a - 1}\right)^{1/\gamma} \tag{2.4}$$

The parameter γ describes the "power" of information sharing by controlling the fraction of participation needed to approach the maximum detection probability. A value of 1 defines a linear increase in probability with participation. Values larger than 1 cause a large increase in detection probability with relatively small participation; values less than 1 require a large fractional participation before the maximum benefit is seen.

A successful attack is assumed to create some cost α at each of the banks attacked. In addition, the attack imposes a cost β on neighboring banks in the financial network. These costs can be due to any of several mechanisms, such as operational interruptions or delays at the attacked bank that inconvenience the neighboring bank or its customers, or propagation of the direct effects of the attack through the business linkages between the banks. Both the cost to the successfully attacked bank and the costs to its neighbors are relative to the bank sizes.

A bank's decision to participate in information sharing is based on the costs they have experienced as a consequence of attack in comparison to the various costs associated with participation in the information sharing system. The model includes three components of cost: initial capital costs associated with installing the system, recurring costs of maintaining the system, and perceived costs due to business risks that might arise in consequence of participation. These latter costs include uncertainty about the impact of incorporating the new system in a bank's existing IT processes and concerns about leakage of business intelligence through the shared information. Although system design (like the one presented in Part II of this book) includes mechanisms to be used in order to prevent such leakage, a lack of experience with the successful performance of this protection may create an important barrier to adoption.

Accumulated experience with the information sharing system, whether by the bank considering adoption or by other banks in the financial system, is assumed to provide public information about the operational impacts of using the system and to alleviate concerns regarding possible loss of sensitive information. This effect is modeled by assuming that the leakage cost that a bank considers when judging whether to participate decays as experience with information sharing accumulates within the financial system:

$$c_l = c_{l\,max} e^{-h_s/(N\tau_m)} \tag{2.5}$$

where h_s is the accumulated experience, up to the current time t_n, with the information sharing system by all financial institutions:

$$h_s = \sum_{k=0}^{n} n_s(t_i) \tag{2.6}$$

where $n_s(t_i)$ is the number of banks participating at time t_i.

2.4.4 Evolution of System State

The information sharing system evolves through a series of time steps. At each step, the economic value captured by the financial system as a whole, v_{Fs}, is first calculated using Eq. (2.1) based on the system's recent experience with attacks, reflected in the current probability of attack $\hat{p}_a$. This total value is then allocated among the individual institutions based on their total size, and on the shifts in business allocation due to contrasts in comparative risk of attack across pairs of banks, using Eq. (2.2).

Next, an attack may be attempted based on the specified attack frequency, with the number of banks attacked randomly chosen between 1 and a specified maximum size. The attacked banks are chosen at random from the entire population. Some of the attacked banks may be participants in the information sharing system. The number of sharing banks attacked determines, via Eq. (2.4), the probability that the attack will be detected and effectively blocked. If the attack is not blocked, it imposes costs on the attacked banks as well as on all neighbors of the attacked banks in the banking system. Each bank then updates its expected probability of attack and the costs it incurs because of attack, using its experience during the time step. The overall probability of attack on any bank, $\hat{p}_a$, which controls the rate of value captured by the banking system, is also updated depending on the success of an attack at any bank. These probabilities retain information about experiences over a time period of τ_m. This represents a "forgetting time" for decision makers in the banking system and the economy.

At the end of the time step, each bank evaluates its participation in the information sharing system. Its recent experience with attacks is used to calculate an expected cost per unit time arising from successful attacks. This cost determines whether the bank joins the information sharing system, if it currently does not participate, or drops out of the system if it does. Banks outside the sharing system decide to join if the expected attack cost is greater than the sum of the (amortized) fixed cost, maintenance cost, and cost of prospective loss of business information. Banks currently in the system continue to participate as long as the expected attack cost is greater than the maintenance cost and cost of information loss.

2.4.5 Output Metrics

Our primary interest is in identifying conditions that maximize benefit to the system. The direct measure of this benefit is the aggregate value generation rate v_{FS}. This is a function of the frequency of successful attacks on the system, which in turn depends on the degree of participation in the information sharing system. The number of participants n_s is therefore an additional important metric. Participation responds to the costs confronted by banks, and so these costs are the natural targets of policies designed to foster the information sharing system benefit.

We examine a financial network consisting of 100 banks. Each bank has links to a number of other banks in the system (uniformly distributed between 2 and 10), representing strong business relationships between the banks or their customers. The size of each bank is proportional to the number of its links to other banks. Each link is assumed to represent a unit of potential economic value created by the banking system. The scale for measuring costs and benefits in the information sharing system is set by the maximum economic value created by the system as a whole (v_{max} in Eq. (2.1)), which is given by the total number of links between banks.

Using the nominal parameter values for the cost of attack and for the information sharing countermeasures, the total economic value captured by the banking system varies in a narrow band around a value of 245 (see Fig. 2.2). The model configuration gives a maximum limit of 300, thus roughly 15% of the potential value to the banking system is lost to the direct and indirect costs of cyber attack. Despite the motivation reflected by this loss, no banks join the information sharing system in this simulation due to the cost values assigned for installation, maintenance, and operational uncertainty.

Reducing the information sharing system maintenance cost by an order of magnitude tips the decision in favor of adopting information sharing. Figure 2.3 shows the resulting trajectory of total economic value captured by the banking system, along with the value function calculated with high cost (see Fig. 2.2) for comparison. In this case the total value captured increases from the reference case by 35 units, or more than 10%. The total maintenance cost in the original simulation if *all* banks had participated would only have totaled 0.1 unit. While these particular results are based on notional parameter values and are not necessarily reflective of the real system, they do illustrate the potential for small changes in *local* costs seen by individual banks to create large *systemic* benefits.

The number of banks participating in the system has an interesting trajectory in this case, as shown in Fig. 2.4. The number of banks does not reach a fixed plateau, but instead fluctuates around a participation level of approximately 80%.

Fig. 2.2 Total economic
value in a system with high
sharing cost and no
participation

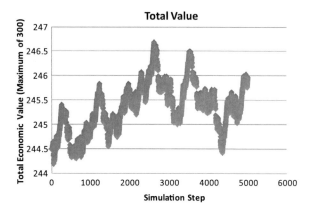

Fig. 2.3 Total economic
value in a system with
lowered maintenance cost

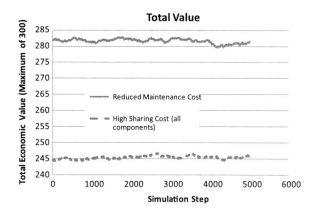

Fig. 2.4 Number of banks
participating in the Semantic
Room with reduced
maintenance costs

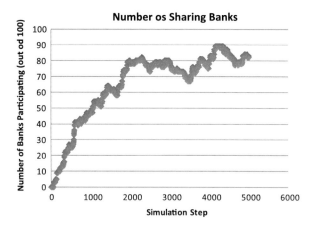

This behavior arises from the way in which banks estimate the costs of successful attack based on their experience of such attacks in the past. As the information sharing system suppresses losses at a bank, that bank reduces its estimate of the potential losses associated with attack, and therefore is led to drop out of the system to reduce cost. This switching behavior occurs in spite of the fact that fixed costs are regarded as sunk, and the participation decision is predicated on recurring costs and leakage costs alone. When banks drop out of the sharing system, the frequency of successful attacks increases, leading to renewed awareness of attack costs, and therefore to increased participation in the sharing system.

2.5 Conclusions: Insights for Policy—Motivating Robust Collective Security

The model proposed in this chapter includes some important basic factors that bear on banks' decisions to adopt new protective technology. Even with a high level of abstraction, the model can provide some insights regarding barriers to good cooperative solutions and possible means of surmounting them. First, if the cost of the system is (or is seen to be) high, then that cost can create a barrier to obtaining an improved *global* state. Some mechanism for spurring coordination is necessary in this condition. Second, with the notional parameter values used here, a reduction in maintenance costs (or equivalently a subsidy offsetting those costs) serves to foster adoption, which subsequently spreads through a large portion of the system. This strategy deters free riding by making the ticket less expensive. Third, the effectiveness of information sharing in reducing the perceived costs of attack (by reducing their success rate) may create a kind of complacency regarding the need to maintain participation. Mechanisms for offsetting a tendency for the financial system to "forget", such as prominent communication of the number of intercepted attacks, might be an especially important element of the information sharing environment.

References

1. Beyeler, W.E., Glass, R.J., Bech, M.L., Soramki, K.: Congestion and cascades in payment systems. Physica A **384**(2), 693–718 (2007)
2. Davey, V.J., Glass, R.J., Min, H.J., Beyeler, W.E., Glass, L.M.: Effective, robust design of community mitigation for pandemic influenza: a systematic examination of proposed U.S. guidance. PLoS ONE **3**, e2606 (2008) doi:10.1371/journal.pone.0002606
3. Glass, Robert J., Ames, A.L., Stubblefield, W.A., Conrad, S.H., Maffitt, S.L., Malczynski, L.A., Wilson, D.G., Carlson, J.J., Backus, G.A., Ehlen, M.A., Vanderveen, K.B., Engi, D.: (Sandia National Laboratories: a roadmap for the complex adaptive systems of systems CA-SoS) engineering initiative, Sandia National Laboratories SAND 2008-4651, September 2008
4. Glass, R.J., Ames, A.L., Beyeler, W.E., Zak, B., Schoenwald, D.A., McKenna, S.A., Conrad, S.H., Maffitt, S.L.: A general engineering framework for the definition, design, testing and actualization of solutions within complex adaptive systems of systems (CASoS) with application to the Global Energy System (GES), Sandia National Laboratories SAND 2008-7952, December 2008

5. Glass, R.J., Ames, A.L., Brown, T.J., Maffitt, S.L., Beyeler, W.E., Finley, P.D., Moore, T.W., Linebarger, J.M., Brodsky, N.S., Verzi, S.J., Outkin, A.V., Zagonel, A.A.: Complex Adaptive Systems of Systems (CASoS) engineering: mapping aspirations to problem solutions. In: Proceedings of the 8th International Conference on Complex Systems, Quincy, MA, 26 June–1 July 2011, Sandia National Laboratories SAND 2011-3354, May 2011

6. Perlroth, D.J., Glass, R.J., Davey, V.J., Garber, A.M., Owens, D.K.: Health outcomes and costs of community mitigation strategies for an influenza pandemic in the U.S., Clin. Infect. Dis. **50**, 165–174 (2010). doi:10.1086/649867

7. Renault, F., Beyeler, W.E., Glass, R.J., Soramaki, K., Bech, M.L.: Performance and resilience to liquidity disruptions in interdependent RTGS payment systems. In: Proceedings of the Joint Banque de France/European Central Bank Conference on Liquidity in Interdependent Transfer Systems, Paris, 9–10 June (2008)

8. Soramaki, K., Bech, M.L., Arnold, J., Glass, R.J., Beyeler, W.E.: The topology of interbank payment flows. Physica A **379**(1), 317–333 (2007)

9. CaSoS Engineering. http://www.sandia.gov/CasosEngineering/ (2011)

10. Straffin, P.D.: Game Theory and Strategy (1993). Mathematical Association of America

Chapter 3
Cyber Attacks on Financial Critical Infrastructures

Mirco Marchetti, Michele Colajanni, Michele Messori, Leonardo Aniello, and Ymir Vigfusson

Abstract This chapter focuses on attack strategies that can be (and have been) used against financial IT infrastructures. The first section presents an overview and a classification of the different kinds of frauds and attacks carried out against financial institutions and their IT infrastructures. We then restrict our focus by analyzing in detail five attack scenarios, selected among the ones presented in the previous section. These attack scenarios are: Man in the Middle (and its variant, Man in the Browser), distributed denial of service (DDoS), distributed portscan, session hijacking, and malware-based attacks against Internet banking customers. These scenarios have been selected because of their distributed nature: all of them involve multiple, geographically distributed financial institutions. Hence their detection will benefit greatly from the deployment of new technologies and best practices for information sharing and cooperative event processing. For each scenario we present a theoretical description of the attack as well as implementation details and consequences of past attacks carried out against real financial institutions.

M. Marchetti · M. Colajanni · M. Messori
University of Modena and Reggio Emilia, via Vignolese 905, Modena, Italy

M. Marchetti
e-mail: mirco.marchetti@unimore.it

M. Colajanni
e-mail: michele.colajanni@unimore.it

M. Messori
e-mail: michele.messori@unimore.it

L. Aniello (✉)
Dipartimento di Ingegneria Informatica, Automatica e Gestionale Antonio Ruberti, Università degli Studi di Roma "La Sapienza", via Ariosto 25, 00185 Roma, Italy
e-mail: aniello@dis.uniroma1.it

Y. Vigfusson
School of Computer Science, Reykjavík University, Menntavegur 1, IS 101 Reykjavík, Iceland
e-mail: ymir@ru.is

R. Baldoni, G. Chockler (eds.), *Collaborative Financial Infrastructure Protection*,
DOI 10.1007/978-3-642-20420-3_3, © Springer-Verlag Berlin Heidelberg 2012

3.1 Introduction

As modern society becomes more and more reliant on networked information systems, cyber attacks on IT infrastructures gain the ability to target crucial services, used by all citizens in their daily activities. Cyber attacks against the IT infrastructure of financial institutions and on their customers are representative of this trend. A large majority of financial activities are carried out by networked computers, and interactions between financial institutions and their customers are usually mediated by the open Internet. This landscape offers new opportunities for attackers. In particular, the ability to compromise the security of online financial transactions is especially alluring, since they give an attacker the opportunity to easily monetize a successful attack.

In this context, several different attack strategies have already been used in the recent past to prepare or to execute frauds and extortions against banks and their customers. These cyber attacks are extremely heterogeneous, ranging from insider threats to network intrusion by an external attacker, from attacks targeted to a specific financial institution to widespread campaigns of spam and phishing, from the exploitation of vulnerabilities in software used by the financial institutions to intrusions in customers' personal computers.

A comprehensive description of all possible attacks that can be carried out against a financial institution by abusing its IT infrastructure is beyond the scope of this book. In this chapter we focus on five different attack strategies: Man in the Middle (Sect. 3.2), portscan activities (Sect. 3.3), distributed denial of service (Sect. 3.4), session hijacking (Sect. 3.5), and malware-based attacks against a financial institution's customers (Sect. 3.6).

All these attacks share a common trait that makes them especially relevant to the context of this book: they involve multiple entities.

Man-in-the-Middle attacks target multiple customers, and possibly multiple financial institutions. Portscan activities are routinely detected by virtually all financial institutions, and are often performed by multiple, coordinated attackers. Distributed denial of service attacks are a well-known threat; they have already targeted several financial institutions in the recent past, and their sources are geographically distributed. Session hijacking techniques can be used to compromise the integrity of financial transactions carried out by multiple customers. Finally, banking malware is usually represented by self-replicating software that attacks hundreds of thousands of vulnerable personal computers, thus targeting a high number of a financial institution's customers.

For each of these strategies we provide a detailed description of how the attack is carried out, and we discuss several case studies that represent recent instances of the described attack against real financial institutions.

Since the activities of the aforementioned attacks involve multiple financial institutions, we highlight how information sharing can provide great benefit by allowing early detection of all these threats. Moreover, cooperation among financial players can result in the early dissemination of information that is useful for preventing new attacks or mitigating their effects.

We emphasize that these benefits can be achieved without the need for sharing sensitive information related to the financial transactions (such as the amount, or the identities of the parties involved in the transaction). Moreover, the heterogeneity of the attacks described in this chapter demonstrates how the information sharing approach proposed here can be beneficial in several different contexts.

3.2 Man-in-the-Middle Attacks

This section describes the preparation and the execution of a Man-in-the-Middle (MitM) attack, as well as the mitigation and prevention activities that can be implemented through information sharing.

MitM attacks are carried out by tricking a legitimate user into starting a connection with a rogue server that is configured to mimic the behavior of the legitimate server. Depending on the nature of the service and its underlying technologies, an attacker can use several different strategies to perform this first step of the attack, ranging from social engineering to the exploitation of software vulnerabilities.

If the fraudster is able to implement a sufficiently good copy of the service to which the user is trying to connect, the user will likely not realize that an attack is in progress. He will then try to log in to the rogue server, thus making his log-in credentials (such as username, passwords, and tokens) available to the attacker. The attacker can then leverage this information to connect to the legitimate server (to which the user intended to connect in the first place) and to initiate a fraudulent transaction by impersonating the legitimate user.

MitM attacks usually target multiple customers and multiple financial institutions. After they have set up the rogue service used as a decoy for the legitimate service of a financial institution, the attackers use it to fraud multiple customers. Moreover, after they develop a new technique for luring users to their fake services, the technique is employed on large-scale attacks that involve multiple, heterogeneous institutions. Hence, the cooperative processing of information gathered from multiple and distributed financial institutions can improve our ability to detect and react to MitM attacks.

3.2.1 Attack Description

A typical Man-in-the-Middle (MitM) attack can usually be performed with minimal hardware requirements. In most cases it is enough to have a server connected to the Internet and reachable through a public IP address. With respect to other attack scenarios (such as distributed denial of service, discussed in Sect. 3.4), the complexity of the preparation phase is significantly lower, since the attacker does not require a complex and distributed attack infrastructure. To set up a successful MitM attack, an attacker needs to overcome two main difficulties:

1. to make the legitimate user send requests to the machine operated by the attacker instead of the server that belongs to the legitimate financial institution;
2. to make the legitimate user believe that the other endpoint of the session is the legitimate server that he intended to interact with.

Several techniques can be used to redirect a user-initiated session to the attacker machine hosting the MitM server. In this section we will limit our analysis to four classes of attacks that have been used in the past to carry out large-scale MitM attacks specifically targeted against financial institutions. These techniques are Domain Name System (DNS) cache poisoning, compromise of an intermediate routing node, phishing, and exploitation of vulnerabilities in the authentication system of the targeted service.

DNS cache poisoning: In this class the attacker compromises the DNS server that one or more customers use to translate the logical name assigned to the server of the targeted financial institution (e.g., www.bankname.eu) to its IP address, which is used by the customer's browser to reach the web server. The most common form of attack involves introducing one or more fake DNS records [8]. These records force the compromised DNS to resolve the logical name of the licit financial institution to an IP address assigned to the rogue server used by the attacker as MitM. This strategy can be very effective, since the customer is transparently redirected to the attacker machine even though the correct hostname has been inserted manually by the user in the address bar of the browser. Moreover, the recent discovery of several vulnerabilities in many DNS implementations [11, 12], as well as in the DNS protocol itself, make this strategy relatively easy to apply.

Compromise of an intermediate routing node: It is enough for the attacker to be able to compromise only one intermediate node performing IP routing operations to execute a MitM attack on all the client machines whose network packets are routed through (and by) the compromised node. A typical example of such an attack, already seen in the real world [13, 14], is the compromise of the settings used by home and small office routers that are configurable through a vulnerable web interface. After the attacker has identified a vulnerability (typically some form of cross-site scripting [45] or cross-site request forgery [46]) in a router that exports a web-based configuration interface, its exploitation can be automated by embedding a web link with a specially crafted URL in web sites that allow users to publish content, such as social networks, blogs, and review sites. The same links can also be included in spam emails. As soon as the unsuspecting customer of a financial institution clicks on the link created by the attacker, the customer's own browser is instructed to send HTTP requests to the router web interface, without further intervention from the customer. These requests aim to change the DNS settings of the router or to redirect connections to specific endpoints to a machine controlled by the attacker. If the attack succeeds, all the subsequent requests directed to the web site of the financial institutions targeted by the attacker will be transparently redirected to the rogue server. An example of a similar attack strategy that was deployed against a financial institution is described in [9]. This particular instance of the MitM attack targeted a Mexican bank and its customers.

Phishing: It is important to highlight that phishing and MitM are two different and independent attack strategies; they require different technical means and are usually performed to achieve different goals. However, several real-life MitM attacks carried out against financial institutions used phishing as the main strategy to lure unsuspecting customers to their rogue servers. Phishing relies on sending high volumes of unsolicited email message spam, on the insertion of rogue links in web sites, and on other similar strategies to make the customer start a connection with a rogue web server. If phishing is used alone, and not as the first phase of a MitM attack, the rogue web site hosts a page that looks similar to the licit web site, to which the customer authenticates, thus disclosing his credentials to the attacker. On the other hand, when phishing and MitM are used together, the rogue web site owned by the attacker pretends to be the licit client and initiates a session with the licit server on behalf of the unsuspecting customer. While this attack was once considered sophisticated, several attack tools are now available on the black market that allow even unskilled attackers to execute frauds based on phishing and MitM. It is difficult to quantify exactly the price of software that is sold on the black market, but several sources report it to be below $1000 [16]. Relevant examples of MitM attacks against financial institution and based on phishing are represented by recent frauds against Nordea and Citibank [15].

Authentication vulnerabilities: It is known that MitM strategies have been used to undermine the authentication solutions deployed by Norwegian banks [10]. In this specific case, the authentication software deployed by the targeted financial institutions was vulnerable, and allowed attackers to change the URL of the licit institution to the one of a rogue server owned by the attacker and used to perform the MitM attack.

After an unaware customer has been lured to a rogue web server used as MitM, the attack is extremely simple. The user authenticates against the rogue server, by sending to it its authentication credentials. The rogue server stores the user credentials and relays them to the licit server, and conveys the response to the user on behalf of the licit server. This mechanism serves a twofold purpose. First of all, it makes the attack much more realistic than a traditional phishing strategy, because the user receives the expected replies from the server. Furthermore, the MitM node is able to analyze all the data that flow between the client and the server, thus obtaining access to a great amount of critical information. Also, the MitM attacker is able to modify on the fly the content of the transaction, e.g., by altering sensitive and critical information.

3.2.2 Attack Detection and Reaction

A single instance of a MitM attack is almost impossible to detect, since it appears as a perfectly normal transaction between a server that belongs to a financial institution and a licit (already known and registered) customer. Rather than focusing on detecting individual transactions, current MitM detection strategies are based on the identification of anomalous traffic patterns that are generated by large-scale MitM activities involving multiple customers and/or multiple financial institutions.

In the case of an extremely simple MitM attack, in which only a very limited number of servers controlled by the attacker (only one, in the simplest possible case) is used to mediate the session of a great number of customers, it is possible for a single financial institution to detect a likely MitM attack by relying on anomaly detection algorithms.

The underlying hypothesis is that customers usually access their financial services from a limited number of devices, and that the same device is not used by a large number of different customers to access the same financial service within a short period of time. Hence, the activities of a MitM server that is starting a high number of connections on behalf of several different customers can be detected as anomalous, and can lead to the generation of a security alert.

On the other hand, MitM detection can become extremely difficult if the attacker uses the same rogue server to execute MitM attacks targeting services provided by different financial institutions. If this is the case, even a high MitM activity might not be easy to detect, because it is distributed among a sufficiently high number of different and non-communicating domains. However, the same MitM attack could be easily detected if the targeted financial institutions cooperated by sharing information related to their observed traffic patterns. Hence, information sharing can be extremely useful in identifying MitM activities that would be impossible to detect otherwise, as well as in speeding up detection of MitM attacks and providing early security warnings.

Once a MitM attack has been detected, reaction and mitigation activities are quite straightforward. It is usually possible for the attacked financial institution to blacklist the IP address of the rogue server used by the attacker to mount the MitM attack, thus preventing it from initiating new fraudulent transactions on behalf of unsuspecting customers.

3.2.3 Case Studies

A typical example of an attack carried out against a financial institution using DNS poisoning was been reported in the news in April 2009 [20]. In this example, the target of the attack was one of the biggest Brazilian banks, Banco Bradesco. According to the news published by several different information sources, attackers were able to steal the authentication credentials of several customers by performing a DNS cache poisoning attack to a DNS server owned by the Brazillian ISP NET Virtua. Hence, the attack was performed without compromising any server owned by the targeted bank. According to a representative of Banco Bradesco, about 1% of their customers have been affected by the attack [21].

DNS poisoning strategies have also been used in a more recent attack against Santander, a well-known banking institution with branches in many countries. In particular, the web site of Santander Brazil was targeted by a DNS poisoning attack in July 2011 [22].

An interesting case in which a financial institution suffered an attack due to vulnerabilities in the home ADSL routers of its customers appeared in the news in January 2008. This attack was limited to customers living in Mexico, and targeted the biggest Mexican bank: Banamex [23]. The attackers managed to hijack the requests of customers who connected to the Internet through several models of modems produced by 2Wire. In particular, these modems were vulnerable to cross-site request forgery attacks that allowed attackers to change several important configurations without express consent (or even awareness) of the end users. Through specially crafted URLs attackers were able to modify the DNS record that the router associates to the Banamex web site, as well as the password that is required to access the router. It is interesting to note that the vulnerability used by the attackers to hijack Banamex's customers had been known and documented by security experts since August 2007, five months before the attack took place; however, no patches were available at that time. The vulnerability is catalogued in the Common Vulnerabilities and Exposures list as CVE-2007-4387.

Perhaps the most common strategy used by attackers to perform MitM attacks against financial institutions is to lure the victim to the rogue web site through a phishing email. Phishing is a well-known attack strategy, and financial institutions are among the preferred targets for this kind of attack.

According to PhishTank [24], a collaborative "clearing house" for data and information related to phishing activities in the Internet, banks and other financial institutions are consistently among the top ten victims of phishing attacks. According to the August 2011 statistics (the most recent month for which PhishTank has published statistics at the time of writing), among the ten most popular targets there are two banks: Santander UK (5th place) and Bradesco (10th place). Other targets that are relevant to the financial world are Mastercard (6th place) and Visa (8th place), while PayPal is by far the most popular target, consistently occupying first place.

Phishing was recently used as a means to deploy MitM attacks against two Finnish banks, Nordea and Osuuspankki, at the beginning of September 2011 [25]. This attack was fairly straightforward: victims received an email pretending to be from their bank that contained a link to the server used by the attacker as MitM. It was an exact copy of the web site of the real banks, and was hosted in France. Similar attacks were also carried out against the Swedish branch of Nordea in October 2005 and against Citibank in July 2006 [15].

A MitM attack against financial institutions that sets itself apart from the other cases described in this chapter is represented by the frauds carried out against customers of several Norwegian banks in 2008. The attack is documented in a research paper titled "Robbing banks with their own software" [10]; the vulnerable software used by the banks to authenticate their customers, called BankID, is part of a security infrastructure built and owned by Norwegian banks themselves for conducting commerce on the Internet. In contrast, all the attacks we have described previously target the end users or some other infrastructure that does not belong to the targeted bank. Since several banks leverage the BankID platform for customer authentication, a single vulnerability in BankID allows an attacker to target multiple independent financial institutions. Full details on the attacks and a technical description of BankID vulnerabilities can be found in [10].

3.2.4 Benefits of Information Sharing

An information sharing approach can be extremely useful in the early detection of MitM attacks targeting multiple financial institutions, as in the case of the ubiquitous authentication applet used by Norwegian financial institutions [10]. When institutions share and correlate information related to the source address from which financial transactions are initiated, it is possible for them to detect traffic pattern anomalies much earlier than any of the individual institutions could do by itself.

After having identified a MitM server, it is possible to immediately spread this information to all the other financial players that collaborate by sharing useful information. Automatic dissemination of MitM addresses can be used to build blacklists (or graylists) of servers that are controlled by attackers, thus preventing a MitM server that has been discovered by some financial institution from initiating rogue sessions toward other institutions.

If information sharing is not restricted to financial institutions, security alerts related to servers that are likely involved in MitM attacks can also be automatically distributed to other interested parties and stakeholders. As an example, it would be useful to automatically distribute security alerts to the Internet service providers (ISPs) that provide connectivity to the collaborating financial institutions. ISPs can make good use of this shared information by verifying the status of the possibly compromised machine with the administrator of the network to which the rogue host is connected. Moreover, ISPs can prevent customers from being lured to MitM servers that have already been detected by blocking the traffic that they generate.

Since ISPs have a vantage point that allows them to detect network anomalies at large scales, it is also possible for an ISP to autonomously detect a server that is likely performing MitM attacks. The ISP can then spread this information among all the other institutions that participate in the collaborative MitM detection effort. The sharing of this information allows financial institutions to add a compromised server that they would not have been able to detect to their blacklist.

Finally, by sharing information about rogue servers used to carry out MitM attacks, it is possible for financial institutions to audit their recent activity logs, thus identifying whether some of their customers have been affected by the attack.

Among the information that can be exchanged by financial institutions in order to facilitate the detection of MitM attacks are: the source addresses of the devices used to access the financial services, the frequency with which the same address has been used to access a financial service, and the number of separate identities that accessed a financial service using the same address.

It is possible that financial institutions will refuse to disclose some of this information (e.g., the IP addresses of machines that access their financial services) in order to protect the privacy of their customers, as well as to prevent other financial institutions from tracking their customers. If this is the case, the financial institutions can apply some form of anonymization to sanitize the required information before releasing it. There is no need to access financial transaction details.

Since MitM attacks target systems that are accessible from the Internet, all this information can be acquired by monitoring systems that are deployed within the demilitarized zone (DMZ) of the targeted financial institutions. Possible sources of information are logs generated by firewalls, routers, and network appliances in general, as well as logs generated by networked applications (such as web servers). Many of the modern network and system monitoring appliances can be configured to relay alerts and logged events to remote machines. Similar techniques can be effectively used to acquire the relevant information through the monitoring equipment already installed in the DMZ.

3.3 Distributed Portscan

This section describes in detail what a distributed portscan is, how it is carried out, and why information sharing can help to improve the detection of such a threat. Generally speaking, a portscan is a reconnaissance activity aimed at discovering and keeping track of the status of Transmission Control Protocol (TCP)/User Datagram Protocol (UDP) ports at target sites. Ports left open can then be used as vectors for launching the actual cyber attack.

3.3.1 Attack Description

The main goal of a portscan is finding out which TCP/UDP ports have been left open at specific target sites. On the basis of the set of open ports, a possible attack could be planned. In fact, an open port signals the presence of a running service waiting for incoming requests. Once this service is identified, an attacker could check whether it exhibits some vulnerabilities and leverage them for malicious purposes.

The simplest way of probing the status of a TCP/UDP port consists in sending some basic requests. For a TCP port, this means issuing a TCP connection and waiting for any reply which would reveal the status of the target port. The situation is slightly different for UDP ports because UDP is a connectionless protocol. In this case the attacker has two options. The first one is to send a probe UDP packet to the target port and wait for any response. If an Internet Control Message Protocol (ICMP) "port unreachable" message is received, then the port can be considered as closed; if no packet is received at all, chances are that the port is open. A weakness of this option is the possibility that the lack of a response packet is actually due to the presence of a firewall that has filtered the UDP packet previously sent, and so the real status of the port cannot be determined precisely. The second option is to directly send an application-specific UDP packet, hoping to generate an application layer response. For example, a DNS server will surely reply to any DNS query sent to port 53, thus revealing the status of this UDP port. In this case we also have the possibility that a firewall could be filtering some packets, but, depending on the specific application we are looking for, we can make a more confident guess. In fact, if we are probing an application that is likely to be reachable on the Internet (e.g., a DNS server again), we can assume that the lack of a response packet is more likely due to the fact that the service is not actually running on the target host than to the presence of a firewall. Another problem of this option is that each port surely requires a different probe packet, because on distinct ports there are distinct services listening.

An important concern about portscan is that of leaving clues. When an application-level request is issued, it is possible that the target service will trace it, together with some types of information about the source host. An analysis of these traces may help in successfully identifying the source of the malicious requests. Due to the connectionless nature of UDP, every malicious packet sent to an application listening on a UDP port is processed by the application itself, hence the source of the packets could be traced. On the other hand, since TCP is connection oriented, services listening on TCP ports are aware of any connection probe only if the three-way handshake phase of a TCP connection is successfully completed. This detail can be leveraged by an attacker to forge probes that attempt to check port status without establishing a connection. In the following discussion we mainly focus on this aspect of portscans, because it turns out to be the most interesting and frequent case.

A portscan aimed at not leaving any clues is said to be a *stealth portscan* [43]. Many different techniques exist for executing stealth portscans. All of them exploit some weaknesses of TCP, using forge packets that make the target host reveal the actual status of a TCP port without having the application layer know anything about what is really happening on the lower layers. The ability of these techniques to correctly reveal the status of TCP ports also relies on the assumption that the target host is compliant with the Request for Comments (RFC) specifications on TCP.

Portscans can also be classified on the basis of what the attacker is looking for. We have two dimensions to explore in this sense. Modeling these dimensions using a Cartesian plane, we have the IP addresses on the x-axis and the ports on the y-axis. If the goal of the malicious host is to discover all open ports at a certain target, we then have a *vertical portscan*, since if we plotted probed ports in that plane we would actually have a vertical line. In contrast, if the attacker wants to check the status of a particular TCP port over a range of IP addresses, we are likely to have a horizontal line, so this kind of probe is called a *horizontal portscan*. We can also experience a hybrid approach, in which a range of ports are checked over a set of hosts. This kind of portscan is called a *block portscan* [40].

3.3.2 Attack Detection and Reaction

Intrusion detection systems (IDSs) usually cope with portscan detection by using techniques based on observations about behavioral aspects that may help in discriminating malicious hosts from benign ones [41, 42]. During a portscan, an attacker is likely to probe either closed/filtered ports or unreachable hosts, since it doesn't know in advance the situation of target hosts. Otherwise, it wouldn't carry out such a portscan. This consideration leads to the consequence that an attacker is usually subjected to more network errors than an honest host. Moreover, an attacker is expected to contact a higher number of distinct ports on different hosts than a normal node, at least within a limited time window, because its goal is to gather as much status information as possible. An IDS commonly leverages these concerns to trace the behavior of the hosts that are generating TCP traffic flowing to the network that the IDS itself is committed to monitor. A few counters are enough to support this kind of tracing, for example, the number of failed connections and the number of distinct probed ports. The IDS keeps updating these counters as specific packet patterns are recognized among monitored network traffic and, whenever any of the counters is found to exceed some configured threshold, an alert is raised to notify the presence of an anomalous situation.

As already mentioned, time windows are commonly used. An attacker is assumed to operate a whole portscan in a single time window whose duration depends on several factors, e.g., how many ports are to be probed and the network load conditions. The point is that the evidence of a portscan is often concentrated in a unique specific segment of the sequence of activities carried out by a host over the time period. This consideration lets the IDS focus only on the last actions performed by a node, disregarding the information older than a certain time bound. In fact, a crucial requirement for IDSs is the ability to detect threats in a timely manner, so that a proper countermeasure can be taken to block the attack or mitigate the damages. Concentrating on more recent events instead of mining a larger set of collected data offline allows the IDS to react earlier to what is currently happening.

Attackers are generally aware of both the thresholds and the time windows adopted by IDSs, so they can accurately tailor their techniques to bypass these security mechanisms. To counter the use of time windows, they can slow down their activities so that the evidence of the portscan is spread over more windows. Since an IDS is always analyzing the last window, the proof of the portscan cannot be obtained. This kind of behavior on the part of the attackers is usually referred to as *distribution in time* of a portscan. The trick that is mostly exploited for circumventing threshold-based controls in horizontal portscans concerns the *distribution in space* of the probes. If target hosts are chosen among several different domains, the IDS monitoring the single domain cannot obtain the evidence of the attack, since the number of suspicious activities it detects is likely to remain below the alert threshold. Another possibility for attackers is to distribute the source of the portscans rather than the destination. In this way the clue of the scan is dispersed over several sources, each of them looking like a benign host for the IDS [44].

3.3.3 Case Studies

As already stated, a portscan is a reconnaissance activity aimed at gathering information about the status of TCP/UDP ports on target sites. This information can then be used to properly plan the actual attack, for example, the sending of an infected payload. The scan and the infection can take place at the same time. This is often the way worm spreading works. An infected node starts sending a malicious payload on a certain TCP/UDP port over a set of targets randomly chosen. If the target runs a vulnerable service, then it becomes infected and also starts scanning for other victims. Using this mechanism, in January 2003, the Slammer worm, the fastest-spreading worm in history, achieved more than 55 million scans per second three minutes from its beginning [36–39].

Regardless of the particular cyber attack that would follow a portscan, the point is that a portscan is a suspicious behavior that could reveal the bad intentions of the attacker. Thus it is worth detecting that it is happening and determining its sources.

3.3.4 Benefits of Information Sharing

For state-of-the-art portscan detection, the new challenges that have arisen concern the distribution of the scans. While the distribution in time can be faced by widening the time windows, the distribution in space turns out to be more problematic. If the sources are distributed, a correlation algorithm could be used to discover whether any connection exists between operations performed by distinct hosts, so that the set of attackers can be identified. What remains outside the possibilities of today's IDS architecture is the detection of portscans whose targets are distributed in space, because each IDS has only a limited vision of what is going on and cannot reveal the presence of the portscan.

Here is where the added value of information sharing comes in. IDSs deployed at different organizations can collaborate, combining the data they have collected to create a common knowledge about the network activities executed by suspicious hosts over several domains. This requires the creation of a collaborative environment which is joined by organizations willing to share part of their network traffic data. In this way, evidence can be reconstructed of portscans whose targets have been spread in order to overcome detection mechanisms.

Moreover, the results of such detection can then be disseminated back to the organizations that are participating in the collaborative environment. These results can be employed to properly tune security mechanisms, for example, by updating firewall rules to prevent any suspected host from further connecting to the organization network.

It would be useful to involve the Internet service providers (ISPs) in these collaborative environments, because they can gather a wider amount of network data and they also have more control over the hosts that are connected to the Internet. The results produced by IDSs often consist of lists of suspected IP addresses. Since portscans are usually issued by infected domestic computers that are assigned different IP addresses over the time period, the involvement of ISPs can help in correctly identifying the users that have generated malicious traffic and then taking the proper countermeasures.

3.4 Distributed Denial of Service Attacks

Another form of cyber attack that has been used against financial (among other) institutions is called *denial of service* (DoS). The goal of this attack is to prevent the IT infrastructure of the attacked institution from delivering the expected services. As an example, a successful DoS attack carried out against the home-banking web site of a financial institution will render it impossible for all the customers of that financial institution to access the home-banking web portal.

While a DoS attack does not intend to perform fraud and does not inflict permanent damage on the attacked financial institution, it is still extremely effective. The unavailability of Internet-facing services causes loss of customers and revenue, undermines the trust relationship between customers and the attacked financial institution, and is usually (and mistakenly) perceived as a threat to the integrity of financial transactions. Moreover, the effects of DoS attacks are often reported by mass media, often with non-technical, incorrect, and exaggerated information that undermines the public image of the attacked financial institution.

Among all the possible forms of DoS attacks, the most dangerous is represented by distributed DoS attacks, which are described in detail in Sect. 3.4.1. The distributed nature of this form of DoS makes it extremely difficult to defend against. Distributed DoS attacks have often been used to extort money from the attacked financial institution.

3.4.1 Attack Description

Distributed DoS (DDoS) attacks are carried out through complex and geographically distributed attack infrastructures, commonly referred to as *botnets*, comprising several machines connected to the Internet and controlled by an attacker.

In order to create the distributed infrastructure, a complex and time-consuming attack preparation phase is required. Within this phase an attacker tries to build the botnet that will be used to generate DDoS attacks and other illicit network activities (such as sending high volumes of unsolicited emails).

The bot recruitment process is carried out through the extensive use of self-propagating malware, such as Internet worms. A worm is a computer program that tries to spread among the highest possible number of Internet-connected hosts by exploiting known vulnerabilities of widespread operating systems (OSs) and software packages. Worms propagate by generating the IP address of the next machine to attack, and by targeting it with one or more remote exploits. In order to increase the chances of generating an IP address belonging to a machine that is currently connected to the Internet, and that shares the same vulnerable configuration of other machines that have already been successfully infected, worms usually start by exploring the IP address space of the network to which the attacking machine (a host that has already been compromised and is now under the control of the attacker) is connected. Once this address space is exhausted, random IP address generation is used to try to infect hosts belonging to different networks.

Once a worm attacks a vulnerable machine, it usually follows a two-step infection procedure. First of all, measures are taken to prevent the compromised machine to be infected again by the same worm, for example, by setting appropriate flags indicating that the machine has already been compromised (like creating a new file or modifying the content of a file already existing on the machine) or even by patching the vulnerabilities used by the worm to propagate (as the infamous Conficker [3] worm does). Then, a fresh (possibly updated) copy of the infective payload is downloaded from a known source, usually by using HTTP, FTP, or TFTP. Finally, the compromised host is turned into a bot by executing the infective payload.

Once executed, the bot code runs silently on the compromised host, waiting for orders from the botnet owner (also known as the herder). Communications between the herder and the bots is usually mediated by a command and control (C&C) infrastructure [19]. The most common communication scheme is based on Internet Relay Chat (IRC) channels. Bots connect to the control channel and interpret the messages sent to that channel as commands from the herder. To increase the flexibility of this centralized communication scheme, botnet herders usually rely on dynamic DNS services, and thus are able to dynamically change the IP address of the IRC server while keeping it reachable from the bots. Moreover, bots can use pseudo-random algorithms to periodically generate new hostnames to contact, thus making it extremely difficult to block the communication through static filtering rules. The problem of backtracking the botnet command chain is further exacerbated by new generations of botnets, able to rely on decentralized communication schemes based on peer-to-peer routing overlays.

Due to their distributed nature and to the difficulties in tracking the C&C chain, it is hard to provide reliable statistics about the number of botnets, their size, and the geographical locations of their bots. It is speculated that the size of the biggest botnets ranges from several hundreds of thousands to some millions of compromised machines. These huge distributed infrastructures can be rented to serve as launch bases for several kinds of attacks and other illicit activities that can generate revenue for the botnet herder. Botnets are the source of virtually all the high-volume DDoS attacks and unsolicited emails (spam). Fast-flux techniques are also used to facilitate the distribution of infective payloads and other illicit contents through an ever-changing chain of bots acting as proxies.

A DDoS attack is executed after a botnet herder distributes to a suitable number of bots orders to attack a target. While the attack preparation phase can be a long and complex process, the attack execution can be extremely fast, depending on the effectiveness of the C&C chain. Depending on the botnet size, several attack strategies can be used to disrupt the target's ability to deliver its services. If the DDoS attack is carried out with a small number of hosts, whose aggregate network throughput is not enough to saturate the network connection of the target, the preferred attack strategy is based on exploiting some execution path in the delivered service that causes high computational load on the attacked systems. For example, in a small-volume attack on a web server, the herder can instruct bots to generate requests for dynamically generated content that cannot be cached and requires heavy run-time computation to be generated. However, this kind of attack is strictly dependent on the nature of the attacked target. More portable attack strategies are based on the exhaustion of other limited resources in the OS of the attacked system. An example of a similar attack is SYN flood, in which a high number of pending connection requests is generated, thus preventing the attacked system from completing the TCP three-way handshake with legitimate hosts.

On the other hand, if the aggregate network traffic generated by the bots is enough to saturate the network connection of the attacked system, a DDoS can be simply generated by instructing the bots to send common and licit requests to the targeted systems. Such high-volume DDoS attacks are the most difficult to defend against, since requests generated by bots are virtually indistinguishable from requests generated by licit clients, making it impossible to apply trivial request filtering and access control schemes. In 2008, a DDoS attack generating an aggregate throughput of 40Gbit/s was reported. Finally, the attack effectiveness can be further increased by leveraging attack amplification techniques. Several amplification techniques can be used to multiply the bandwidth generated with a small number of hosts. A traditional attack amplification scheme is smurf [11], executed by broadcasting to an entire network an ICMP echo-request packet having the IP address of the attacked system as the spoofed source IP address. As a consequence, all the hosts connected to the network send a reply to the targeted system, which is reached by a multitude of network packets. Countless variations of this attack scheme exist, based on different ICMP messages or on completely different protocols.

A more recent amplification technique is DNS-based amplification [17], which can theoretically be used to amplify the bandwidth of a DDoS attack up to a factor of 73 (up to now, the highest amplification factor achieved in real attacks is between 16 and 19). The effectiveness of this amplification strategy is increased by the traditional traffic filtering rules applied by border routers and firewalls, usually configured to allow all DNS traffic.

In contrast to other cyber attacks that are carried out against the IT infrastructure of financial institutions, and that are usually based on the exploitation of some software vulnerability on the systems used by the financial institutions' customers or by the financial institutions themselves, DDoS attacks are based on the sheer volume of traffic that a sufficiently high number of bots is able to generate. The lack of a vulnerability to correct often leaves the administrators of the IT infrastructure of a financial institution powerless, since there is nothing they can do to stop or limit the flow of requests that is overloading their systems.

3.4.2 Case Studies

DDoS is one of the most common forms of attack that is routinely carried out against financial institutions. Moreover, the effect is evident to all the customers of the attacked institutions, and DDoS attacks also receive a lot of attention from the media. A simple query to common search engines with the keywords "DDoS" and "bank" suffices to reveal countless examples of attacks to renowned financial firms and credit card companies.

Among the most recent DDoS attacks against European financial institutions, a well-known one targeted Rabobank, one of the biggest Dutch banks [26]. Rabobank's web site was deliberately overflowed by a massive amount of data on the 19th and 20th of February 2011, and the attack resulted in extended periods of service downtime during which customers were unable to conduct Internet-banking and web-banking transactions. As a consequence of the countermeasures taken by the ISP used by Rabobank to connect to the Internet, several customers were unable to resume normal use of the home-banking web application until a few days later.

Moreover, the Rabobank case highlights the need for novel, automatic strategies for information sharing among financial institutions. Even though Rabobank detected the DDoS attack, they failed to inform some of their key business partners, perhaps because they were too busy trying to recover from their technical difficulties. Among these business partners is iDEAL, a major Dutch payment service. This lack of information resulted in dramatic impacts on the iDEAL business. According to an iDEAL spokesman [26],

> With notification, or even just monitoring of its vendor's online posture, iDeal would have been able to avoid the major service outage they suffered that went well beyond the Rabobank situation. Outreach to key processors/partners/government needs to be part of any response plan where there's a major compromise or loss of service.

DDoS attacks have also been used to extort money from the owner of web-based businesses, such as home-banking web sites, online bookmakers and casinos, and online gaming platforms. A DDoS extortion usually starts with an email sent by the attacker to the administrator of the targeted business, announcing that the mail will be followed by a sample DDoS attack. After that, a short-lived DDoS attack is executed, demonstrating the attacker's ability to disrupt the target's business. This demonstration of power is then followed by a second email that threatens the victim with a new, longer DDoS attack unless a certain amount of money is received (typically through an off-shore bank account).

A typical example of such an extortion letter was published in a whitepaper by Prolexic [28] in 2004 [27]:

> Your site is under attack and will be for this entire weekend. You can increase your pipe all you want and it wont help. You have a flaw in your network that allows this to take place. You have two choices. You can ignore this email and try to keep your site up, which will cost you tens of thousands of dollars in lost (business) and customers, or you can send us $40k to make sure that your site experiences no problems.
> If you send the $40k your site will be protected not just this weekend, but for the next 12 months. This will let you enjoy business with no worry. If you choose not to pay for our help, then you will probably not be in business much longer, as you will be under attack each weekend for the next 20 weeks, or until you close your doors.
> You can always choose to wait, see what happens, and then contact us for our help when you realize you cant do it yourself, however, then it will cost you more and your site will still be down.
> The choice is yours as we await your response.
> P.S. The sites that were attacked and paid last weekend are happy that they paid and are protected

Finally, several powerful DDoS attacks have been motivated by religious, political, and ideological reasons. As an example, consider the string of DDoS attacks against financial institutions and payment services that were carried out by the so-called Anonymous as a retaliation toward all the institutions that stopped processing donations to the Wikileaks web site (the "operation Avenge Assange"). These DDoS attacks took out of business for extended periods of time companies such as Pay-Pal [29], Mastercard [31], Visa [30], the Swiss bank PostFinance [32], and Bank of America [33].

3.4.3 Benefits of Information Sharing

The detection of a DDoS attack is usually extremely simple, since even trivial and centralized system and network monitoring tools can report a sharp and unexpected increase in resource consumption resulting in the inability of the attacked system to correctly deliver their services. Once the attack has been detected, it is important for the attacked system to log all the possible information about the traffic that is causing the DDoS.

If multiple financial institutions cooperate by sharing information, then all this data can be processed together, thus allowing for better and more precise assessment of the real nature of the attack. Cooperation through information sharing can be extremely useful, especially if the attack is hitting multiple systems at the same time (such as replicated and redundant web servers of the same financial institution).

If there is a low variability in the source addresses and protocols of the network packets used to carry out the DDoS attacks, then it is possible to effectively cluster them in a limited number of classes characterized by specific features. This classification information can then be disseminated to all the interested parties (both within the same financial institution and across different domains) to help define appropriate filtering rules able to mitigate low-volume DDoS attacks.

For high-volume DDoS attacks, which rely on network packets that are indistinguishable from licit requests, the information collected by the network monitoring system and shared among collaborative financial institutions can be aggregated with the aim of identifying the network prefixes from which the largest part of the attack traffic originates. It is also possible to leverage geo-location techniques of the originating networks, to attempt to identify the countries from which the attack originates.

All the information related to the source addresses from which the attack appears to be generated can be automatically distributed to the ISP of the attacked financial institution. ISP involvement is known to be the most effective means to counter DDoS, because it allows filtering of the offending traffic when it is near to its source. However, the common best practices do not provide for an automatic communication channel between institutions and ISPs, thus requiring human intervention. Typically, network security experts within the attacked institution directly contact the technical personnel of their ISP (e.g., by phone), asking for collaboration in setting up new filtering rules whose parameters are transmitted manually. This process is prone to human error, introduces unnecessary delays in the application of

DDoS mitigation procedures, and is slow to react to possible changes in the attack pattern. All these issues can be effectively tackled by the CoMiFin communication infrastructures.

Another benefit of cooperation through information sharing is the dissemination of event information to financial institutions and ISPs that have not been directly involved in the attack. While these parties cannot do anything to mitigate the attack while it is happening, the knowledge of past DDoS attacks can be effectively used to help in early identification of known attack sources (amplifiers, bots, entire networks, or subnetworks) that participate in subsequent illicit activities. ISPs can use this information to backtrack the attack sources, contacting their service providers and the owners of originating networks in order to notify them of systems that have been compromised with very high probability.

In particular, information sharing can prove very useful to counter traffic amplification. DDoS carried out by different botnets through different means can still leverage the same amplification techniques (for example, the same ill-configured DNS servers). By correlating events generated by several distributed sources, it is possible to identify these invariants among distributed attacks targeting heterogeneous financial infrastructures, thus allowing ISPs to filter the traffic generated by known DDoS amplifiers as near to the source as possible.

One can identify different kinds of information that collaborative financial institutions can share in order to improve the effectiveness of DDoS detection and mitigation activities:

- source addresses of network traffic received during the attack;
- transport layer protocol of the network traffic received during the attack;
- application layer protocol (if applicable) of the traffic received during the attack;
- size of network packets received during the attack;
- any information related to the network traffic received during the attack that is flagged as suspicious by commonly deployed network-based intrusion detection systems, or NIDSs (such as unusual flags in the TCP headers).

This information can hardly be defined as critical, since they reveal details about the attack without leaking any knowledge about a financial institution's inner network structure or business processes. Addresses and other details related to the attacked systems can be anonymized without reducing the mitigation and prevention effectiveness.

Possible information sources are the logs generated by firewalls, routers, NIDSs, and applications (such as web servers). Since DDoS attacks target systems that are accessible from the Internet, all this information can be acquired by monitoring systems that are deployed within the DMZ of the targeted financial institutions. In particular, there is no need to access financial transaction details or any monitoring information related to the financial networks.

3.5 Session Hijacking Attacks

To facilitate repeated user interactions over prolonged periods, the HTTP/1.1 protocol defined key-value text strings to be issued by a server and handed to a client; these are called *cookies*. When the client's browser next communicates with the server, all cookies that have been handed to the client by that server are automatically submitted as a part of the HTTP request. The most common use of cookies is to provide a unique, hard-to-guess *session identifier* (session ID) to each client. When a user submits a request along with the appropriate session identifier, the server will be able to retrieve the state pertaining to the user, such as the user's name, whether she has been authenticated, her credit card information, and so forth.

The security of the session ID relies entirely on it being hard to guess. Various attacks are based on snatching a valid session ID from a victim (such as cross-site scripting or snooping attacks), but what about the direct brute-force approach? It turns out that several implementations of widely used session ID generators have been shown to provide inadequate security, and these can be exploited by botnets (see Sect. 3.4.1). In this section, we discuss how large botnets can be used to compromise web sessions. In particular, we focus on the session IDs generated by servers running the current version of PHP (5.3.6). The security of PHP session generation was hardened following the discovery of a weakness in versions 5.3.1 and below [5]. While these countermeasures effectively prevent a lone attacker from compromising the web sessions, they prove insufficient against a determined adversary who commands an army of bots.

3.5.1 Attack Description

Security experts and academics have demonstrated that botnets are not only numerous but appear to have become gargantuan in size (Table 3.1). To illustrate the scale of the problem, the Mariposa botnet was estimated to be running on 12.7 million infected hosts when it was infiltrated and taken down in December 2009 [18]. Between April and June 2010, Microsoft alone removed known bots from 6.5 million of the roughly 600 million computers enrolled in Microsoft's various update and anti-malware services [20]. The black market for botnets is thriving and even competitive, as witnessed by their low prices ($200 per week for 6000 infected computers) and the availability of advanced features such as "verified sellers" and 24/7 technical support for the botnet customers [20]. Money attracts talent, so it is natural to contemplate what attacks may be launched with tomorrow's botnets.

The attack we will focus on is speculative yet feasible against session IDs. The observation is that session IDs generated by many web sites rely on a few true bits of randomness, such as a hash of the time of day, the client's IP address, or even just a counter. Let the *bits of entropy* denote the number of bits that the attacker, after factoring in all his knowledge, needs to guess in order to produce the correct session ID. For example, a scheme which hashes the time of day and the client's

Table 3.1 *Botnet sizes.*
Estimated total number of
infected nodes (footprint) in
various botnets whose size
exceeded 100,000 hosts in the
past. We use the estimate
from the most recently
published source when
multiple ones exist

Botnet name(s)	Estimated size
Mariposa/Rimecud [18]	12,700,000
Conficker [3]	6,000,000–12,000,000
Rustock/R,000Rustok/Costrat [1, 7]	1,100,000–1,700,000
Cutwail/Pandex/Mutant [1, 7]	560,000–840,000
Mazbeen [7]	510,000–770,000
Grum [7]	310,000–470,000
Bobax [1, 7]	250,000–370,000
Kraken [6]	318,000
Srizbi/Cbeplay/Exchanger [1]	315,000
Clickbot.A [12]	100,000
Storm [1]	85,000

IP address provides 32 bits of entropy if the adversary knows the log-in time and potentially less if the IP address can be narrowed down. Note that the adversary is guessing the *input* values to the generator and then simulating the generator to produce the session ID—not guessing the hashed output values directly. Using a botnet to guess all combinations for the unknown bits can prove remarkably efficient against weak session ID generators.

Claim Consider a web site that hosts c concurrent sessions and provides k bits of entropy for the session IDs. An attacker whose botnet can sustain x requests per second to the web site without overloading it can guess *some* session identifier within $\frac{2^k}{x \cdot c} \log \frac{1}{\varepsilon}$ seconds with probability at least $1 - \varepsilon$.

Proof We assume the k random bits in each new session ID are uniformly chosen and ensured to be distinct. A random guess will match a session ID in use with probability $1 - \frac{c}{2^k}$. Then a series of n guesses succeeds with probability

$$1 - \left(1 - \frac{c}{2^k}\right)^n \geq 1 - e^{-\frac{nc}{2^k}}$$

which is at least $1 - \varepsilon$ when $n \geq \frac{2^k}{c} \log \frac{1}{\varepsilon}$. $\square$

For example, an attack at a rate of $x = 1000$ HTTP request pairs per second against a web site with $c = 10,000$ active sessions and $k = 32$ bits of entropy in session IDs will match some identifier in 17 minutes with at least 90% probability.

Modern Session ID Generators

The session ID produced by modern web servers is typically a hash (SHA1 or MD5) of a pseudo-random number manipulated by some *salt*—a random value based on the client, such as his IP address or the timestamp of the log-in, or both. Thus the bits of entropy now depend on the output of the pseudo-random number generator (PRNG) as well as the salt extracted from the client. The botnet operator can still attempt to guess these bits by brute force, but the claim above shows that the attack takes exponentially longer with more bits of entropy. A different approach is required.

It turns out that if the attacker can produce a valid session ID while essentially knowing the value of the salt used (e.g., the time of the log-in and the IP address used), he can launch a two-stage attack.

- *Stage 1*: Perform an offline computation to find what seed of the PRNG would produce the valid session ID. Note that the scan requires no interaction with the server. PRNGs are deterministic when the seed or internal state is known, so the only source of entropy in a future session ID is the salt.
- *Stage 2*: The adversary launches an online brute-force attack against the server to guess the bits of entropy in the salt for authenticated clients and thus determine valid session IDs.

Exploits of this kind have been conducted in the past. For example, Gutterman and Malkhi [4] showed that the supposedly secure 128-bit session IDs in Apache Tomcat 5 used only 64 bits for the PRNG seed (so Stage 1 takes 2^{64} computation steps) and no salt whatsoever, so all future session identifiers could be deterministically predicted. In 2010, Samy Kamkar [5] showed that the 64-bit seed for the PRNG in PHP 5.3.1 and below provides only 37 bits of entropy (and less if the PHP process ID is known) due to a weakness in the timestamp manipulation. The original seed for the PRNG could be brute-forced in less than a minute on a typical laptop, although the duration depends linearly on the number of session IDs that have been issued by the PHP server. Kamkar did not discuss salt, and the weakness he identified was fixed in PHP 5.3.2. Andreas Bogk [2] pointed out that a brute-force attack could be done to guess the PRNG seed in the new version of PHP, assuming that information is either leaked by the server or that sufficient computational resources are available. We refine his analysis and investigate how an attack on PHP could be mounted by a botnet in the next section.

Session ID Generation in PHP

In the current version of PHP (version 5.3.6), the following 148 pseudo-random bits are hashed to create a 128-bit session ID:

1. current timestamp $(32 + 20$ bits),
2. IP address of the client (32 bits), and
3. a pseudo-random value from a PRNG (64 bits).

PRNG input As outlined before, let us begin by investigating the PRNG, which is a linear congruential generator (LCG). The LCG is seeded by `lcg_seed()` with two 32-bit integers `s1` and `s2` as follows:

```
//from ext/standard/lcg.c
gettimeofday(&tv, NULL);
LCG(s1) = tv.tv_sec ^ (tv.tv_usec <<11);
LCG(s2) = (long) getpid();
//Add entropy by checking again
gettimeofday(&tv, NULL);
LCG(s2) ^= (tv.tv_usec <<11);
```

We must now estimate the bits of entropy produced by this process, which constitutes two timestamps and a process ID. First, we can assess the effect of calling `gettimeofday()` twice in rapid succession. In an experiment on PHP 5.3.6, we found that the difference between the timestamps is between 3 and 10 μs over 99.74% of the time, giving about 3 bits of entropy. We measured the difference d between the value of `tv.tv_usec` in the second call and that of the first in PHP 5.3.5 on an idle 2.5 GHz Intel Core Duo 2 laptop over 100,000 trials. While d takes values between 2 and 3432 μs, the mode is 4 μs, the mean is 4.587 μs and 99.74% of the values lie between 3 and 10 μs (over 99.9% lie between 3 and 18 μs). However, the last line in the code snippet XORs the 5 most *variable* bits of `tv.tv_usec` with the high-order bits of the unknown 16-bit process ID. Thus, with high probability, the operation cancels out the 3 bits of entropy that were supposedly added to `s2`.

We are thus left with a timestamp and a process ID. Let's assume that the attacker knows the first k bits of the time when PHP seeded the LCG (i.e., within 2^{31-k} seconds). If $k \leq 15$, then the same guess for the top k bits in `tv.tv_usec` can be applied in both `s1` and `s2` with high probability. Thus the bits of entropy in the LCG is $62 - k$ bits, ranging from 47 bits (seed time known within 9 hours) to typically about 50 bits (seed time known within 12 days). If $k \geq 20$, the attacker will have information about the low-order 11 bits of `tv.tv_sec` and thus `s1`; the bits of entropy are $67 - k$.

A determined attacker can flood an Apache process via an HTTP keep-alive connection, causing the process to respawn and thus the PHP to be reseeded at a known point in time. A less aggressive adversary could instead continuously `ping` the server and wait for it to be rebooted by observing the `epoch` value in the options of a TCP session when it comes back up. While the latter method requires more patience, it has the additional benefit that the process ID value from `getpid()` lands in a short range of common values, reducing the bits of entropy by another 15 bits on Linux or 17 bits on OS-X [5]. With this approach we assume that the timestamp is known within a second, giving 36 bits of entropy.

PRNG output   We now understand how the LCG is seeded, but how can we know when we find the appropriate seed? Despite the large internal state, the LCG generator `php_combined_lcg()` has only has 2^{31} distinct outputs (it converts an `int` to a `double`). This means that by viewing an output value (or two) from the target LCG, we will be able to determine the correct LCG seed in the offline scan of Stage 1 with high probability.

Let's look back at the sources of entropy. As seen in `lcg.c`, PHP computes the session ID for a user as the MD5 hash of a buffer consisting of `LCG(s1)` and

LCG(s2). Thus in order to determine what LCG output value was used to generate the attacker's session ID, he must try 2^{20} possibilities for the microsecond times 2^{31} values corresponding to the LCG output, run it through MD5, and compare the resulting hash to the session ID. If they match, he can proceed to crack the internal state of the LCG as described above. The value of the bits of entropy within the LCG is larger than its output value, so multiple candidates for the values of the internal space produce a valid output. To narrow down the list of options, the attacker may repeat the exercise on a new session ID. In total, this gives 2^{51} MD5 computations.

Botnet Attack Against PHP

In summary, the botnet herder could proceed as follows. Here, s should be set to bound the number of times the LCG has been called on the server, which is usually the number of sessions that have been created.

- *Stage 1.1*: One bot waits for PHP to be reseeded, obtains a valid session ID, recording the server timestamp and own IP address, and disseminates to other bots.
- *Stage 1.2*: Each bot repeatedly guesses random microsecond and LCG output values, constructs a buffer, and computes an MD5 hash. If the session ID matches the MD5 hash, send the value ℓ of the LCG to all other bots to begin Stage 2.
- *Stage 1.3*: Each bot repeatedly guesses a random seed, and iterates the LCG s times. If the LCG output value matches ℓ, output candidate values for s1 and s2.
- *Stage 1.4*: Terminate when a handful of candidates have been collected. One bot establishes another valid session ID, determines the correct LCG seed, and disseminates it to other bots.

With the LCG seed in hand, the attacker now waits for a victim client to log in to the PHP server. If the attacker knows the time of the log-in within a second accuracy (if the site displays "users online," for instance, like Facebook) and the IP address range of the victim (suggesting a targeted attack).

- *Stage 2*: Each bot repeatedly guesses microsecond and IP values for the victim, constructs a session ID using the correct LCG value, and tries the session ID on the target PHP server.

Stage 1.1 takes at most a second after the server is reseeded. Stage 1.2 takes at most $\frac{2^{51-30}}{n} = \frac{2^{21}}{n}$ seconds with n bots, assuming each bot performs 2^{30} MD5 computations per second [2]. A million bots will complete the stage in 2 seconds. To compute all possible candidate seeds, Stage 1.3 will take at most $\frac{0.03 \cdot 2^{36}}{n}$ seconds, assuming the seed time to be known to within a second, thus taking a little more than 30 minutes on a million-node botnet with each bot running 33 LCG computations per second [2]. Note that the expression is independent of s by using a memory-time tradeoff [5]. Stage 1.4 takes at most one second. The duration of Stage 2 depends on the information known about the victim, and is lower bounded by the time it takes the PHP server to receive 2^{20} packets when only the microsecond information is missing. If the server is able to keep up with 1000 HTTP requests/response pairs per second, Stage 2 takes on average less than 10 minutes per victim.

3.5.2 Case Studies

Botnet herders are acutely aware of the tremendously powerful artillery at their disposal, and continuously seek out new profitable venues. A hijacked web session of an email or bank account (or a shopping site) can give access to substantial sensitive information. Fortunately, to the best of our knowledge, no large-scale botnet attacks against session IDs have been reported.

Nevertheless, in a similar vein, botnets that try to guess common passwords against servers have been around for years [47]. They exploit the fact that users often do not change default passwords, and that passwords are rarely stronger than what the password policy dictates as a minimum [13]. Commanding more bots also implies that more attempts in aggregate can be made to guess the password for a single user, because security policies often restrict the number of guesses from an IP address instead of temporarily blocking a given username when too many attempts have been made.

3.5.3 Benefits of Information Sharing

The brute-force attack against PHP web session IDs we have detailed here shows how large botnets can be used to overcome protection based on something being "hard to guess." The category includes session IDs, cookies, hidden URLs, and passwords. For session IDs, the problem can be solved by using sufficient entropy when seeding security-critical PRNGs. For instance, /dev/urandom on Linux generates bits generated from random activity on peripheral devices and drivers. PHP supports additional entropy sources for session IDs, but unfortunately disables them by default. It is also prudent to expire sessions faster and periodically regenerate IDs used in persistent session cookies.

While it is easy to fix particular vulnerabilities (such as patching up PHP), the real challenge is to protect against new vulnerabilities. The botnet attack we described has a general structure that cooperating financial institutions can use as a template to nip novel botnet attacks in the bud.

While the first stage of the PHP attack is mostly conducted offline, the second stage involves presenting the server with a large number of invalid session IDs. This kind of behavior should immediately raise red flags with the help of anomaly detection techniques. In fact, the large influx of requests will look similar to a DDoS attack, and so the same kind of information logging and sharing discussed in Sect. 3.4.3 applies in this scenario.

If multiple financial institutions cooperate to create and enforce a blacklist of IP addresses involved in the attack, then the probability that the botnet operator successfully guesses a valid session ID diminishes quickly. In particular, each bot can only be used a limited number of times against any participating financial institute, so very large botnets (on the order of millions) are required to launch a successful attack.

We can further assume that logs collect information about the type of activity encountered in each request. As before, this does not reveal critical information as long as the activity is tagged as "invalid session identifier" rather than including more details. Now it could be understood that an abnormally large fraction of requests present an invalid session identifier. When this is discovered, it could be a matter of policy to dictate that all valid session IDs are henceforth revoked and that all previously authenticated users at the cooperating financial institutions must be reauthenticated. While reauthenticating is inconvenient for the users, it improves the security of their bank accounts.

3.6 Malware-Based Attacks Against Customers

Malware, and especially Internet worms and Trojans, represent a well-known threat to the security of networked information systems; this is not limited to the scenario of financial institutions. However, in the last few years computer security researchers witnessed a steep increase in the number of malware that are specifically designed to target banks.

An example of an attack to a financial institution conducted through a malware has already been described in Sect. 3.2—the example of MitM attack through the compromise of home ADSL routers carried out by a worm that targeted the Brazilian bank Bradesco. In this case the attack was limited to a particular bank and relied on a specific network appliance that is owned by only a minority of the bank's customers.

However, the more recent (and definitely more successful) malware variants known as Zeus, SpyEye, and Tatanga represent a much worse threat, since they exploit vulnerabilities in common web browsers that have a very wide install base, and are programmed to target a high number of different home-banking web sites.

3.6.1 Attack Description

Since home-banking applications are always made available through a web-based interface, access to a home-banking account has to be mediated by a browser, such as Internet Explorer, Firefox, Opera, or Chrome, among others. Attackers soon realized that by exploiting the vulnerabilities of a browser it is possible to design a malware that is able to take control of a home-banking session that has been initiated by a legitimate customer. In particular, a malware that successfully compromises a customer's browser has direct access to the customer's credentials (including one-time tokens) and to a home-banking session that has already been opened by the unsuspecting customer.

The first phase of the attack through banking malware is the infection. This step of the attack does not present anything new with respect to other generic (not bank-oriented) malware that infects common personal computers and spreads over the Internet. Banking malware can be installed on a personal computer or on a mobile computing device as the infective payload that is loaded by an Internet worm. Moreover, an attacker may try to exploit different infection vectors, such as social engineering through spam and phishing email.

Once the banking malware is installed, it tries to compromise the browser that is used to browse the Web. If the infection succeeds, the malware stays silent, waiting for the user of the compromised personal computer to connect to one of the known home-banking web sites. Home-banking web sites of different financial institutions can have different internal structures, can be based on different server-side and client-side technologies, and can adopt different measures to protect the security of their customers. Hence banking malware is shipped with a list of known home-banking web sites (uniquely identified by their URL) and with the code that is necessary to attack each of them. Since the design of a home-banking web site is subject to changes over time, the most sophisticated banking malware are able to constantly update the attack code through the Internet. Moreover, this feature can also be used by an attacker to increase the number of home-banking web sites that are "supported" by the malware.

When the user points the compromised browser to a known home-banking web site, the malware activates and starts to perform a *Man-in-the-Browser* (MitB) attack. While a MitM attack (see Sect. 3.2) is performed by sitting "in the middle" of the connection between the customer and the server of the financial institution, in a MitB attack the malware has full control of the browser that is one of the two endpoints of the connection. This vantage point offers a new avenue to the attacker and greatly simplifies the execution of frauds. To perform a MitM the attacker needs to build an exact copy of the targeted home-banking web site, while in the MitB case the customer reaches the true home-banking web site. Moreover, nowadays virtually all the home-banking web sites leverage SSL and HTTPS protocols to authenticate themselves. Since it is extremely difficult for an attacker to obtain the digital certificates of a financial institution, in most cases the connection to the MitM server fails HTTPS authentication, thus giving a security-conscious customer the ability to recognize that something fishy is happening. On the other hand, with MitB the customer connects to the legitimate web site, hence HTTPS authentication does not pose any problem.

While active, the banking malware has access to all the information that the customer inputs into the browser to access its bank account. This information includes normal authentication credentials (usernames, PINs, and passwords), one-time tokens generated through RSA keys, and security codes sent to the customer through emails, SMSs, or phone calls. All this information is stored, and possibly sent to the criminal organization that controls the malware for later use.

To prevent keyloggers from gathering the credentials and the codes that customers use to authenticate themselves, some financial institutions implemented "software keyboards" or "software numpads" that allow customers to input the required information by clicking with the mouse on letters and numbers drawn on the monitor. This defense strategy has been overcome by modern banking malware that is able to take a screenshot of the monitor (or of the region of the monitor that is near the mouse pointer) and collect the required information even though the keyboard is not used.

After the customer has successfully authenticated to the home-banking web site, the banking malware leverages its capability to take over the browser to issue money transfer orders over the authenticated connection that was initiated by the customer. Typically the malware executes short batches of money transfer orders as soon as possible. Since MitB strategies allow the malware to take full control of the browser, the malware is also able to alter the content of the web page before it is rendered and displayed on the monitor. This feature is commonly used to hide the amount of money stolen from the bank account and the records of money transfer that have been ordered by the malware.

3.6.2 Case Studies

Recently, two main families of banking malware have been detected in the wild, and they have been able to infect several thousands of users: Zeus [34] and SpyEye [35].

Both Zeus and SpyEye do not limit themselves to performing the MitB attacks described in the previous section. They come with built-in rootkit functionalities, which allow them to stay hidden and make it more difficult for antivirus software to remove them, and they implement a communication infrastructure that is typical of botnets. Moreover, both of them are able to receive updates, thus representing a continuous threat that is difficult to eradicate completely.

Zeus is the first (or at least the first one that reached worldwide diffusion) banking malware to implement advanced features for information stealing, such as the ability to take screenshots of virtual keyboards. SpyEye is mostly known for its ability to infect mobile devices based on the Android operating system.

While old specimens of Zbot and SpyEye are detected by all major antivirus software, new variants that try to evade detection are produced continuously. Moreover, the public availability of Zbot source code makes it easy to build a custom malware while inheriting all the most advanced features of Zbot.

3.6.3 Benefits of Information Sharing

Information sharing, together with continuous analysis of the events that are related to the activities of home-banking customers, can be of great help in allowing early detection of banking malware.

Banking malware tries to infect the highest possible number of customers in the shortest period of time; hence financial institutions will soon start to handle home-banking transactions that are controlled by the malware from different customers and IP addresses. Since these transactions are the result of browsing sessions that are controlled programmatically, they always exhibit similar features, such as the order with which some activities are performed and the time interval between them. By analyzing a high number of transactions, it is possible to outline these features, and to build patterns of anomalous activities that can be used to detect if a customer browser is being controlled by the malware.

Moreover, if procedures and infrastructures for automatic dissemination of these patterns are used, this information can be shared among different financial institutions. Information sharing at this level would allow financial institutions to build a common database of anomalous behavior that could be used to reduce the time needed to detect MitB attacks.

References

1. Stewart, J.: Top spam botnets exposed, April (2008)
2. Bogk, A.: Advisory: weak PNG in PHP session ID generation leads to session hijacking, March (2010)
3. BBC News: Botnet hacker caught in Slovenia, July (2010)
4. Gutterman, Z., Malkhi, D.: Hold your sessions: an attack on java session-id generation. In: Menezes, A. (ed.) CT-RSA. Lecture Notes in Computer Science, vol. 3376, pp. 44–57. Springer, Berlin (2005)
5. Kamkar, S.: phpwn: Attacking sessions and pseudo-random numbers in PHP. Las Vegas, NV, USA, July 2010. Blackhat
6. Moscaritolo, A.: Kraken botnet re-emerges 318,000 nodes strong. SC magazine June (2010)
7. MessageLabs Intelligence: Annual security report, December (2010)
8. Davies, K.: DNS cache poisoning vulnerability, available online at http://www.iana.org/about/presentations/davies-cairo-vulnerability-081103.pdf (2008)
9. Espiner, T.: Symantec warns of router compromise, available online at http://www.zdnetasia.com/news/security/0,39044215,62036991,00.htm
10. Espelid, Y., Netkand, L.-H., Klingsheim, A.N., Hole, K.J.: Robbing banks with their own software, an exploit against Norwegian online banks. In: Proceedings of the IFIP 23rd International Information Security Conference, September 2008
11. Klein, A.: BIND 9 DNS cache poisoning. Available online at http://www.trusteer.com/files/BIND_9_DNS_Cache_Poisoning.pdf
12. Microsoft Corporation: Microsoft Security Bulletin MS07-062 Important. Available online at http://www.microsoft.com/technet/security/bulletin/MS07-062.mspx
13. Smith, D.: Link router based worm? Available online at http://isc.sans.org/diary.html?storyid=4175
14. SecurityFocus: Cross Site Request Forgery in 2wire routers. Available online at http://www.securityfocus.com/archive/1/476595/100/0/threaded
15. TriCipher: The perfect storm: man in the middle attacks, weak authentication and organized online criminals. Available online at http://www.infosec.co.uk/ExhibitorLibrary/634/The_Perfect_Storm_-_TriCipher_MITM_Whitepaper2_20.pdf
16. Wilson, T.: For Sale: Phishing Kit. Available online at http://www.darkreading.com/security/management/showArticle.jhtml?articleID=208804288

17. Vaughn, R., Evron, G.: DNS amplification attacks. Available online at http://packetstorm. linuxsecurity.net/papers/attack/DNS-Amplification-Attacks.pdf, March 2006
18. Kumar, S.: Smurf-based distributed denial of service (DDoS) attack amplification in internet. In: Second International Conference on Internet Monitoring and Protection (ICIMP 2007) (2007)
19. Cooke, E., Jahanian, F., McPherson, D.: The Zombie Roundup: Understanding, Detecting, and Disrupting Botnets. USENIX Step to reducing unwanted traffic on the internet Workshop (SRUTI'05)
20. http://www.eweek.com/c/a/Security/Report-Claims-DNS-Cache-Poisoning-Attack-Against-Brazilian-Bank-and-ISP-761709/, last visited: September 2011
21. http://www.theregister.co.uk/2009/04/22/bandesco_cache_poisoning_attack/, last visited: September 2011
22. http://forums.cnet.com/7726-6132_102-5169711.html, last visited: September 2011
23. http://www.wizcrafts.net/blogs/2008/01/hackers_exploit_vulnerability_in_2wire_modem. html, last visited: September 2011
24. http://www.phishtank.com/, last visited: September 2011
25. http://www.f-secure.com/weblog/archives/00002235.html, last visited: September 2011
26. http://news.idg.no/cw/art.cfm?id=3F6822FF-1A64-6A71-CE67724BB606D61C, last visited: September 2011
27. Paulson, R.A., Weber, J.E.: Cyberextortion: an overview of distributed denial of service attacks against online gaming companies. Issues in Information Systems **VII**(2) (2006)
28. Prolexic home page. Available online at http://www.prolexic.com/, last visited: September 2011
29. http://www.theregister.co.uk/2010/12/06/anonymous_launches_pro_wikileaks_campaign/, last visited: September 2011
30. http://www.readwriteweb.com/archives/ddos_attacks_take_down_mastercard_and_visa_website.php, last visited: September 2011
31. http://www.itproportal.com/2010/12/08/anonymous-ddos-mastercard-site-wikileaks-revenge-attack/, last visited: September 2011
32. http://www.computerworld.com/s/article/9200098/WikiLeaks_furor_spawns_rival_DDoS_battles, last visited: September 2011
33. https://www.infosecisland.com/blogview/10542-Bank-of-America-Hit-By-Anonymous-DDoS-Attack.html, last visited: September 2011
34. http://www.symantec.com/security_response/writeup.jsp?docid=2010-011016-3514-99
35. http://www.symantec.com/security_response/writeup.jsp?docid=2010-020216-0135-99
36. CERT Advisory CA-2003-04, MS-SQL Server Worm. Available online at: http://www.cert. org/advisories/CA-2003-04.html
37. Moore, D., Paxon, V., Savage, S., Shannon, C., Staniford, S., Weaver, N.: Inside the Slammer Worm. IEEE Security & Privacy (2003)
38. Microsoft Security Bulletin MS02-039. Buffer Overruns in SQL Server 2000 Resolution Service Could Enable Code Execution (Q323875). Available online at: http://www.microsoft. com/technet/security/bulletin/MS02-039.mspx
39. Government of Canada OCIPEP. Microsoft SQL Server 2000 Slammer Worm—Impact Paper (2003)
40. Lee, C.B., Roedel, C., Silenok, E.: In: Detection and Characterization of Port Scan Attacks, vol. 2004, San Diego, CA (2003)
41. Bro: an open source Unix based Network intrusion detection system (NIDS). http://www. bro-ids.org/ (2010)
42. Snort: an open source network intrusion prevention and detection system (IDS/IPS). http://www.snort.org/ (2010)
43. Staniford, J.A.H.S., McAlerney, J.M.: Practical automated detection of stealthy portscans. In: Proceedings of the 7th ACM Conference on Computer and Communications Security (2000)
44. Aniello, L., Lodi, G., Baldoni, R.: Inter-domain stealthy port scan detection through complex event processing. In: 13th European Workshop on Dependable Computing (EWDC 2011) (2011)

45. OWASP page on Cross-site Scripting attacks, https://www.owasp.org/index.php/Cross-site_
    Scripting_(XSS), last visited: September 2011
46. OWASP page on Cross-site Request Forgery attacks, https://www.owasp.org/index.php/
    Cross-Site_Request_Forgery_(CSRF), last visited: September 2011
47. Goodin, D.: Server-based botnet floods net with brutish SSH attacks. http://www.theregister.
    co.uk/2010/08/12/server_based_botnet/ (accessed on 01/24/11) (2010)

Part II
CoMiFin Collaborative Platform

The only real security that a man can have in this world is a reserve of knowledge, experience and ability.
Henry Ford

As we argued in Part I, critical infrastructures (CIs), such as financial, air traffic control, and power grid systems, are undergoing profound technological and usage changes. Globalization, new technological trends, increasingly powerful customers, and intensified competition have brought about a shift in the internal organization of the CI IT from being confined within the organizational boundaries to becoming a truly global ecosystem featuring numerous cross-domain interactions and heterogeneity of systems and data. These trends, along with the increased prevalence of off-the-shelf hardware and software, reliance on open communication infrastructures (such as the Internet), and growing "webification" of customer-facing services are making the CIs increasingly vulnerable to sophisticated Internet-based security attacks.

The complex proprietary infrastructures that "no hackers knew" are now being replaced by open systems whose vulnerabilities are documented and well known. Although the sophistication of cyber attacks has been increasing over time, the technical knowledge required to exploit the existing vulnerabilities has been declining (H.F. Lipson, Tracking and Tracing Cyber-Attacks: Technical Challenges and Global Policy, 2002.). Today, attacking tools are often fully automated, and the technology employed in many attacks is simple to use, inexpensive, and widely available. This leads to rapid expansion of the attacker communities, amplifying the damages that they inflict upon the CIs (In the Crossfire—Critical Infrastructure in the Age of Cyber War, McAfee, 2010.). Furthermore, the resulting massive scales of the attacks complicate their detection and prevention by individual CI organizations, making cross-organizational cooperation and collaboration an imperative.

In Part II of the book, we introduce a middleware platform, called *CoMiFin*, facilitating collaborative protection of the financial CI. At the core of CoMiFin is the abstraction of *Semantic Room (SR)*, allowing the interested participants to share information and combine their computing powers to collectively resist massive scale attacks against their IT assets. We describe the SR abstraction, a software architecture for realizing it in a distributed system, and the implementation of its various components. We demonstrate how the resulting system can be utilized to build full-stack end-to-end protection mechanisms against the attack scenarios described in Part I.

Chapter 4
CoMiFin Architecture and Semantic Rooms

Roberto Baldoni, Vita Bortnikov, Gregory Chockler, Eliezer Dekel,
Gennady Laventman, Giorgia Lodi, and Luca Montanari

Abstract We present the architecture of a middleware platform, called *Collabo-rative Middleware for Monitoring Financial Critical Infrastructure* (*CoMiFin*), that facilitates collaborative protection of the financial critical infrastructure (CI). At the core of CoMiFin is a new abstraction of *Semantic Room* (*SR*), allowing the in-terested participants to share information and combine their computing powers to collectively resist massive scale attacks against their IT and business assets. We de-scribe a full stack of software components aiming at realizing SR in a distributed setting. At the lowest level, the SR functionality relies on a customizable event pro-cessing platform, which can be supported through a variety of event processing and analytics containers. The containers abstract away the intricacies of the distributed environment, and allow the application developers to focus on implementing the processing logic at hand. The higher level aspects of the SR abstraction are sup-ported by the SR Management layer, which includes components to control the SR

V. Bortnikov · G. Chockler (✉) · E. Dekel · G. Laventman
IBM, Research Division, Haifa University Campus, Mount Carmel, Haifa 31905, Israel
e-mail: chockler@il.ibm.com

V. Bortnikov
e-mail: bortnikov@il.ibm.com

E. Dekel
e-mail: dekel@il.ibm.com

G. Laventman
e-mail: laventman@il.ibm.com

R. Baldoni · L. Montanari
Dipartimento di Ingegneria Informatica, Automatica e Gestionale Antonio Ruberti, Università
degli Studi di Roma "La Sapienza", Via Ariosto 25, 00185 Roma, Italy

R. Baldoni
e-mail: baldoni@dis.uniroma1.it

L. Montanari
e-mail: montanari@dis.uniroma1.it

G. Lodi
Consorzio Interuniversitario Nazionale Informatica (CINI), Via Ariosto 25, 00185 Roma, Italy
e-mail: lodi@dis.uniroma1.it

R. Baldoni, G. Chockler (eds.), *Collaborative Financial Infrastructure Protection*,
DOI 10.1007/978-3-642-20420-3_4, © Springer-Verlag Berlin Heidelberg 2012

lifecycle and deployment, inter-SR connectivity, and the contract compliance monitoring. The proposed architecture is modular and flexible, allowing the developers to easily create and customize the processing logic according to the SR business goals, plug in different types of processing platforms, and deploy the implementation in a variety of realistic settings.

4.1 Introduction

We present the architecture of a middleware platform, called *Collaborative Middleware for Monitoring Financial Critical Infrastructure (CoMiFin)*, that facilitates collaborative protection of the critical infrastructure (CI) of financial institutions (and other CI operators) in the face of massively scoped attacks and other threats against their IT and business assets.

The CoMiFin service model allows its clients to form business relationships, called *Semantic Rooms* (*SRs*), which they can leverage for information sharing and processing purposes. Each SR is associated with a *contract* determining the set of services provided by that SR along with the data protection, isolation, trust, security, availability, fault tolerance, and performance requirements. The CoMiFin middleware incorporates the necessary mechanisms to share the underlying computational, communication, and storage resources both across and within each of the hosted SRs to satisfy the requirements prescribed by their contracts.

The processing within an SR is accomplished through a collection of software modules, called CoMiFin Applications, hosted within the SR. The architecture for the application hosting support is derived based on the types of hosted applications and on their resource management requirements.

The design of the CoMiFin middleware faces many challenges stemming from the need to support on-line processing of massive amounts of live data in a timely, wide distribution, as well as resource heterogeneity and diverse service level agreement (SLA) constraints imposed by the SR contracts. In this chapter, we address these challenges by following a top-down approach wherein the system is first broken down into a collection of high-level components whose functionality and interaction with each other are clearly specified. The design and implementation of each of the individual components of the proposed architecture are discussed in the ensuing chapters of the book (Chaps. 5–9). Chapters 8 and 9 demonstrate how the proposed architecture can be leveraged for implementing protection mechanisms against the attack scenarios described in Part I.

The rest of this chapter is organized as follows. Section 4.2 introduces the CoMiFin service model, Sect. 4.3 describes the CoMiFin principals, and Sect. 4.4 introduces the Semantic Room (SR) abstraction. The CoMiFin architecture overview appears in Sect. 4.5, followed by more detailed discussions of its main constituent pieces in Sects. 4.6, 4.7, and 4.8. Section 4.9 concludes the chapter.

4.2 CoMiFin Service Model

The primary functionality supported by the CoMiFin middleware is to facilitate information exchange and processing among participating principals for the sake of identifying threats against their IT infrastructure and business. The information sharing is facilitated through the *Semantic Room* (*SR*) abstraction, which provides a trusted environment in which the participants can contribute and analyze the input data. The input data can be real-time security events, historical attack data, logs, etc. This data can be generated by local monitoring subsystems (such as system management products, IDS, and firewalls) installed within the IT of the participating principals as well as provided by external sources, e.g., Computer Emergency Response Teams (CERTs).

The processing within the SR is accomplished through various types of data processing *applications*, which support the following functionalities:

- data preprocessing, which may include filtering and anonymization;
- on-line data analysis for real-time anomaly detection (such as complex event processing);
- off-line data analysis;
- long-term data storage for future off-line analysis and/or ad-hoc user queries.

The processing results can be either disseminated within the SR, or exported to other SRs and/or external clients. The output will typically include a description of the suspected illicit activities along with their identifying attributes, such as transaction identifiers, user identities, network addresses, and attack signatures. The rules for information sharing and resource provisioning within the SR are governed by the SR contracts discussed in Sect. 4.4.1.

4.3 CoMiFin Principals

The CoMiFin middleware recognizes three main *principals*, referred to as *CoMiFin Provider*, *CoMiFin Authority*, and *CoMiFin Partner*, respectively, whose responsibilities, rights, and trust relationships are summarized below:

- *CoMiFin Provider* is the organization that offers various types of IT resources (computing, storage, network, etc.) to support runtime operation of the CoMiFin middleware;
- *CoMiFin Authority* is an organization that is trusted by all the principals. The CoMiFin Authority is responsible for deploying and operating the entire CoMiFin system, and can host some of the system's management components. Typically, a CoMiFin Authority is a trusted third party, such as a central bank, a regulatory body, or an association of banks. Its primary responsibility is to serve as a mediator of contractual processes.
- *CoMiFin Partner* is a business entity or organization interested in the SR services. A CoMiFin Partner becomes a *member* of the SR by signing a basic contract, and can be any entity interested in the CoMiFin services (such as a financial institution), or a CoMiFin Provider.

Fig. 4.1 Semantic Room
abstraction

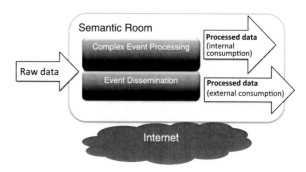

4.4 Semantic Room Abstraction

Semantic Room (*SR*) is a federation formed by a collection of CoMiFin Partners
for the sake of information sharing and processing. The Partners participating in a
specific SR are referred to as the *members* of the SR.

Each SR is characterized through the following three properties:

- *Objective*: specifies functionality and services exposed by the SR, such as port
  scan detection, Man-in-the-Middle attack detection, etc.
- *Contract*: defines the set of processing and data sharing services provided by the
  SR along with the data protection, privacy, isolation, trust, security, dependability, and performance requirements. The contract also contains the hardware and
  software requirements a member must provision in order to be admitted into the
  SR.
- *Deployment*: SR software and its instantiation in the production system. The SR
  information processing and sharing logic can be supported through a variety of
  approaches, for example, centralized (e.g., Esper [2], which is a centralized event
  processing engine), decentralized (e.g., MapReduce [3]), or hierarchical.

Figure 4.1 illustrates the main components comprising the SR internal structure.
SR members can inject raw data into the SR, which may include real-time data,
inputs from human operators, stored data (e.g., historical data), queries, and other
types of dynamic and/or static content. The injected raw data is processed within
the SR to extract the information and produce security alerts as prescribed by the
SR objectives. The raw data can undergo preprocessing steps, during which it is
converted to the format consumable by the processing logic as well as sanitized to
meet the privacy constraints imposed by the SR contract.

The SR processing results (e.g., derived events, models, profiles, blacklists,
alerts, and query results) are primarily consumed by the SR members (the dotted
arrows in Fig. 4.1), who can use it to feed their internal protection systems. In addition, a subset of the output data can be offered for consumption (see Fig. 4.1) by
other SRs or by external entities interested in the services provided by the SR.

4.4.1 Semantic Room Contract

An SR contract is used to define the set of rules for accessing and using raw data shared within the SR. There is a contract for each SR, which must be signed by all CoMiFin Partners willing to participate in the SR.

Following the structure defined in [1], an SR contract includes the following four components: information on the parties bound by the contract, a list of contractual statements, a list of service level specifications (SLSs), and finally, the signatures of the involved parties. In the following, we describe the various components comprising the SR contract in more detail.

1. Parties involved in the contract, which include the identities of the SR members, SR administrator (see below), and external SR clients (if they exist).
2. Signatures: signatures of the involved parties.

The rest of the SR contract is a service level agreement (SLA), which can vary depending on the services offered by the SR and the requirements specified by the SR members. In particular, the contractual statements section of the contract specifies:

3. Name of the SR: a descriptive name in natural language;
4. SRID: an identifier that uniquely identifies the SR;
5. Services: a description of the services offered by the SR and the rules for obtaining the services. In addition, if the contract allows the processing results to be consumed by the external clients, it may also incorporate the pricing scheme as well as other rights and obligations regulating this type of relationship;
6. Penalties: the actions to be performed in case members, clients, or other business entities violate the contract.

The SLS section of the contract includes all the technical requirements and the associated metrics. In particular, this section can be thought of as divided into two principal parts: the requirements related to the quality of the information processed and disseminated by the SR, and the requirements related to the SR performance. These are described in order as follows.

7. *Data format* determines which raw and processed data formats are to be required by the SR (attributes, types, etc.);
8. *Rules* governing data sharing, processing, and storage within the SR and for outgoing/incoming data, which are as follows:

   - *Information security and data disclosure rules* determine the policies required for data encryption within the SR and for data leaving the SR boundaries;
   - *Anonymization rules* determine the degree of sanitization required for data that enter and leave the SR;
   - *Processing rules* regulate data exposure to the processing engines;
   - *Dissemination rules* govern data exchange and sharing within and outside the SR as well as across multiple SRs;

- *Storage rules* control recording data and logs within the SR.

9. *Minimum join requirements* specify the minimum amounts of computation resources and data that must be contributed by a joining Partner;
10. *Processing QoS* specifies the quality-of-service (QoS) goals that must be met by the processing activities within the SR;
11. *Dissemination QoS* specifies the QoS goals to be met by the data dissemination logic;
12. *Storage QoS* specifies the QoS goals for data stored within the SR.

4.4.2 SR Schemas and Instances

In order to support implementation and deployment independence, we distinguish between an *SR schema* and an *SR instance* (similarly to the object-oriented approach). An SR schema determines the high-level services provided by the SR. For instance, an SR can have a predefined schema with a generic objective (e.g., detection of intruders that perform stealthy scan activities) and contract.

An SR instance is a specific instantiation of the SR schema. The SR instances can vary according to a number of different aspects, such as the software used to implement the SR logic, the geographical locations of the SR members, the software used for data dissemination, and specific QoS requirements imposed by the contract. Different instantiations of the same SR schema can differ in the internal organization of their processing logic (e.g., centralized vs. distributed), or can have distinct data protection requirements as dictated by the local governments.

Analogously, we distinguish between a *contract schema* and a *contract instance*. In particular, an SR schema is associated with a contract schema that defines a set of basic contract requirements for that schema (e.g., the minimum QoS requirements and the penalties to apply in case of violations of the contract). An SR instance is associated with a contract instance, which could extend the base schema with more refined QoS requirements.

We model the SR contract instance as an XML document and the contract schema as an XML schema, which specifies how the XML document has to be structured.

4.4.3 Semantic Room Principals

Each SR is associated with a collection of *principals*, which are assigned different responsibilities and privileges with respect to accessing SR and managing its lifecycle. The two special principals, called *Central Authority* (*CA*) and *SR Creator*, are responsible for handling administrative tasks. Specifically, CA is in charge of managing the middleware that supports the construction of all possible SRs and is allowed to activate a fixed number of SR Creators. The SR Creator is responsible for creating new SR schemas and SR contract schemas.

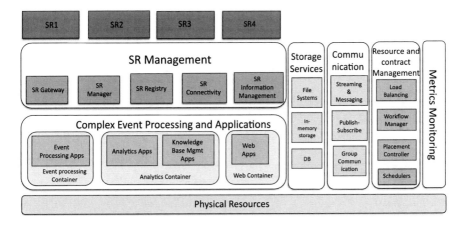

Fig. 4.2 The framework for building Semantic Rooms

A Partner can then join one of the specialized SRs that have been previously created by the SR Creators. A Partner in an SR can be assigned any one of the following roles:

- *SR administrator* is responsible for managing the lifecycle of the SR;
- *SR member* is eligible to contribute raw data to the SR, and consume the processing results;
- *SR client* is an external entity eligible to consume a subset of the processing results generated by the SR.

In addition, each Partner (either SR administrator, SR member, or SR client) can specify additional accounts whose responsibilities and access rights are local to that Partner's organization.

4.5 Architectural Overview

The CoMiFin middleware layering and component breakdown is depicted in Fig. 4.2, and the high-level Unified Modeling Language (UML) representation appears in Fig. 4.3.

The *SR Management* layer is responsible for managing the lifecycle of the SRs and the interactions with the rest of the Partners and users of the CoMiFin system (see Sect. 4.7). It exposes interfaces for managing the SR contracts and lifecycle and inspecting various configuration parameters thereof (e.g., trust metrics). These interfaces are consumed by the SR Complex Event Processing and Applications, SLA Management, and Metric Monitoring components.

The *SR Complex Event Processing and Applications* layer is responsible for managing the resources allocated to that SR by the SR Management layer and for processing the input events it receives (see Sect. 4.6). It exposes interfaces to consume normalized input events produced by the SR Gateway (which is a part of the

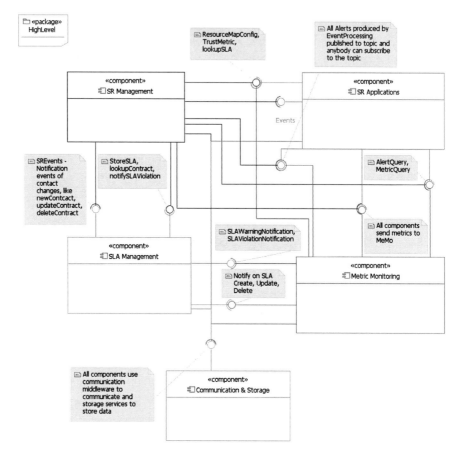

Fig. 4.3 High-level model of the CoMiFin framework: components and interfaces

SR Management component and further described below), generate alerts resulting
from processing the SR input events (consumable by SR Gateway), and produce
various sensor data to enable monitoring of the SR internal infrastructure (e.g., for
SLA compliance) by the Metric Monitoring component.

The *SLA Management* component is in charge of monitoring the SLA compliance within each of the deployed SRs. It provides interfaces for registering SLAs
specified as a part of the SR contract, and for listening to the SLA-related violation
and warning alerts. It interacts with the SR Management layer to stay apprised of the
SLAs specified by the currently active SRs and with the Metric Monitoring component to request monitoring for metrics required for checking the SLA compliance.

The *Metric Monitoring* component offers interfaces allowing various components of the framework to supply monitoring and configuration data, query the current metric readings, and subscribe and receive alerts in response to the violation of
the target objectives.

The *Communication and Storage* component aggregates various communication and storage middleware functionality used by all other components of the CoMiFin framework (see Sect. 4.8).

4.6 Complex Event Processing and Applications Layer

The Complex Event Processing and Applications layer is responsible for managing the applications implementing the data processing and sharing logic required to support the SR services. A typical application being hosted in an SR will need to fuse and analyze large volumes of incoming raw data produced by numerous heterogeneous and possibly widely distributed sources, such as sensors, intrusion and anomaly detection systems, firewalls, and monitoring systems, etc. The incoming data will be either analyzed in real time, possibly with the assistance of analytical models, or stored for the subsequent off-line analysis and intelligence extraction.

The applications are managed at runtime through different types of containers, which we discuss below:

- *Event Processing Container*: This container is responsible for supporting event processing applications in a distributed environment. The applications manipulate and/or extract patterns from streams of event data arriving in real time, from possibly widely distributed sources, and they must be able to support stringent guarantees in terms of the response time and/or throughput. We further distinguish the following types of event processing that should be supported:
  - *Simple event processing* (SEP) [4] will perform simple preprocessing operations over the event data such as filtering.
  - *Mediated event processing* (MEP) [4] is SEP extended with the ability to perform simple transformations over the individual events and event streams. These include enrichment (i.e., adding new attributes), translation, aggregation, split, etc.
  - *Complex event processing (CEP)* [6] is MEP extended with an ability to identify complex correlation patterns in possibly disjoint event streams.
- *Analytics Container:* This container is responsible for supporting parallel processing and querying massive data sets on a cluster of machines. It will be used for supporting the analytics and data warehousing applications hosted in the SR for the extraction of analytical models to be used to assist in the on-line event processing. The models are important for (i) correlating the activity patterns involving multiple remote sites to prevent coordinated attacks (e.g., inter-domain port scan activities) and (ii) calibrating individual patterns based on their likelihood of being abnormal to reduce the rate of false alarms [5];
- *Web Container:* This container provides basic web capabilities to support the runtime needs of the web applications hosted within an SR. These applications support the logic enabling the interaction between the client side presentation level artifacts (such as web browser-based consoles, dashboards, widgets, rich web clients, etc.) and the processing applications.

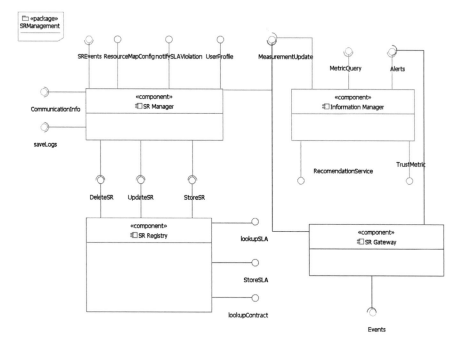

Fig. 4.4 The internal structure of the SR Management layer: components and interfaces

The SR applications can interact with each other in a variety of ways. For example, the event streams submitted to an SR can first be preprocessed by a SEP application, which would then forward the derived stream to either a MEP or CEP application. The latter can be subscribed to the model updates coming from an offline analytics application and the results of processing and/or analytics can be stored in a data warehousing application.

The architecture is flexible to accommodate CEP applications designed according to diverse styles in paradigms. Specifically, the SR examples described in Chaps. 6, 8, and 9 incorporate distributed processing containers, whereas the container used by the SR implementation in Chap. 7 is centralized.

4.7 SR Management Layer

The SR Management layer is responsible for supporting the SR abstraction on top of the individual processing and data sharing applications provided by the Complex Event Processing and Applications layer. It embodies a number of components fulfilling various SR management functions, as shown in the UML diagram of Fig. 4.4. The functionalities of each component are summarized as follows.

SR Manager is responsible for managing the lifecycle of the SRs and all the interactions with the Partners and users of the CoMiFin system (as discussed in the previous chapter). In particular, it is in charge of:

- managing Partner registration to the system and related access control restrictions;
- managing the entire SR lifecycle, which includes mechanisms for:
  - creating an SR schema and the associated SR contract schema;
  - instantiating a previously created SR schema;
  - disbanding an SR;
  - managing the SR membership through voluntary joins and leaves as well as forced leaves in response to SLA violations.
- SR configuration, which includes selecting the applications to implement the SR services and specifying interconnections among the applications and resources.

SR Registry exposes directory services consumed by SR Manager for SR location and registration purposes. In particular, SR Registry provides the necessary mechanisms for registering new SR contracts, updating and deleting existing SR contracts, and discovering the contracts when a lookup of an SR is required.

SR registry is also used as a directory service for locating, registering, and canceling the SR SLAs. To this end, the SLA Management component interacts with SR Registry to store the SLAs derived from the SR contracts. The stored SLAs are made available through a lookup interface, which is mainly used by the Metrics Monitoring component. Whenever an SR contract is removed from SR Registry, its corresponding SLA is also removed.

SR Gateway allows SRs to interact with the outside world. In particular, it acts as an access point for Partners' local network management systems. It is responsible for converting the incoming raw data to the formats consumable by the SR processing applications, and sanitizing the data according to the privacy constraints specified in the SR contract. The gateway is typically hosted within the Partners' IT boundaries.

A wrapper subcomponent of SR Gateway is used to interface the local network management systems (see Fig. 4.5). It is designed in a modular fashion wherein Partner-specific data conversion policies are implemented by *plugins*.

The wrapper dispatches the normalized data to the preprocessing stack, which supports the following three functions: (1) filtering, which selects only the data of interest for meeting the SR objective, (2) aggregation, which can reduce the amount of data being sent to the SR by creating batches of data, and (3) anonymization, which sanitizes sensitive data before it leaves the internal network of the SR member. Chapter 6 introduces an example of SR in which anonymization is performed by the SR Gateway.

The final output of the preprocessing is then sent to the communication module of the gateway, where it is injected into the SR (Fig. 4.5).

SR Information Manager aims to provide suitable assurance of the goodness of the data being injected, processed, and disseminated into the SR. To this end, this component provides the capability of evaluating and monitoring the trust levels of each SR member, which can then influence the SR complex event processing itself. A full chapter of this book (see Chap. 6) is devoted to a detailed description of this framework component.

Fig. 4.5 The SR Gateway

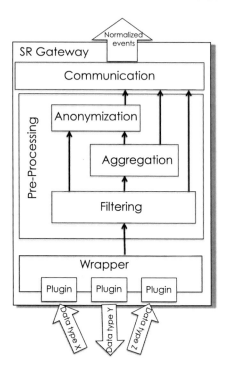

Metrics Monitoring is responsible for monitoring the architecture in order to assess whether the requirements specified by the SR contract are effectively met. As the Metrics Monitoring is a transversal layer of the framework, it operates at both the SR Management and Complex Event Processing and Applications layers. A detailed description of the principal functionalities offered by this component of the framework can be found in Chap. 5.

SR Connectivity is responsible for enabling information exchange between multiple SRs. It consists of the following building blocks:

- *Web GUI* a web interface through which interested SR administrators can request specific data services from other SRs, taking into consideration the applicable SLAs.
- *Data spigot* is a subcomponent that acts as a filter that decides which data must be exported to which SRs.
- *Configuration repository* is the subcomponent that stores the data requirements of the SR clients, i.e., the data specifications made by the SR administrators through the web GUI during the registration to the SR data services.
- *Configurator* is the subcomponent that reads from the repository, updates the configuration data, and notifies the data spigot about modifications. In other words this building block of SR Connectivity is responsible for managing the configurations lifecycle of the configuration repository and for notifying the data spigot about every modification.

4.8 Auxiliary Services

The following auxiliary services are utilized by both of the layers discussed above:

- *Java Message Service (JMS)* is used internally by the SR Gateway component in order to implement the wrapper layer. Each Gateway plugin publishes raw events to the JMS provided by the wrapper. Events are received by all the Gateway preprocessors that subscribe to the JMS provided by the wrapper.
- *Simple Object Access Protocol (SOAP)* is a de facto standard for web service communication, defining a simple XML "envelope" for sending remote messages. It can be extended to support nonfunctional requirements (e.g., encryption) and can be transported over multiple protocols, such as HTTP, JMS, etc. SOAP messages are exchanged among different framework components like the SR Manager, SR Registry, Metric Monitoring, and SLA Management.
- *Nagios* is a widely used open source IT monitoring system, which offers a range of sensors (plugins) which collect standard OS and network level metrics. Nagios is also accompanied with a number of additional plugins and can be extended with custom ones written, e.g., in Perl. Nagios by default uses its own protocols (NSCA, NRPE) for communication, but can be extended to support other means of communication as well. In our framework, we developed custom plugins for log file parsing (see Chap. 5 for further details about the use of Nagios in our framework).
- *FreePastry* is a distributed hash table (DHT) implementation offering both communication and storage services among peer nodes. It is used inside the DHT-based SR (see Chap. 9) to store events and to enable the distribution of messages among peers in the overlay network.
- *Hadoop Distributed File System (HDFS)* is a distributed file system for storing large amounts of data intended for batch processing. It is used by both the Agilis and privacy-based SRs (Chaps. 8 and 6, respectively) for storing historical data.
- *IBM WebSphere eXtreme Scale (XS)* is a memory-based data grid system. It is used by the Agilis SR as a low-latency storage facility to buffer incoming event streams (see Chap. 8).

4.9 Conclusions

In this chapter, we presented a comprehensive software architecture of the CoMiFin middleware, which facilitates collaborative protection of the financial CI through a novel abstraction of Semantic Room (SR). The presented architecture builds upon the requirements derived from the CoMiFin service model as well as those derived from the analysis of the application workloads and service level objectives. Our approach emphasizes modularity by focusing on the functionality of each of the proposed components and their interaction with each other. The internals of the individual components of our design will be described in more detail in the following chapters.

References

1. Lamanna, D., Skene, J., Emmerich, W.: SLAng: a language for defining service level agreements. In: FTDCS '03: Proceedings of the Ninth IEEE Workshop on Future Trends of Distributed Computing Systems, p. 100. IEEE Comp. Soc., New York (2003)
2. Where complex event processing meets open source: Esper and NEsper. http://esper.codehaus.org/ (2011)
3. Jeffrey, D., Ghemawat, S.: MapReduce: simplified data processing on large clusters. Commun. ACM **51**(1), 107–113 (2008)
4. Etzion, O.: Semantic approach to event processing. Keynote at DEBS2008. Available online at http://www.debs.msrg.utoronto.ca/etzion.pdf (2011)
5. Hall, D.: Mathematical Techniques in Multisensor Data Fusion. Artech House, Boston (1992)
6. Luckham, D.: The Power of Events: An Introduction to Complex Event Processing in Distributed Enterprise Systems. Addison-Wesley, Reading (2002)

Chapter 5
Monitoring and Evaluation of Semantic Rooms

László Gönczy, György Csertán, Gábor Urbanics, Hamza Ghani,
Abdelmajid Khelil, and Neeraj Suri

Abstract   The CoMiFin framework can be considered as a highly dynamic controlled system that evolves over time according to SR interactions and the event
processing activities performed within SRs. SR event processing requires the ability
to allocate and manage online the resources that are necessary for the processing
itself, and for meeting the SR business level objectives. These objectives are usually
specified in the SR contracts as service level agreements. Accordingly, it is crucial
to continuously monitor the operation of the CoMiFin framework in order to ensure its compliance with the specifications of the expected behavior. This chapter
describes an efficient monitoring system that (a) collects vital infrastructure metrics
(e.g., CPU/memory utilization) and application data (e.g., the number of processed
events) from the set of resources and services used for event processing purposes,
and (b) processes those metrics to detect violations of the SR contract. The monitoring architecture is model-driven so that changes in the resources or the system
objectives can be automatically mapped to monitoring assets. It is implemented in a
plugin-based fashion, which enables the flexible extension of evaluation features to
capture the complex behavior of the system.

L. Gönczy (✉) · G. Csertán · G. Urbanics
OptXware Research and Development Ltd., Budapest, Hungary
e-mail: laszlo.gonczy@optxware.com

G. Csertán
e-mail: gyorgy.csertan@optxware.com

G. Urbanics
e-mail: gabor.urbanics@optxware.com

H. Ghani · A. Khelil · N. Suri
Technical University of Darmstadt, Darmstadt, Germany

H. Ghani
e-mail: ghani@cs.tu-darmstadt.de

A. Khelil
e-mail: khelil@cs.tu-darmstadt.de

N. Suri
e-mail: suri@cs.tu-darmstadt.de

R. Baldoni, G. Chockler (eds.), *Collaborative Financial Infrastructure Protection*,
DOI 10.1007/978-3-642-20420-3_5, © Springer-Verlag Berlin Heidelberg 2012

5.1 Introduction

As a facility for sharing confidential data and performing critical analysis tasks, CoMiFin is a critical service. Consequently, CoMiFin should be protected against external attacks and internal faults by a carefully designed IT infrastructure, and the runtime operation should be driven by the required service level for the participating entities. The defining of several dedicated metrics, whose calculations require partly real-time measurements from the sensing nodes, constitutes the basis for monitoring the operation of the CoMiFin infrastructure. Though sensing nodes and overlays are used in multiple scenarios to realize critical protection mechanisms, there is a dearth of approaches to quantitatively evaluate the protection enhancement [6, 7]. The use of quantitative measures is important for designers to maximize the resilience of protection mechanisms, for users to increase their trust in the system, and for managers to assess their investment [1]. Therefore, it is crucial to ensure that CoMiFin itself is working safely; that is, its operation is resilient (e.g., the availability and performance of the overall system is satisfactory) and it automatically ensures a certain level of trust among participants. Moreover, resources of a CoMiFin installation may contribute to multiple Semantic Rooms (SRs), which necessitates a thorough design of the monitoring.

We define monitoring as (a) the collection of data on the operation of the system, at the level of both IT infrastructure components and applications, and (b) the processing of this data to continuously evaluate whether the system meets specific requirements. This assumes an architecture in which a (centralized or distributed) data collector receives measurements from different software sensors (agents). The agents are either deployed at the measured assets (e.g., a server) or gather data by using standard interfaces of the measured objects (e.g., by executing operating system level commands or running a ping). In the course of designing such an architecture, one has to address both the business goals of the particular system as well as the technicalities of the concrete implementation. Requirements and goals are expressed as service level agreements (SLAs) that are attached to the contracts created during the initialization of the SRs, whereas the implementation is captured by a *configuration* (*resource map*) of the middleware.

In this chapter, we primarily investigate the fundamental question of how to evaluate and assess the operation of CoMiFin from different aspects. We introduce (a) a method to determine the metrics needed to measure the operation of CoMiFin, and (b) a model-driven approach to develop a monitoring system which delivers and evaluates the runtime information needed to maintain CoMiFin compliance to the SLA requirements. We illustrate our approach using the requirements, measurements, and architecture of the CoMiFin prototype.

The remainder of the chapter is organized as follows. Section 5.2 discusses the motivation behind the proposed model-driven approach. Section 5.3 focuses on how the monitoring of the trustworthiness of CoMiFin participants is accomplished using the metrics-based SLA. This section also discusses the details of our metamodel along with an example showing how the monitoring configuration can be derived from the clauses of the SR contract. In Sect. 5.4, we describe the monitoring architecture and its current implementation in CoMiFin. Related work is discussed in Sect. 5.5.

5.2 Monitoring Challenges and Our Model-Driven Approach

In CoMiFin, an SR contract defines various requirements as an SLA. SLAs are composed of service level specifications (SLSs) that describe the requirements to be met in the specific SR. As we detail in Sect. 5.3, an SLA consists of SLSs which may describe requirements of different logical levels or even for different actors. For instance, some SLSs are directly related to the *trust level* of the client, whereas others express constraints on the *performability*. In the CoMiFin middleware, the tasks of system monitoring are performed by the Metric Monitoring (MeMo) component, while SLA adherence is tracked by the SLA Management component. To this end, we derive a *monitoring configuration* from the SLA.

5.2.1 Creation of Monitoring Configuration

The resulting monitoring configuration contains:

- Measurable attributes for all (physical and logical) components in the SR, e.g., the response time of all physical hosts and the message throughput of applications implementing the Analytics Container,
- The metrics calculated based on the collected measurements corresponding to the defined SLAs, e.g., the minimum/average/maximum of the throughput, and
- Thresholds and penalties of SLA violations and thresholds of warnings when the system is endangered. For instance, if the trust level of a CoMiFin participant drops below a specific threshold, a gradual penalty is applied; first a warning is issued to the participant, followed by a forced leave if the participant continues to misbehave.

The process of deriving such monitoring configurations from SLAs raises several challenges. One challenge is to address the abstractional gap between the SLSs defined in the SR contract and the corresponding monitoring details, i.e., to decide which physical and logical components should be monitored if the SR contract includes a requirement on the trust level of the participants. Besides the identification of the relevant components, the attributes and measurement mode have to be determined.

Furthermore, it is desirable to automate the configuration creation process. Performing this manually is error-prone and ineffective, and requires any change in the SR contract or membership to be propagated to the monitoring configuration, resulting in frequent manual updates. Finally, in a complex system, there could be multiple requirements on the same resource instance which are difficult or even impossible to satisfy simultaneously. Although not detailed here, virtualization techniques and provisioning of resources among different SRs complicates this task, which needs a strong support of (a) reusability of knowledge on system monitoring, and (b) validation of monitoring requirements.

5.2.2 Model-Driven SLA Management and Monitoring Configuration

In order to address the challenges above, we propose a model-driven approach to manage the metric-based SLA and the underlying monitoring configurations. Our approach is inspired by model-driven architectures (MDAs) and has the following advantages. First, the monitoring configuration, which is essential for checking the adherence to the defined SLAs, can be treated independently from the underlying monitoring platform, thus increasing *portability across various monitoring platforms*.

However, note that additional metamodels describing each target platform are necessary to carry out the transformations.

Since a typical monitoring configuration is not a simple "one-to-one" mapping of the higher level concepts defined in the SLA, but rather includes a set of interrelated configuration elements (e.g., configuration files, database entries, agent configurations, evaluation rules, and database triggers), the creation and maintenance of this set of configurations can be a tedious and error-prone task. This is particularly interesting if the monitored infrastructure is subject to frequent changes or the requirements defined in the SLA are rather complex; however, both the system model and the related *IT monitoring and management need to be maintained in a consistent and coherent manner*. Additional optimization of this process, such as updating only the part of the monitoring configuration that really needs to be changed, can also be implemented.

Though it is possible to create a monitoring configuration based on an existing metric-based SLA model in a fully automatic way, creating a *sensible SLA model from high-level requirements* in the same manner is a more complex task. A semi-automatic solution, also depicted in Fig. 5.1, could be the following:

1. Based on the SLA part of an SR contract, manually create a partial SLA model (an instance of the SLA metamodel) by using a domain-specific tool, or create it automatically based on some predefined rules.
2. Extend the model with non-functional requirements, such as high availability, encrypted communication, periodic backup, etc. Most of these requirements obviously affect what items should be monitored on the services and how they should be monitored. Some of these requirements can also be derived from the SR contract.
3. Using predefined rules, this additional information, i.e., the additional requirements, can be used to populate the same model with more elements to obtain a

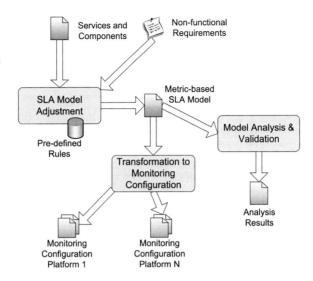

Fig. 5.1 Transformation of the SLA model with non-functional requirements into monitoring configuration

complete SLA model. The rules correspond, for instance, to "best practices" or are derived from regulations. Additional information could be metrics from the metrics library or measurements supported by the particular component.

Further processing of the complete SLA model, such as generating monitoring configurations for various platforms or validation/analysis of the model, can still be performed. Some examples are to check if various (anti)patterns are present in the model or if complex constraints are satisfied in a particular model.

Finally, an additional transformation (with loss of abstraction of some specific details) can *create the SLA model from existing monitoring configurations* where the same analysis and validation procedures can be applied. This also raises some traceability concerns which are out of the scope of this chapter. Note that these models also enable the multiaspect analysis of SLAs and requirements themselves.

5.3 Systematic Trustworthiness Monitoring in CoMiFin

The main motivation behind the CoMiFin middleware is to provide a platform for detection and protection against various attacks targeting critical infrastructures (CIs). Since it is a collaborative approach, the trustworthiness of the participating members, detailed in [13], is a crucial aspect. Therefore, attributes and events contributing to trust evaluation must be monitored. Additionally, in order to be able to pinpoint problems in CoMiFin, one must have a decent picture of the status of the entire infrastructure, which would include all the components comprising the CoMiFin platform regardless of their role or responsible partner.

5.3.1 Metrics in CoMiFin

Determining adequate metrics to monitor is highly dependent on the platform and the operational profile. This process can be driven by regulations and best practices, but it generally requires a good understanding of both the given application domain and the technical environment. This knowledge should be captured in a tangible form. In order to create metrics for CoMiFin, we applied the goal-question-metric (GQM) [2, 3] approach, which is a user-centric, widely accepted metrics definition methodology. As a result, we identified the following six categories of metrics.

1. Resource-level metrics include elementary resource usage metrics, such as CPU, memory, disk, or network usage. The metrics monitoring framework is able to correlate these "low-level" metrics with other "high-level" metrics in order to detect important, but otherwise hidden patterns of misbehavior.
2. The availability metrics allow the measuring of classical availability attributes in CoMiFin; for example, mean uptime, availability, reliability, and mean repair time of each component. These are the most typical metrics to be included into SLAs.
3. The attributes of the applied communication mechanisms represent essential communication metrics, since information sharing among the CoMiFin partners or among SRs has strict security requirements (confidentiality, non-repudiation). These are, for example, the selected encryption key length, the ratio of encrypted/signed content, the time required to transfer messages, or the communication latency.
4. Application-specific metrics describe the applications implementing the CoMiFin platform, e.g., the version of the running application, the number of available but not installed security updates for that particular version, or the performance of each application type in CoMiFin.
5. SR Connectivity metrics encompass metrics that describe the attributes of the connection among the SRs. For example, K-connectivity, proximity properties of the SR, or the properties and amount of the messages transferred among SRs are included.
6. Trust metrics include trust-level measurements for CoMiFin participants. The interested reader is referred to [13] for further details.

The following list enumerates some of the metrics used in MeMo:

- The packet loss and round trip time of PING Internet Control Message Protocol (ICMP) messages are two of the resource-level metrics. The domains of these metrics are [0, 100] and (practically) [0, 60000], while the measurement units are percentage and milliseconds, respectively. In the current implementation, the average of these metrics within the last 30 minutes, 1 hour, and 4 hours is available. The packet loss also serves as a basis for availability metrics.
- In the group of application-level metrics a tangible one is the throughput of the Analytics Container components, which is defined as the average number of messages processed within the last 30 minutes, 1 hour, or 4 hours. Its measurement unit is $1/second$.

- In the trust metrics group the most representative examples are the trust score and the trust confidence metrics. The trust score's domain is the $[-0.5, 0.5]$ interval, while the confidence takes its value from the interval $[0, 1]$. Both are unitless metrics, and again the averages of 30 minutes, 1 hour, and 4 hours are calculated. Another good example in this group is defined as the number of SLA violations within the last 5 minutes. This metric is calculated based on the actual measurements and the configured thresholds in MeMo (its domain is $[0, \infty]$ and it is also unitless).

5.3.2 Metrics and SLA Metamodel

In order to manage the metrics-based SLA, which captures both the SLSs defined in the contract and the metrics that monitor the compliance with the requirements, a formal representation of these concepts is needed. Consequently, we have defined a metamodel representing the metric-based SLAs. The model is rich enough to capture not only the SLSs and metrics but also the lower level details of how the metrics are calculated at runtime. The metamodel includes and extends some concepts from the web service level agreement (WSLA) [11] specification. We illustrate the model with its two main metaclasses *SLA* and *MetricCalculationLibrary* in Fig. 5.2. An *SLA* typically embodies:

- *Service*s available in the monitored system,
- The *SLAParameter*s that describe the measurable attributes of each *Service*, and
- *ServiceLevelObjective*s that encapsulate the expected behavior (e.g., thresholds) and the applicable penalties.

The *MetricCalculationLibrary* represents a reusable container of *Metric* and *Function* classes, which can be maintained independently of the particular SLA model. The container simplifies extending the set of metrics/functions or creating metric libraries for certain domains. The details of calculating a particular metric can be described using the rest of the classes: the *Component* class represents a physical component of the system measuring one or more *SLAParameter*s, i.e., the source of measurements with the desired technical details, while the subclasses of *Calculation* allow for composing simple expressions to be evaluated at runtime using the functions defined in the library. For example, the expression $avg(sliding\_window(CPUUsage_{processing}, 30))$ can be created with the instances of these classes, which translates to the average of the CPU utilization (of a service) within the last 30 minutes. Using a well-defined metamodel to capture metric-based SLAs provides several advantages that are mentioned in Sect. 5.2.2.

5.3.3 Example Requirements and Their Monitoring

As described before, the lifecycle of the SR instance begins with the instantiation step, where, in compliance with the SR contract schema, the SR contract contains

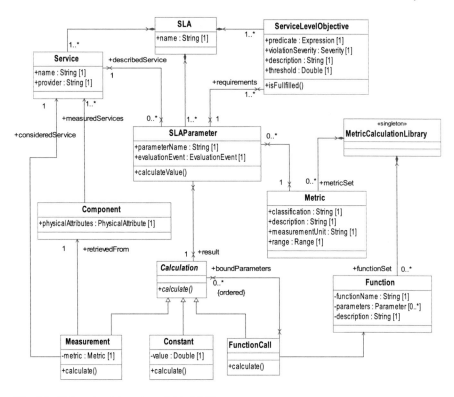

Fig. 5.2 SLA and metric metamodel in MeMo

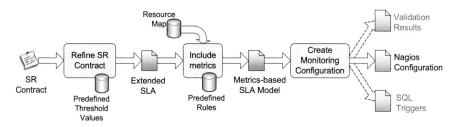

Fig. 5.3 From SR contract to monitoring configuration

information specific to the particular SR instance. Additionally, an extension point for the SLA is created in the high-level SR contract to be further extended by the SLA Management (see also in Chap. 4). Figure 5.3 illustrates the process in which the SR contract and its SLA part are step-by-step converted to a deployable monitoring configuration. First, in the *Refine SR contract* step, the SLA Management adjusts the SLA part of the contract: the thresholds are set to predefined values (or values retrieved from other parts of the SR contract, if available), and all service level specifications (SLSs) are created. SLSs capture the requirements in a more refined and complete form than originally available in the SR contract; e.g., besides the violation thresholds, the warning thresholds are set. This extended SLA serves as input for the *Include metrics* step, where the MeMo further processes the SLA model. The result of employing metrics along with the predefined simple rules is a metrics-based SLA model complying with the metamodel described in Sect. 5.3.2. MeMo takes the description of the infrastructure as an additional input (*Resource Map*) in order to have a full model. The rules applied here are based on practical best practices adjusted to CoMiFin context.

For example, the availability of all SR Gateways will be checked. In addition, the performance of the Analytics Containers has to be measured by evaluating metrics related to their throughput. The processing time is measured only in the case of the DHT-based Container. After creating this model, the *Create Monitoring Configuration* step transforms this model to Nagios [8] configuration files. In parallel with these steps, early model validation and analysis can guarantee that the monitoring configuration is correct and complete, and "overmonitoring" of the system can also be prevented by analysis of the thresholds and metrics (see the dashed arrows in the figure).

In the following, we present a concrete example of translating the SLS part of an SR contract into the corresponding monitoring configuration. The SR contract contains basic information about the SR, such as the involved parties and their roles or the description and objective of the SR. Additionally, the contract includes an SLS section (see the example in Listing 5.1) where some values are missing (e.g., trust).

For instance, the parameter "signature" has a value of 70 (one could also use other notation). This value means that at least 70% of all transmitted messages have to contain a digital signature. The SLA Management, having been notified about the presence of an SR contract, populates the SLS part of the contract with predefined values as described above. For example, Listing 5.2 illustrates the SLA pertaining to the security and trust category where the concrete threshold values are now set.

In this example, we consider trust scores in the interval $[-1, 1]$; for a confidence value of 0.5 the threshold value for a "warning" message is -0.2 and -0.5 for a "violation". The populated SLA is then retrieved by the MeMo component, which creates its own representation complying with the metrics-based SLA metamodel (see Sect. 5.3.2) and creates the monitoring configuration. One relevant entry from the Nagios configuration is presented in Listing 5.3.

Since the trust is calculated by the SR Information Manager, the active check (periodic measurement collection initiated by Nagios) is disabled for the corresponding Nagios service. Note that the entry contains an identifier designating the host of the member with which this metric is associated. There are several such entries in the entire configuration, one for each participating member in the SR. The collected measurements are then processed by MeMo, and the average trust value is calculated and stored in the database.

5.4 The CoMiFin Monitoring Architecture

The SLA Management and MeMo components together provide the functionalities of system monitoring and, based on the requirements defined in the SR contract,

```
<sls>
 <category name="resource-sharing-schema"></category>
 <category name="data-quality">
  <information-share></information-share>
  <compliance-degree type="FI-GW"></compliance-degree>
  <compliance-degree type="GW-SR"></compliance-degree>
 </category>
 <category name="security-and-trust">
  <trust-relationship></trust-relationship>
  <anonymization>95</anonymization>
  <signature>70</signature>
  <encryption>99</encryption>
 </category>
 <category name="data-processing">
  <event-throughput>5000</event-throughput>
  <dissemination-time>5</dissemination-time>
  <processinng-time>2</processinng-time>
 </category>
 <category name="resource-requirements">
  <minimum-number-of-machines>4</minimum-number-of-machines>
  <minimum-available-storage-capacity>30
  </minimum-available-storage-capacity>
 </category>
 <category name="intra-sr-communication-qos">
  <reliability></reliability>
  <throughput></throughput>
 </category>
 <category name="storage">
  <availability></availability>
  <reliability></reliability>
  <capacity></capacity>
  <throughput></throughput>
 </category>
</sls>
```

Listing 5.1 The empty SLA part of the contract with SLS entries

```
<sla-parameter-category name="security-and-trust">
<!--
trust-score: Minimal trust level.
For score: [-1, 1], thresholds: -0.2, -0.5
Confidence: [0,1], thresholds: 0.4, 0.5
-->
<trust-score-warning id="sec_and_trust1">-0.2</trust-score-warning>
<trust-score-violation id="sec_and_trust2">-0.5</trust-score-violation>
<confidence id="sec_and_trust3">0.5</confidence>
...
</sla-parameter-category>
```

Listing 5.2 The portion of the SLA populated with concrete values

```
define service{
   use                     local-service ; Name of service template to use
   host_name               member
   service_description     bank1-trust
   check_command           null_command
   active_checks_enabled   0
   notes                   BUSINESS_TRUST
}
```

Listing 5.3 The Nagios configuration entry corresponding to the trust SLS

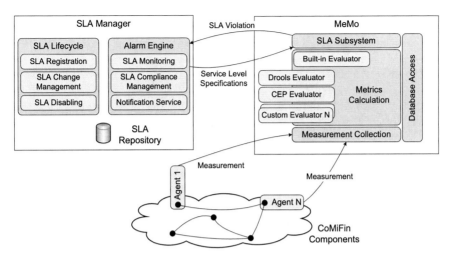

Fig. 5.4 Reference architecture for SLA Management and metrics evaluation

create a metrics-based SLA model and corresponding monitoring configuration. Figure 5.4 illustrates both components in the context of CoMiFin. The following subsections describe the functionality of each block in detail.

5.4.1 Architecture of SLA Management

Our approach envisages the implementation of an SLA Management responsible for managing SLAs throughout their whole lifecycle (Fig. 5.4). As a proof of concept, we have implemented an SLA Manager, the key component of SLA Management layer, that is interacting with MeMo in order to monitor the degree of compliance with the defined SLSs. The interaction with MeMo can be triggered if an SLA is violated. The monitoring activities of MeMo allow the detection of SLA violations, which can be directly reported to SLA Manager. This notification is accompanied by a suggestion of appropriate countermeasures that can be taken according to the penalties stated in the SLA (e.g., forcing a specific participant to leave the SR). In Fig. 5.4 the two main subcomponents are responsible for providing the functionalities of *SLA Manager*. The *SLA Lifecycle* is responsible for managing SLAs throughout their lifecycle (from creation to modification to expiration). Furthermore, the *Alarm Engine* ensures the compliance with the SLAs through its interaction with MeMo, which is monitoring the degree of compliance of each participating member. Finally, SLAs are stored in a dedicated *SLA Repository*.

5.4.2 Metrics Monitoring

The main tasks of the MeMo component include:

- Collecting low-level measurements at runtime,

- Calculating the metrics based on these measurements, and
- Emitting the appropriate notifications when an SLA violation occurs.

The layered architecture of the MeMo component appears on the right-hand side of Fig. 5.4. The lowermost layer, *Measurement Collection*, receives measurements from the components of the CoMiFin platform according to the monitoring configuration. Each measurement is determined by the metrics definition and is implemented by agents deployed into the components themselves, or the measurements are extracted from the component by external means. Agents in this sense are small, simple applications capable of measuring the necessary attribute locally on the node; e.g., a CPU usage agent measures the utilization of the CPU of the machine.

The next layer, called *Metrics Calculation*, calculates the defined metrics based on the collected measurements. MeMo supports either one of the following two ways to calculate the metrics:

- Built-in mechanisms, which allow for simple and relatively fast arithmetic calculations, e.g., totaling, averaging, minimum or maximum calculation, or
- Evaluator plugins, which are utilized if advanced or complex functionality is required (e.g., the collected measurements are the basis for a complex metric or the amount of data is large).

Evaluator plugins have access to the collected measurements and the previously calculated metrics. In the current implementation, a *rule engine*-based plugin is used for correlating the received measurements to effectively process metrics and detect meaningful patterns by performing complex event processing (CEP). In this plugin-based monitoring architecture the SR Information Manager (IM) is also used as a plugin with enhanced trust calculation features. The trust maintenance algorithm is implemented in the IM while MeMo keeps track of system status information, both for low-level security metrics and trust values computed by the IM (the trust issues are further elaborated in [13]).

The *SLA Subsystem*, the topmost layer of the architecture, is responsible for collaborating with the SLA Manager. Internally, it is responsible for processing SLAs, deriving the configuration of the other two subcomponents, and tracking the adherence/violation of these SLAs. In the case of an SLA violation, this component notifies the SLA Manager as described above.

All three layers of the reference architecture use the *Database Access* subcomponent to persistently store measurements, metrics, SLA descriptions, and notifications.

5.4.3 Current Implementation Status

Preliminary implementations of both the SLA Manager and the MeMo component are available. In the following sections we briefly summarize their current status.

SLA Manager Preliminary Implementation

The current prototype implementation of the SLA Manager focuses on the core functionalities, which are creating, modifying, and deleting SLAs from the repository. The current implementation includes: (a) a web application permitting the management of SLAs throughout their lifecycle, (b) a database component where the SLA Manager can store the SLAs, and (c) a set of communication interfaces (web services and JMS message queues) ensuring the interaction with MeMo. The web services provided by the SLA Manager are SLAViolationNotification and SLAWarningNotification. They can be called by MeMo if the latter has detected an SLA violation (ViolationNotification) or if it has proactively detected that an SLA is close to being violated (WarningNotification). JMS message queues are used to communicate information related to the SLA lifecycle from SLA Manager to MeMo: the SLA Manager notifies MeMo about any SLA status modification (SLA creation, modification, expiration, and disablement).

MeMo Preliminary Implementation

The preliminary implementation of MeMo integrates several open source components. The Measurements Collection component is implemented by the Nagios [8] monitoring server along with its agent framework to collect specific measurements. The component has been designed to support the easy replacement of the underlying monitoring system in later development phases against industry standard monitoring tools, such as Tivoli Monitoring or HP OpenView. The built-in Metrics Calculation functionality is provided by database triggers of MySQL database, which provides simple but effective arithmetic calculations on metrics. As mentioned before, a rule engine-based evaluator plugin has been developed which utilizes the Drools [4] rule engine. Communication between the evaluator plug-ins and the Metrics Calculation subcomponent is implemented by Java Remote Method Invocation (RMI) and through JMS queues using the JBoss MQ JMS implementation. As for the metrics, we rely on measurements that the built-in Nagios plugin could provide. These include basic resource-level metrics, such as *availability*, *average round trip time* of PING ICMP messages, *statistics of network* interfaces, *CPU utilization*, *hard disk attributes*, and *memory consumption*. In addition, we created Nagios plugins that monitor the execution of components (e.g., the SR Gateway log analysis plugin) and provide measurements specific to the considered application, e.g., *throughput of processed messages*, *number of malformed messages*, and *time of message processing*. Additionally, MeMo calculates *higher level metrics*, such as the *number of SLA violations* for each component, by comparing the thresholds defined in the SLSs and the actual measured values for each SLA Parameter.

Regarding the implementation of SLA metamodel and model transformation related functionality, we use Eclipse Modeling Framework and subprojects of Eclipse Modeling Projects (e.g., Java Emitting Templates and Xpand) for modeling and also for automatically generating Nagios configuration settings. Our current implementation still needs manual intervention, yet it is:

- able to help runtime validation of the SLA model and synthesize configurations on the basis of high-level requirements,
- logically independent from the concrete platform, as stated before.

5.4.4 Evaluation of the Current Implementation

This section shows the functionalities of the CoMiFin demonstrator by taking an example where there is an SR being deployed and running. The graphs focus on a single member of this SR, called "Bank of Noldor".

Figures 5.5(a), 5.5(c), and 5.5(e) (the column on the left in Fig. 5.5) depict three metrics monitored by MeMo when there is no input sent by the members to the Semantic Room. Consequently, there are no messages processed by the Analytics Container (Fig. 5.5(a)) and, since each member should send input to the Semantic Room (the exact number is defined in the SLA), there are SLA violations for each partner (Fig. 5.5(c)). Furthermore, the trust score of the same member is also very low, as the member does not send input. After the members start sending messages, there is a change in each metric. The throughput rises (Fig. 5.5(b)), the number of SLA violations decreases (Fig. 5.5(d)), and the trust score of the same member (Fig. 5.5(f)) ascends.

5.5 Related Work

Modern societies increasingly rely on CIs such as power grids and communication, financial, and transportation networks. These CIs are increasingly interconnected and therefore highly dependent on computing and communication infrastructures. Logically, the need exists to secure CIs against threats (operational or deliberate) arising from the whole spectrum of interconnected entities, as their disturbance can cause considerable material, financial, and even (in extreme cases) human loss. As a consequence, the accurate and quantitative assessment of the security level of these CIs constitutes a key objective for both the public and private sectors. The need to protect CIs reveals the necessity to quantify trustworthiness (i.e., dependability and security) metrics to determine their exact level [15]. A first step toward CI protection (CIP) is accomplished through CI monitoring and control, provided by a monitoring infrastructure using multiple sensing nodes.

Measuring and controlling IT security through metrics is a less explored research field. Such metrics are a prerequisite for understanding, improving, and validating/certifying the security of CIs. As it is almost impossible to survey all the existing metrics in this chapter, we provide an insight into the various existing classes with a particular emphasis on security metrics.

There exist some approaches that aim at categorizing the existing security metrics. "Most of the resulting taxonomies have been developed for practitioners, and therefore, do not cover the whole spectrum of existing security metrics as they are

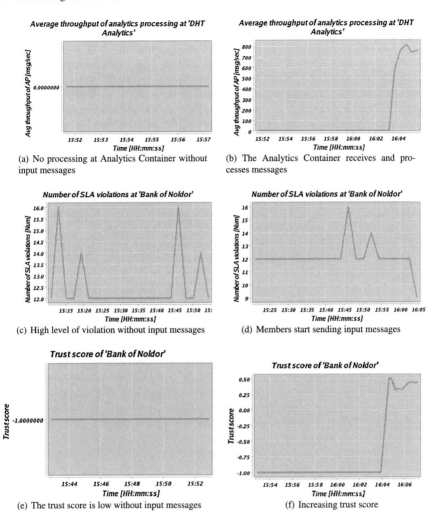

(a) No processing at Analytics Container without input messages

(b) The Analytics Container receives and processes messages

(c) High level of violation without input messages

(d) Members start sending input messages

(e) The trust score is low without input messages

(f) Increasing trust score

Fig. 5.5 Results of input messages arriving from members to the Semantic Room

industry oriented and try to fulfill the requirements of the market" [9, 19]. Savola [17] presents a high-level taxonomy containing metrics for both organizational information security management and product development. The National Institute of Standards and Technology (NIST) [16] has proposed a different security metrics taxonomy from the perspective of an organization. It contains three distinct categories: management, technical, and operational metrics. Each of these categories contains several subcategories (17 in total). The Institute for Information Infrastructure Protection (I3P) [10] proposed a further taxonomy [19]. Driven by the process control system perspective, this taxonomy consists of three different metrics classes (technical, operational, and organizational metrics), which are further subdivided into several subcategories. Vaughn et al. [20] have proposed a taxonomy consisting of two categories: organizational security metrics and metrics for technical target of assessment. Seddigh et al. [18] introduce a taxonomy for information networks: security, quality of service (QoS), and availability. Each of these three categories consists of technical, organizational, and operational metrics. The technical metrics consist of subcategories for product rating, incident statistics, and security testing. The organizational security metrics include metrics for information assurance, program development, and resources. The operational security metrics comprise metrics for technical readiness, susceptibility, and effectiveness. Savola [17] introduces a high-level information security metrics taxonomy incorporating metrics for both organizational information security management and product development. It begins with Level 0: security metrics for business management, which form the highest category in this taxonomy. It contains five subcategories: (a) security metrics for cost-benefit analysis containing economic measures such as return on investment (ROI), (b) trust metrics for business collaboration, (c) security metrics for business-level risk analysis, (d) security metrics for information security management (ISM), and (e) security, dependability, and trust (SDT) metrics for ICT products, systems, and services. Savola's taxonomy covers the new emerging field of economics-driven security metrics, which targets an audience of managers and decision makers without an information security background. The taxonomies we have mentioned here constitute a considerable effort to bring order to the myriad of existing security metrics. They consider the existing metrics from different perspectives: organizational management, product development, and operational assessment.

A similarly important research field deals with how high-level (business) requirements, e.g., in the form of SLAs, can be transformed to monitoring configurations and related artifacts. Momm et al. [14] present a model-driven approach to reduce the complexity and maintain coherency of components in service-oriented architecture in the face of the changing requirements. Similarly, in [5] an SLA metamodel, which is independent of the functional design of the component in hand, and the related metrics and indicators are defined. However, the instrumentation of the monitored infrastructure is out of the scope of their approach. In [12] the authors present a new approach to service-delivery management systems supporting heterogeneity and collaboration. Integral parts of their proposal are the performance and service delivery metrics, and the management of the key performance indicators (KPIs).

5.6 Conclusions

In this chapter, we presented a systematic metric-driven, model-based approach for monitoring the trustworthy operation of the CoMiFin middleware. This approach addresses high-level contractual requirements described in the form of SLAs, infrastructural elements of the supporting IT systems captured by resource maps, and the technical constraints of the underlying monitoring environment. This model-based approach can be extended by additional validations to support early detection of faults and misconfigurations of the monitoring system. Moreover, the proposed method can be extended to incorporate domain-specific knowledge and industrial best practices by modeling sample metrics of requirements on the basis of existing frameworks, e.g., Control Objectives for Information and related Technology (COBIT).

The approach uses a plugin architecture where the evaluation of monitoring results can be performed at multiple levels. This currently includes trustworthiness evaluation as implemented in the Information Manager component of the middleware. However, complex event processing engines or even the CoMiFin approach itself could be used to achieve a higher scalable online evaluation of monitoring data generated by different software sensors, i.e., a "CoMiFin for CoMiFin" concept. This could be implemented, e.g., by setting up an SR for collecting data from other SRs and performing enhanced evaluation.

References

1. Acquisti, A.: Essays on privacy, anonymity, and tracking in computer-mediated economic transactions. Ph.D. thesis, UC Berkeley (2003)
2. Basili, V.: The goal question metric approach. In: Encyclopedia of Software Engineering, pp. 528–532 (1994)
3. Berander, P., Jönsson, P.: A goal question metric based approach for efficient measurement framework definition. In: Proc. of the 2006 ACM/IEEE International Symposium on Empirical Software Engineering, pp. 316–325 (2006)
4. JBoss Community: Drools, Dec 2010. http://www.jboss.org/drools/
5. Debusmann, M., Kroger, R., Geihs, K.: Unifying service level management using an MDA-based approach. In: Network Operations and Management Symposium, 2004. NOMS 2004. IEEE/IFIP, vol. 1, pp. 801–814. IEEE, New York (2004)
6. Ghani, H., Khelil, A., Suri, N., Gönczy, L., Csertán, G., Urbanics, G., Clarke, J.: A metrics based approach for assessing the quality of critical infrastructure protection (The CoMiFin Project Approach). In: Proc. of the 1st International Workshop on the Security of the Internet of Things (SecIoT) (2010)
7. Khelil, A., Jeckel, S., Germanus, D., Suri, N.: Towards Benchmarking of P2P technologies from a SCADA systems protection perspective. In: Proc. of the 2nd International Conference on Mobile Lightweight Wireless Systems (MOBILIGHT) (2010)
8. Nagios Enterprises: Nagios—The Industry Standard in IT Infrastructure Monitoring, Dec 2010. http://www.nagios.org/
9. Grance, T., Hash, J., Stevens, M., O'Neal, K., Bartol, N.: Security metrics guide for information technology systems. In: NIST report 800-35 (2003)
10. Institute for Information Infrastructure Protection. I3P: Institute for Information Infrastructure Protection (2010)
11. Keller, A., Ludwig, H.: The WSLA framework specifying and monitoring service level agreements for web services. J. Netw. Syst. Manag. **1**, 57–81 (2003)
12. Kumaran, S., Bishop, P., Chao, T., Dhoolia, P., Jain, P., Jaluka, R., Ludwig, H., Moyer, A., Nigam, A.: Using a model-driven transformational approach and service-oriented architecture for service delivery management. IBM Syst. J. **46**(3), 513–529 (2007)
13. Lodi, G., Baldoni, R., Csertan, G., Elshaafi, H., Gonczy, L., Mulcahy, B.: Trust management in monitoring financial critical information infrastructures. In: Proc. of the 2nd International Conference on Mobile Lightweight Wireless Systems—Critical Information Infrastructure Protection Track (2010)
14. Momm, C., Detsch, T., Gebhart, M., Abeck, S.: Model-driven development of monitored web service compositions. In: 15th HPSUA Workshop (2008)

15. Naqvi, S., Riguidel, M.: Quantifiable security metrics for large scale heterogeneous systems. In: Proc. of the 40th Annual IEEE International Carnahan Conferences Security Technology, pp. 209–215 (2006)
16. National Institute of Standards and Technology (NIST). National Institute of Standards and Technology (2010)
17. Savola, R.: A novel security metrics taxonomy for R&D organizations. In: Proc. of the Innovative Minds Conference (ISSA), pp. 379–390 (2008)
18. Seddigh, N., Pieda, P., Matrawy, A., Nandy, B., Lambadaris, I., Hatfield, A.: Current trends and advances in information assurance metrics. In: Proc. of the Second Annual Conference on Privacy, Security and Trust (PST), pp. 197–205 (2004)
19. Stoddard, M., Haimes, Y., Bodeau, D., Lian, C., Carlson, R., Santos, J., Glantz, C., Shaw, J.: Process control system security metrics, state of practice. Technical report, Institute for Information Infrastructure Protection Research (2005)
20. Vaughn, R.B., Henning, R., Siraj, A.: Information assurance measures and metrics state of practice and proposed taxonomy. In: Proc. of the 36th Annual Hawaii International Conference on System Sciences (HICSS), vol. 9, pp. 331–340 (2003)

Chapter 6
Trust and Privacy

Jimmy McGibney, Hisain Elshaafi, Barry P. Mulcahy, Dmitri Botvich, Giorgia Lodi, Davide Lamanna, and Hani Qusa

Abstract In this chapter we demonstrate how to increase the value of shared information by providing context on its quality via trust metrics. In order to evaluate the achieved level of trust, a trust evaluation system is described. This system assesses the quality of information based on past behaviour, direct experience, recommendation, referral, and roles. This management process filters and prioritises information provided by Semantic Room (SR) members while dynamically adjusting the trust level of members.

Sharing of sensitive information in a commons requires that precautions be taken to safeguard the interest of members and to uphold codes of privacy. In the case of financial institutions, the requisites for security and privacy place demands on the CoMiFin platform that are satisfied using advanced modelling techniques, rigorous data analysis, and information management.

J. McGibney · H. Elshaafi · B.P. Mulcahy (✉) · D. Botvich
Waterford Institute of Technology, Waterford, Ireland
e-mail: bmulcahy@tssg.org

J. McGibney
e-mail: jmcgibney@tssg.org

H. Elshaafi
e-mail: helshaafi@tssg.org

D. Botvich
e-mail: dbotvich@tssg.org

G. Lodi
Consorzio Interuniversitario Nazionale Informatica (CINI), via Ariosto 25, Roma, Italy
e-mail: lodi@dis.uniroma1.it

D. Lamanna · H. Qusa
Dipartimento di Ingegneria Informatica, Automatica e Gestionale Antonio Ruberti, Università degli Studi di Roma "La Sapienza", Roma, Italy

D. Lamanna
e-mail: lamanna@dis.uniroma1.it

H. Qusa
e-mail: qusa@dis.uniroma1.it

R. Baldoni, G. Chockler (eds.), *Collaborative Financial Infrastructure Protection*,
DOI 10.1007/978-3-642-20420-3_6, © Springer-Verlag Berlin Heidelberg 2012

To this end, in this chapter we present a distributed SR architecture which is capable of correlating events coming from SR members while preserving the privacy of sensitive data items. The SR consists of SR Gateways deployed at each financial institution and a set of private clouds forming the SR collaborative processing system (CSP). SR Gateways perform data pre-processing and anonymize data items, as prescribed by the SR contract, using the Shamir secret sharing scheme. Anonymous data are sent to the CPS, which aggregates information through MapReduce-based computations. The anonymous data resulting from the collaborative computation are revealed to the SR members only if suspicious activities are detected. We show how this SR can be leveraged for detecting Man-in-the-Browser attacks.

6.1 Introduction

Providing protection to the financial infrastructure in the face of faults and malevolent attacks is vital to the stability, availability, and continuity of key financial markets and businesses worldwide. Traditional protection approaches have focused on protecting individual financial institutions (FIs) while ignoring the threats arising from cross-domain interactions as well as those originating from other critical infrastructures. With the growing complexity of inter-organisational boundaries and their increasing interdependence, such isolated approaches are no longer adequate. However, sharing information between FIs relating to critical events and relying on others' quality of service attributes such as security requires varying levels of trust between them, depending on the requirements of each individual FI and the sensitivity of exchanged information. It also requires mechanisms for the protection of the privacy of organisations and individuals while sharing information.

In order to allow detection and proactive response to threats against financial critical infrastructures and thus ensure business continuity, the CoMiFin [3] research project has developed a prototype solution to facilitate information exchange and distributed event processing among groups of federated participants. These federated groups are called Semantic Rooms (SRs) [1]. The SRs are set up based on common interest, for instance for collaborative protection against distributed denial of service, intrusion, or Man-in-the-Middle attacks. The SRs are enabled through a common middleware infrastructure (Fig. 6.1), allowing sharing and processing of information through a secure and trusted environment for the participants to contribute and analyse data. Exchanged data can include e.g. real-time security events, historical attack data, and logs that concern other SR participants. Processed data can be used internally by the SR members. In this case, derived events, models, profiles, blacklists, and alerts are made available for the members.

This chapter describes a trust management system developed as part of the CoMiFin system to allow the evaluation, monitoring, and management of trustworthiness levels of FIs exchanging critical events and information. The CoMiFin *Information Manager* allows the composition of the trust context that indicates the focus of the trust semantics, for instance; integrity, privacy, competence. Trustworthiness levels are used to assure FIs of each other's reliability and to filter events

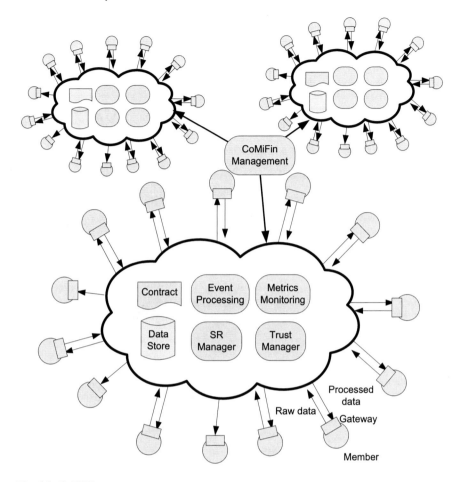

Fig. 6.1 CoMiFin system

and data being processed. This chapter introduces a novel reusable architecture that allows flexibility and extensibility of trust metrics and trust algorithms, thus providing the ability to refocus the weighting of trust algorithms to prioritise different sets of requirements such as compliance and privacy.

Sharing and processing of data among FIs could lead to the disclosure of potentially sensitive information relating to people and/or organisations. Therefore, protecting the privacy of such information becomes an imperative requirement. In this chapter we describe a specific architecture of the SRs whose goal is to allow distrusting SR members to execute collaborative computations on massive sets of input raw data while preserving the privacy of some sensitive data.

The rest of this chapter is organised as follows. Section 6.2 describes the design of the information management architecture. Section 6.3 investigates the privacy issues inherent to information sharing between organisations. Finally, Sect. 6.4 provides the conclusions of the chapter.

6.2 Trust Management

As illustrated in Fig. 6.1, in addition to the Information Manager described in this chapter, members share common resources that include:

- SR Management: manages the group lifecycle from creation to disbandment, including configuration of the SR and maintaining logs of the SR activities.
- Event Processing and Data Mining: provides simple to complex event filtering and processing services to the SR, depending on the SR and the types of events. SR data mining applications mine a large number of events and other data accumulated over time to extract analytical models to be used to assist the online event processing.
- Metrics Monitoring: monitors the middleware to assess its status in meeting the requirements specified in the SR contract.
- Data Store: supports storage needs of the SR, its events, and knowledge base.
- SR Contract: regulates participation and the relationship between members. The contract also governs the services available in the SR, and access to those services and requirements in relation to data protection, isolation, trust, security, availability, fault tolerance, and performance.

Note that in this chapter we use the words "member" and "agent" to indicate the SR participants. An agent is a principal whose trust is managed by the Information Manager and it can be a current, past, or future member of the SR.

Since the members of an SR share potentially sensitive and mission-critical information, SR management needs to provide suitable assurance to each of those members indicating their trustworthiness levels. To that end, we developed the CoMiFin Information Manager. Trust evaluation is based on past behaviour and the reputation of each agent through direct experience, recommendation, and referral. We define trust as a relationship between two entities that indicates the contextual expectations from one entity towards another in relation to reliance in accomplishing a certain action at a certain quality. Trustworthiness level is the level of trust that the trusting entity has in another entity. The trustworthiness level consists of a trust score that is calculated based on weighted ratings given to different types of metrics and events. It also includes a confidence degree which indicates the quantity and variability of the ratings on which the trust score was based. The weighting mechanism of events and metrics allows the enquiring party to determine the context of trust.

A CoMiFin SR member may request information from the Information Manager regarding the trustworthiness of another member when sending new events and data or when receiving them from other members. This assures each of the SR members of the trustworthiness of other members and provides a mechanism for fine-grained access control in the dynamic environment in which the SR membership operates.

6.2.1 Trust Background

In the past decade there has been extensive research on the area of trust in various aspects of multi-agent systems [5, 6], web services [7, 8], e-commerce [9], and information filtering [2]. The concept of trust varies, with those works frequently interpreting trust in the context of security as a way of achieving authentication and access control, as in [10]. However, the CoMiFin Information Manager allows its administrator to customise the system to measure trust based on reputation for an adaptable context; therefore, the trustworthiness levels can reflect security, integrity, competence, predictability, etc., of the agents based on weights. However, the Information Manager builds upon, and extends from, the results of previous research, particularly systems and algorithms developed in ReGreT [11], FIRE [5], and TOPAS [2]. The CoMiFin Information Manager is developed to suit the requirements of a set of nodes collaborating in information exchange in relation to security threats to their assets and infrastructure.

Distributed Trust: Between Semantic Rooms

In previous work [2], an overlay of a distributed trust management infrastructure on top of a service delivery infrastructure for unstructured networks was proposed. This provides a closed-loop system where live distributed trust measures are used to modify access control settings in a changing threat environment. This can also be used to assist collaboration *between* SRs. It can be expected that a member of one SR will be a member of other SRs, and the idea is to share information between SRs on the behaviour of common members.

With this architecture, illustrated in Fig. 6.2, a distributed trust management overlay operates separately from normal SR activity (including local trust management). Two message passing interfaces are defined between the operational layer and the trust management layer and another between the distributed information managers of individual SRs.

The interfaces are as follows:

- *Experience reports*: *SR local information manager* → *SR distributed information manager*.
- *Trust updates*: SR_i *distributed TM* ↔ SR_j *distributed TM*.
- *Filter tuning*: *SR distributed TM* → *SR local TM*.

In a peer-to-peer network, such as the inter-SR case, information is not stored centrally. In any case, trust by its nature is subjective and thus best managed by the SR doing the trusting. There is no global view: any given SR will be aware of the existence of, and can share information with, zero or more other SRs.

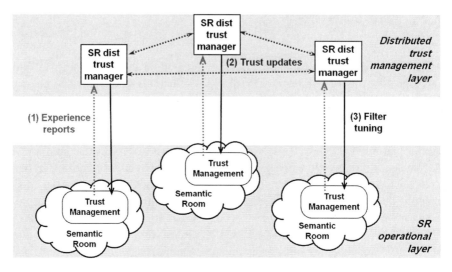

Fig. 6.2 Distributed trust management overlay

6.2.2 Information Manager

This section describes a trust system we call the *Information Manager* developed to allow the evaluation, monitoring, and management of trustworthiness levels of FIs exchanging critical events and information in CoMiFin. Trustworthiness levels are used to assure FIs participating in SRs of the reliability of each other and for filtering events and data being processed. The system is a novel reusable architecture that allows flexibility and extensibility of trust metrics and trust algorithms.

Trust Events

Trust events refer to the notifications received by the Information Manager from the Event Processing and Metrics Monitoring components (Fig. 6.1). CoMiFin SRs are governed by contracts that define requirements for processing and data sharing services. Trust events received by the Information Manager indicate violations or adherence to those contracts. Those trust events can be classified into two types:

- *Metrics*: Metrics measure how quality of service (QoS) requirements are adhered to by the SR member. Those metrics are classified into categories including security, performance, and availability. The Information Manager allows the administrator to customise the weight of each category of metrics in calculating the overall trust. Each category includes one or more metrics. For example, the performance category includes the response time metric, and availability includes uptime.
- *Alerts*: Alerts are received from the Event Processing component in relation to events that indicate the level of collaboration of the members in supporting the

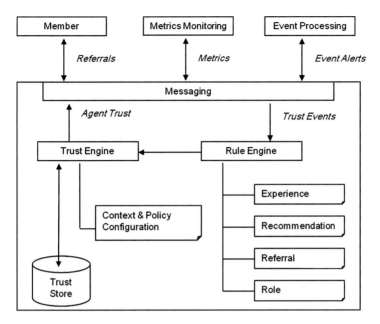

Fig. 6.3 CoMiFin Information Manager

functioning of the SR, such as contributing to blacklists and threat detection. The alerts are also classified by the Information Manager into categories including competence, integrity, and willingness of an SR member. These categories can be extended and modified for each SR.

Trust Evaluation, Monitoring, and Management

Figure 6.3 illustrates the architecture of the Information Manager. Each SR shares a common infrastructure that includes an Information Manager. Agents can dynamically join or leave the membership of an SR. The Information Manager stores, monitors, and updates trust of each of the agents it has knowledge of. It determines the trustworthiness level of an agent using:

- *Direct experience*: It receives alerts (from Event Processing) and metrics (from Metrics Monitoring) indicating the level of adherence or violation of a member to the SR's contract.
- *Recommendation*: It requests recommendations from Information Managers in other SRs regarding the reputation of an agent.
- *Referral*: A trusted agent can provide another with a reference certifying its reputation. An agent can use the reference to improve its trust; this is especially useful for new members and those with little or no interactions.
- *Role*: Each agent is assigned to a role which gives it a default trustworthiness level that can be improved or reduced through direct experience, recommendations,

Fig. 6.4 System combines
rules-based filter with trust

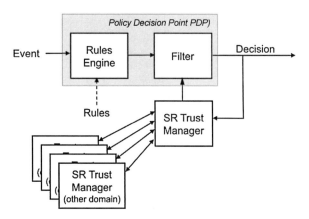

and/or referrals. In CoMiFin there are currently a number of roles in an SR that
include owner, member, and client. The SR owner is one SR member who is
responsible for setting up, managing, and disbanding the SR. An SR member is
a CoMiFin partner that participates in an SR. It can input data into the SR and
can use the output of the SR. A client cannot contribute data directly to the SR,
but can only act as a consumer of the processed SR data that can be shared with
clients.

A trust query can be received from a member, the Metrics Monitoring system, or
other CoMiFin SR's Information Managers, etc. The query invokes the calculation
of the trustworthiness level from existing ratings. The SR operations are enhanced
by combining classical policy-based management with distributed trust management. As illustrated in Fig. 6.4, incoming events are evaluated by a rules engine
within a policy decision point. A filter takes the outcome of these rule evaluations
and makes a (binary) decision on whether the event is to be allowed, for example,
by comparing some function of these rule outcomes with a threshold. This threshold is a function of trust in the event's originator, evaluated by a local information
manager. This local information manager is influenced by (i) previous experience
(hence closed-loop feedback in Fig. 6.4) and (ii) reputation information from third
parties.

Figure 6.5 depicts a use case diagram for the system. Table 6.1 contains descriptions of the use cases. The diagram shows the capability to allow the Information
Manager's administrator to make a variety of customisations and updates to the system.

As depicted in the diagram, in CoMiFin there are two internal systems that can
feed trust events to the Information Manager. One is the Event Processing system,
responsible for filtering and complex event processing (CEP) of critical financial infrastructure events and data [13]. The other is the Metrics Monitoring system, which
monitors QoS and other related metrics including contract violations/adherence.
A trust query can be received from a member, the Metrics Monitoring system, or
other CoMiFin SR's Trust Managers, etc. The query invokes the calculation of the

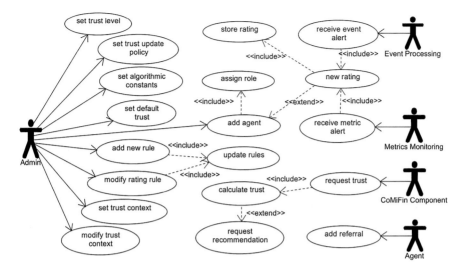

Fig. 6.5   A use case diagram for the Information Manager

trustworthiness level from existing ratings and based on the configured policy and context.

Ratings Computation

The system utilises the Drools [4] rule engine to specify business rules for processing different categories of trust events and the calculation of the resulting ratings. The rules calculate the rating for the event and add other attributes including the recency value (when the event occurred) and the type of event. Ratings are then stored by the Information Manager and can be used for calculating the overall trustworthiness level of each agent.

A trust event e can be represented as

$$e = (a, g, v_x, v_y, t),\tag{6.1}$$

where a is the agent; g is the category of trust event, e.g., performance, security; v_x is the value agreed to in the contract; v_y the actual value measured, which may or may not be adhering to the limits in the agreed contract value; and t is the time at which the event took place. Additional parameters may be added to v_x to indicate the type of measurement, e.g., real number, percentage, and how it is compared to the actual value v_y, e.g., minimum, maximum, range. For example, the contract may refer to a minimum uptime accepted as 95%.

The rating score s is calculated using the function

$$s = f(v_x \circ v_y),\tag{6.2}$$

where $\circ$ is an operator determined by the type of measurements and how they are compared. A simple formula would be v_x/v_y, applicable for example when real

Table 6.1 Use case descriptions

Use case	Description
Set trustworthiness level	Set a static trustworthiness level to an agent
Set trust update algorithm	Specify which available trust update algorithm to use or add new policy
Set algorithmic constants	Some algorithms use constant parameters; their values can be set in the configuration
Set default trust	Default trust is required for an agent whose trust is unknown through normal mechanisms such as experience. It may also be required by some trust update algorithms and policies
Add new rule	Create or add a new rule to the existing rules for the ratings
Modify rating rule	Existing rules can be modified to suit changing requirements
Update rules	Commands for new rules or modifying existing rules result in updating the Information Manager for the rule sets that can be fired due to an event
Set trust context	The Information Manager has preconfigured set of contexts emphasising competence, integrity, etc. Each of those contexts assigns different weights to each category of events. Administrator can switch between trust contexts
Modify trust context	A trust context can be modified by changing the weights of categories of events; e.g., a category can be assigned to weight $= 0$ if it needs to be ignored in calculating trust
Add agent	An agent is added automatically when a new trust event is received concerning the agent. An agent can also be added by the administrator
Assign role	Adding a new agent requires assigning the agent to a role. Each role implies an initial trust value and the trust sensitivity to the effect of new events
Receive event alert	Event Processing component sends a new trust event
Receive metric alert	Metrics Monitoring component sends a new trust event
Add referral	An agent sends a new referral signed by a trusted agent
New rating	A trust event can result in a new rating of the agent
Store rating	Each rating is persistently stored
Request recommendation	The system requests recommendations from other groups' Information Managers regarding the trustworthiness level of an agent
Request trust	The Information Manager receives requests concerning the trustworthiness level of an agent
Calculate trust	Trust is calculated using chosen and/or customised policy

numbers are used for measuring the event, v_x is the maximum allowed value in the contract, and $v_y \neq 0$. Function f provides the rating score taking into consideration penalty or reward given as a result of violation or adherence to the contract, respectively. The function can be specified in the Information Manager's configuration. Each rating is stored in the database in the form of a tuple $R = (a, g, s, t)$ where s is the rating score.

Trust Computation

The trust engine is responsible for providing a snapshot of the current trustworthiness level of an agent. A trust context provides a way to answer the question: "what to trust the agent for?". For instance, an agent may be trusted for its security and integrity but may not be trusted for its competence. Therefore, the Information Manager can be customised to emphasise a specific context. A context requires providing more emphasis to certain types of trust events, e.g., metrics relating to performance and reliability categories, by giving them higher weights. The trust engine has default algorithms but allows for substituting or modifying existing algorithms through plugins. In addition to configuration files, an administrative web interface aims to allow system administrators to access and modify those configurations in a user-friendly manner.

Experience trust is a tuple $T = (a, S, C)$, where S is the score for agent a and C is the confidence in the score. The default algorithms used to calculate the experience trust are described here. The trust score for agent a, S_a is calculated through a weighted mean of the rating scores:

$$S_a = \sum_{i \in n} \frac{w_i \cdot s_i}{\sum_{i \in n} w_i}, \tag{6.3}$$

where n is the number rating for agent a and w is the weighting of the rating score s. The weighting is based on the recency of the rating and the category of event that triggered that rating. w is always between 0 and 1. Recency weight w_t is calculated using the exponential decay formula

$$w_t = \left(\frac{1}{2}\right)^{\frac{\Delta t}{\tau}}, \tag{6.4}$$

where Δt is the age of score s, i.e., the difference between the current time and the time when the rating took place; and τ is the half-life of the rating as set in the configuration.

Category weight w_g is set in the configuration as a value between 0 and 1. The rating score's weight w is calculated as follows:

$$w = \frac{w_t \cdot w_g}{\sum_{i \in n} w_{ti} \cdot w_{gi}}. \tag{6.5}$$

The confidence value of agent a, C_a, is calculated using the formula

$$C_a = c_\eta \cdot c_\delta, \tag{6.6}$$

where c_η is the rating quantity confidence and c_δ is the rating quality confidence. The value of c_η is calculated as follows:

$$c_\eta = 1 - e^{-\frac{\alpha \cdot n}{10}}, \tag{6.7}$$

where α is a constant parameter that can be used to adjust the slope of the relationship between the total number of ratings and the quantity confidence. The higher the value of α, the faster the full confidence (i.e., 1) is reached. It can be set to any positive value, but for gradual increase in confidence it should typically be set to a value

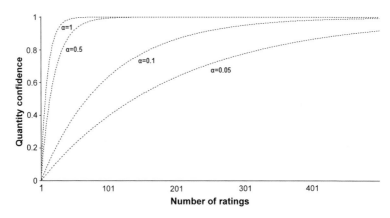

Fig. 6.6 Quantity confidence

between 0 and 1. Figure 6.6 illustrates the relationship between c_η, the number of ratings, and the value of α. The confidence increases proportionately to the number of ratings.

The quality confidence c_δ is calculated using the following formula:

$$c_\delta = 1 - \frac{1}{2} \cdot \frac{\sum_{i \in n} w_i \cdot |S - s_i|}{\sum_{i \in n} w_i}, \tag{6.8}$$

$|S - s_i|$ is the absolute difference between the agent's trust score and the individual rating score. The quality confidence indicates the deviation of the rating scores around the overall trust score and ranges between 0 (highest deviations) and 1 (lowest deviations). The deviations (range between 0 and 2) are weighted to allow varying degrees of confidence based on the weight of the deviating rating score.

6.2.3 Evaluation

The Information Manager is written in Java and runs as a JBoss Server application with a MySQL database for storing ratings and other trust management data. JBoss clustering is used to support load balancing and scalability and to protect from a single point of failure. Figures 6.7 and 6.8 show a demonstration of the Information Manager at work, where it sequentially receives 500 trust events for members A and B, respectively.

Member A is set to trigger more negative trust events and hence more frequent negative ratings than those of member B. A request for the trustworthiness level is also received every 10 member events and the trust score and confidence are consequently calculated. The trust computation uses the default algorithms that are described in the previous section. The trust context is configured to reflect security, reliability, performance, and willingness categories. As can be seen in the diagrams, trust scores change according to the past ratings including those received after the

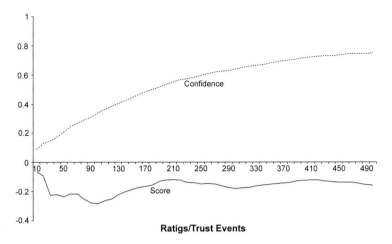

Fig. 6.7 Ratings and trust changes (member *A*)

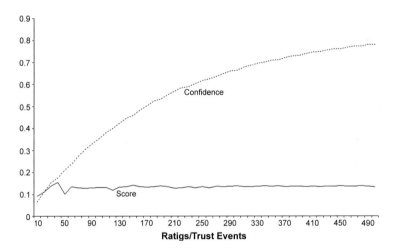

Fig. 6.8 Ratings and trust changes (member *B*)

last trust score calculation. As expected, trust confidence grows as new ratings are made. As the confidence constant α is set to 0.05, the confidence gradually levels off and its change then becomes more dependent on deviations between the rating scores.

Discussion

The Information Manager provides a feedback and control system for information exchange, a part of its role is in establishing and improving the quality of information being provided to CoMiFin. The emphasis placed by CoMiFin in trust provides an explicit incentive for members to participate positively; thereby ensuring accurate reporting of emerging threats. As a consequence, SR members must strive to achieve and maintain a high level of trustworthiness as measured by the Information Manager in order to gain the most benefit from their membership. This exhibits a strong positive effect on the integrity of the overall system. Members that are inaccurate or misleading with their intelligence contributions will be rated negatively by the Information Manager and may be penalised by the SR Manager. This approach to trust is further reinforced by the application of formalised SLAs that establish a minimum level of trust to be maintained in a given SR for its members.

To a lesser extent, the Information Management system and approach to trust adopted in CoMiFin provides a further incentive for SR members to ensure that their contributions are timely. If SR members provide information that is consistently lagging in comparison to other comparable members, then their information will not be rated as highly, and they may be in danger of violating SLA trust requirements. Leveraging trust in this manner helps ensure the overall availability of information in the CoMiFin system.

In addition, simply knowing that members are being evaluated provides an implicit incentive to not only comply with SLA requirements but to exceed them. As a result, the trust users can place in the alerts generated by CoMiFin is greatly increased. Since the context of trust can vary, the novel rule-based rating system used by the Information Manager allows adaptation of the trust context based on the requirements and goals of each SR. This includes compliance with regulatory requirements and the need for preserving privacy in an SR.

6.3 Privacy

As already demonstrated in this book, sharing information among organisations is a key factor in increasing their productivity with consequent benefits for customers, such as improved competitiveness and cost reduction [12]. This is particularly confirmed in the context of cyber security, where information sharing and processing is required in order to detect and prevent frauds and other cyber crimes (e.g., cyber money laundering, phishing, Man-in-the-Browser schemes). However, on the other side, sharing and processing of data typically related to a person and/or organisation (i.e., personal identifiable information) could lead to the disclosure of potentially sensitive information concerning single individuals and organisations. Therefore, protecting the privacy of such information becomes an imperative requirement.

In the following sections, we describe a classification of data, the specific architecture of an SR whose goal is to allow distrusting financial institutions (FIs) participating in the SR to execute collaborative computations on massive sets of input raw data while preserving the privacy of some sensitive data. In this SR, we assume that the FIs have established service provision relationships with their customers through specific contracts. These contracts include privacy guarantees that customers may require and FIs can ensure that are then mapped into a number of SR contract clauses which allow financial members of the SR not to violate their own

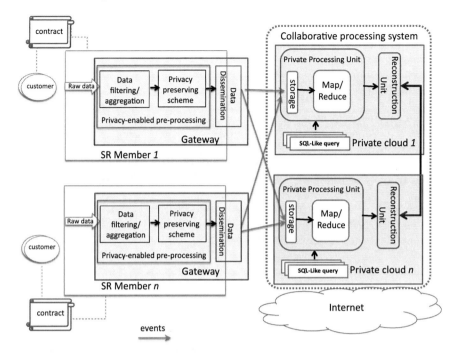

Fig. 6.9 SR privacy-preserving architecture

contracts with their customers. For example a contract may specify requirements related to the non-disclosure of sensitive information (e.g., customers' identities) to any third party provided that customers do not carry out suspicious activities.[1] In the case that suspicious activities are performed by customers, FIs can be relieved of any privacy obligations and can disclose information concerning those customers and their related activities.

In order to show the effectiveness of the proposed privacy-preserving SR, we introduce the case study of Man-in-the-Browser attacks detection while preserving the privacy of sensitive customers data.

6.3.1 Privacy-Preserving Semantic Room Architecture

Figure 6.9 illustrates an SR privacy-preserving architecture capable of preserving the privacy of sensitive data during collaborative events processing. The architecture consists of two components: the SR Gateway previously introduced, and the *collaborative processing system* (CPS). As already described, the SR Gateway transforms raw data into *events*, whereas the CPS detects anomalous behaviours.

---

[1]Suspicious activities have different meanings according to the legislation of different countries.

These components are used in three different phases of the data processing. The phases work as in a pipeline and are described next.

Pre-processing Phase

The SR Gateway is located at the SR member side. It is responsible for (i) protecting sensitive data items, as prescribed by contracts SR members may establish with their own customers (see Fig. 6.9), and (ii) injecting anonymized data to the CPS. In our privacy-preserving SR we have designed the SR Gateway component to embody two principal modules: the *privacy-enabled pre-processing* and *data dissemination* modules.

Privacy-Enabled Pre-processing Module

In the privacy-enabled pre-processing module, raw data of SR members are pre-processed by filtering unnecessary data and/or aggregating data according to specific formats necessary for the successive private event processing phase (see Sect. 6.3.2 for details). In addition, aggregated data are given to a privacy-preserving algorithm which anonymizes sensible data according to specific contractual clauses.

The algorithm is based on Shamir's (k, n) secret sharing scheme [15], which permits sharing a secret s among n participants in such a way that the secret can be easily reconstructed if and only if any k out of the n participants make their shares available, where $k \leq n$ provides the strength of the scheme. This is achieved by generating a random polynomial f of degree $k - 1$ defined over a prime field $\mathbb{Z}_p$, with $p > s$ and such that $f(0) = s$. The polynomial is used to generate n different shares, $s_1, s_2, \ldots, s_n$, where $s_i = f(i)$. The vector of shares is denoted by $[s]$. The secret can be reconstructed by exploiting the Lagrange interpolation technique.

Our architecture assumes that a certain number $w < n$ of SR members are semi-honest; that is, they do follow the collaborative processing protocol, but they are "curious" and attempt to infer as much information as possible from the computation itself. In principle, semi-honest members can even coordinate themselves in order to increase the chances of getting private data. In order to neutralise the semi-honest activities, we set $k = w + 1$.

The privacy-preserving scheme embodied in the SR Gateway first divides the aggregated data into two parts, a sensitive data part s and a non-sensitive part u.

Shamir's scheme is then applied to s and the produced list of shares $[s]$ is sent to the data dissemination module together with the u part.

Data Dissemination Module

This module is in charge of disseminating private data to all the SR members in the form of events. The dissemination occurs periodically, i.e., every fix time window. The beginning and end of each period is demarcated through special signalling messages. The module sends elementary information in the form of a triple

$(hash([s]), s', u)$, where $hash()$ is a perfect hash function, i.e., a function with no collisions. Note that the hash function takes all the shares as its argument: for any two secrets s, t, $hash([s]) = hash([t])$ iff $s = t$.

For the purpose of data ordering, the data dissemination module of SR member i manages a vector seq_{ij} of sequence numbers associated with the member j, which is reset at the beginning of a new dissemination phase. The entry seq_{ij} represents the sequence number of the last pair sent by i to j, and it is increased by one unit before each transmission.

Each triple $(hash[s], s_j, u)$ sent by the data dissemination module of SR member i to SR member j is tagged with the pair (i, seq_{ij}). We assume that all the communication channels are secure, FIFO, and reliable. The tuple $(i, seq_{ij}, hash[s], s_j, u)$ defines an *event*.

Private Processing Phase

The CPS is responsible for (i) collecting private data sent by SR Gateways of SR members, (ii) properly aggregating and processing the private data, and (iii) sending back a result of the computation in an unanonimyzed form to SR members.

The CPS can be thought of as a federation of private clouds. Each private cloud is owned by an SR member and deployed for the sake of collaborative complex data processing. A private cloud consists of the set of hardware and software resources made available by the member. It communicates with other private clouds in the federation only during the reconstruction phase (see below) using secure channels. Within a private cloud two processing units can be identified, as shown in Fig. 6.9: a *private processing unit* and a *reconstruction unit*.

Private Processing Unit

The goal of this unit is to aggregate and correlate private large data sets coming from the SR Gateways and to notify anomalies to all the SR members.

In our design, the jth private processing unit receives events $(i, seq_{ij}, hash[s], s_j, u)$ from SR Gateway i, $i = 1, \ldots, n$. The private processing unit is constructed from a distributed network of processing and storage elements hosted in the private cloud. As a share acts as a shadow of the original secret, any SR member has all the necessary data to make correlations. The processing elements manipulate and aggregate those data as follows. The processing elements are components of the MapReduce framework [19]: a centralised Job Tracker coordinates the execution of mappers and reducers on each resource of the private cloud through a collection of Task Trackers deployed on those resources. Mappers and reducers process the data according to a specific processing logic. We use a high-level query language to define the processing logic. The language compiles into a series of MapReduce jobs. Specifically, the language supports SQL-like query constructs that can be combined into flows and specify the *data patterns* to be discovered on the set of input data.

A query engine is in execution inside each private processing unit: the engine retrieves the data in the storage elements and aggregates them according to one or more SQL-like queries.

The final result from the reducers is an ordered sequence of shares. The ordering is carried out by exploiting the "order by" constructs made available by the majority of SQL-like languages for data processing (e.g., Hive [14], Jaql [16]). An external protocol could also be used as an alternative; it first orders the shares in groups, according to the lowest ID of the participant from which the shares were sent, and then inside a group it orders according to the sequence number of the shares.

Reconstruction Unit

The reconstruction unit is responsible for communicating with the other reconstruction units of the private clouds of the federation in order to rebuild the secret. Each reconstruction unit sends the output of the query, i.e., an ordered list of shares, and waits to receive a similar list from all the other members. Each unit then applies the Lagrange interpolation algorithm to reconstruct the original secret. The reconstruction algorithm is organised as a sequence of reconstructions. The first interpolation is applied using the first share in the lists received from the SR members, the second interpolation is applied using the second shares, etc.

6.3.2 Case Study: Privacy-Preserving Semantic Room for Man-in-the-Browser Detection

We instantiated the architecture of Sect. 6.3.1 to discover Man-in-the-Browser attacks, as described in Chap. 3 of this book. We recall here that for Man in the Browser we are interested in discovering if a bank's licit servers are receiving a high number of connections on behalf of different customers from the same device. The underlying hypothesis is that customers usually access their financial services, also provided by different banks, from a limited number of devices, and that the same device is not used by a large number of customers to access financial services in a short time period. The attack is then detected by identifying statistical anomalies related to the activities of a single source of network traffic that successfully logs into several services (such as home banking web sites) provided by different banks and using different identities. Once identified, the source IP addresses are included in a blacklist.

Processing Steps

At the first step, data coming from sources (i.e., web server logs) deployed at the network of each bank participating in the SR are collected and forwarded to the

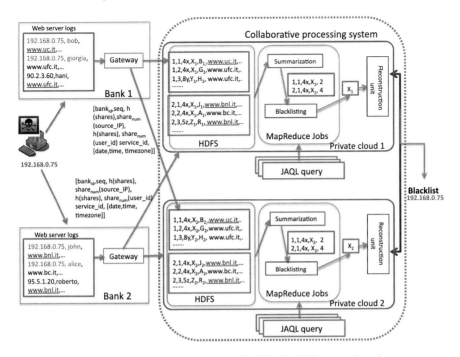

Fig. 6.10 Processing steps of the SR for collaborative Man-in-the-Browser detection

bank's SR Gateway (see Fig. 6.10). We have implemented the SR Gateway component as a Java program that pre-processes the incoming data by filtering and aggregating them (for instance, we filter the HTTP code of the request). These data are then anonymized through the secret sharing privacy scheme. In our case study, we consider the example in which contracts state that the source IP address and the user_id are the most valuable data items and must be maintained private during the computation.

The SR Gateway produces shares (and hash of shares) for each IP address and user_id of the filtered and aggregated data. In particular, in the example of Fig. 6.10 two banks participate in the Man-in-the-Browser SR processing system: two shares are thus produced by the Gateways for each IP address and user_id. All the remaining data (e.g., financial web site, date, time, time zone) that the Gateways manipulate are unchanged, as knowing their values during the computation cannot compromise the privacy of customers.

At the end of the pre-processing phase the SR Gateway produces a stream of data in the form: $\langle bank\_id, seq_{bank\_id,shareNum}, hash(all\_shares(sourceIP)),$ $share_i(SourceIP), hash(all\_shares(user\_id), share_i(user\_id), service\_id, [date, time, timezone]\rangle$ where $i \in [1, n]$. The data dissemination component of the SR Gateway sends these data to each corresponding private cloud in the SR, as described in Sect. 6.3.1. The data is stored in a portion of the Hadoop Distributed File System (HDFS) deployed at each private cloud.

The data is then processed by a collection of Hadoop's MapReduce jobs [20] handled by our architecture. The processing logic for Man-in-the-Browser detection is expressed in Jaql [16]. With Jaql we divide the processing logic into two flows. The first flow is named Summarization flow; it is responsible for correlating the data and further aggregating them according to statistical anomalies that can be discovered. In our case study, for each IP address, the Summarization flow counts the number of distinct accesses done by distinct customers (distinct shares of user_id) to different financial services (distinct service_id) in the fix time window. The output of this step, as shown in Fig. 6.10 is a collection of summary data in the form $\langle bank\_id, seq_{bank\_id,shareNum}, hash(all\_shares(sourceIP)), share_i(SourceIP),$ $Num\_Access\rangle$ where $i \in [1, n]$.

The data are then injected into the Blacklisting flow, which counts the number of accesses and verifies whether that total number exceeds predefined thresholds. If the check is positive, the Blacklisting produces a stream of data in the form $\langle share_i(SourceIP)\rangle$ where $i \in [1, n]$. This result is ordered according to the ordering protocol (or SQL-like ordering constructs) previously described.

The ordered shares are then passed to the reconstruction unit of the private cloud. We have implemented a Java distributed protocol for reconstruction purposes that takes the ordered shares and starts the reconstruction algorithm as described above.

6.4 Conclusions

This chapter presented a trust management system that can monitor and evaluate the trustworthiness levels of members in groups of financial institutions (FIs) sharing critical events and data relating to financial infrastructure protection. We also presented sets of requirements for compliance and methods for preserving the privacy of sensitive data in SRs. This provides a basis for information to be controlled according to each member's data sharing policy and in compliance with the SR contract. The aim of the cooperation and information exchange between FIs is to protect those institutions against threats and attacks that would otherwise be unavoidable using the existing isolated protection mechanisms.

Trust means different things in different contexts. The Information Manager allows the composition of the trust context to indicate the focus of the trust semantics, e.g., integrity, privacy, competence. The CoMiFin Information Manager allows its administrator to customise the system to measure trust based on reputation for an adaptable context, and therefore the trustworthiness levels can reflect security, compliance, predictability, etc., of the agents based on weights. The Information Manager is developed to suit the requirements of a set of nodes collaborating in information exchange in relation to security threats to their assets and infrastructure. The dashboard described in this chapter provides a visualisation on trust metrics that facilitates the system administrator in making trust-based decisions and to intuitively control and formulate the rules, algorithm, and contexts at runtime.

Another important feature of the Information Manager is that future and existing trust models and algorithms such as those mentioned in Sect. 6.2 can be made as add-ons to the CoMiFin Information Manager; consequently changing how the trustworthiness is calculated and what trust means. The Information Manager therefore introduces novel ideas that allow flexibility and extensibility of the trust metrics and trust algorithms based on the requirements. Trust metrics can be added or modified in the system configuration files, and trust algorithms can be added as system plugins. This provides the ability to refocus the weighting of trust algorithms to prioritise different sets of requirements such as compliance (Sect. 1.12 of Chap. 1) and privacy (Sect. 6.3).

The Information Manager is developed with a focus on financial infrastructure protection. However, the solution itself is generic and is applicable to other business and technical domains. The Information Manager has a reusable architecture that is highly flexible and extensible, allowing the composition and modification of rules, policies, and trust contexts. The rules engine receives trust events and, based on the customisation of the categories of events, it fires specific extensible rules. Those rules then generate the rating including a new score resulting from the event. The trust engine allows choosing between multiple algorithms for calculating the overall trustworthiness level.

In the design of collaborative environments it is worth considering that possibly competitor distrusting organizations (e.g., different FIs) can be reluctant to fully adopt the approach offered by the SR abstraction, as this implies sharing information that can be potentially sensitive. In these competitive contexts, stringent data privacy requirements are to be continuously met. In this chapter we also proposed an SR architecture capable of collaboratively correlating raw data coming from web logs of FIs with the aim of detecting Man-in-the-Browser attacks while preserving the privacy of specific data items.

Such data can be revealed if and only if a set of specific conditions is verified corresponding to some contractual conditions. The architecture includes SR Gateways, co-located at each SR member, executing a first level of aggregation and filtering, and a collaborative processing system (CPS) formed by a set of private clouds that correlate events in a batch way. This SR introduces a novel combination of MapReduce-based distributed parallel processing to support massive data processing and Shamir's secret sharing schema to guarantee the privacy of sensitive data (as in [17, 18]).

Once a batch has been completed, a MapReduce [19] computation starts at each cloud; this computation is instrumented by one or more complex queries, the same at each cloud, that are specified in the Jaql high-level language. The shares that satisfy the query are ordered and passed, one at a time, to a reconstruction unit that collects necessary shares of a data item from other clouds. When a sufficient number of shares is received, the cloud is able to reconstruct the secret.

References

1. Lodi, G., Querzoni, L., Baldoni, R., Marchetti, M., Colajanni, M., Bortnikov, V., Chockler, G., Dekel, E., Laventman, G., Roytman, A.: Defending financial infrastructures through early

warning systems: the intelligence cloud approach. In: Proc. 5th Annual Workshop on Cyber Security and Information Intelligence Research, Knoxville, TN, USA (2009)

2. McGibney, J., Botvich, D.: A trust overlay architecture and protocol for enhanced protection against spam. In: Proc. 2nd Int. Conf. on Availability, Reliability, and Security (ARES), Vienna, pp. 749–756 (2007)

3. CoMiFin (Communication Middleware for Monitoring Financial Critical Infrastructures). http://www.comifin.eu

4. Drools, http://www.jboss.org/drools

5. Huynh, T., Jennings, N., Shadbolt, N.: An integrated trust and reputation model for open multi-agent systems. J. Autonom. Agents Multi-Agent Syst. **13**(2), 119–154 (2006)

6. Xiong, L., Liu, L.: PeerTrust: supporting reputation-based trust for peer-to-peer electronic communities. IEEE Trans. Knowl. Data Eng. **16**(7), 843–857 (2004)

7. Singh, M.P.: Trustworthy service composition: Challenges and research questions. In: Proc. of the Autonomous Agents and Multi-Agent Systems, Workshop on Deception, Fraud and Trust in Agent Societies, pp. 117–135 (2002)

8. Malik, Z., Bouguettaya, A.: RATEWeb: reputation assessment for trust establishment among web services. VLDB J. **18**(4), 885–911 (2009)

9. Reiley, D., Bryan, D., Prasad, N., Reeves, D.: Pennies from Ebay: the determinants of price in online auctions. J. Ind. Econ. **55**(2), 223–233 (2007)

10. Blaze, M., Feigenbaum, J., Keromytis, A.: KeyNote: trust management for public-key infrastructures. In: Security Protocols Int. Workshop, Cambridge, England, pp. 56–63 (1998)

11. Sabater, J.: Trust and reputation for agent societies. Departament d'Informàtica, Universitat Autònoma de Barcelona (UAB), Ph.D. Thesis (2002)

12. Cate, F., Staten, M., Ivanov, G.: The value of information sharing. In: Protecting Privacy in the New Millennium Series, Council of Better Business Bureau (2000)

13. Luckham, D.: The Power of Events: An Introduction to Complex Event Processing in Distributed Enterprise Systems. Addison-Wesley, Reading (2002)

14. Hive. http://wiki.apache.org/hadoop/Hive (2011)

15. Shamir, A.: How to share a secret. Commun. ACM **22**, 612–613 (1979)

16. Jaql. http://www.jaql.org/ (2011)

17. Burkhart, M., Strasser, M., Many, D., Dimitropoulos, X.: SEPIA: privacy-preserving aggregation of multi-domain network events and statistics. In: USENIX Security Symposium, USENIX (2010)

18. Bogdanov, D., Laur, S., Willemson, J.: Sharemind: a framework for fast privacy-preserving computations. In: Proc. of the 13th European Symposium on Research in Computer Security: Computer Security, ESORICS '08, pp. 192–206. Springer, Berlin (2008)

19. Jeffrey, D., Ghemawat, S.: MapReduce: simplified data processing on large clusters. Commun. ACM **51**(1), 107–113 (2008)

20. Hadoop. http://hadoop.apache.org/ (2011)

Chapter 7
Collaborative Inter-domain Stealthy Port Scan Detection Using Esper Complex Event Processing

Leonardo Aniello, Giuseppe Antonio Di Luna, Giorgia Lodi, and Roberto Baldoni

Abstract This chapter describes a specific instance of a Semantic Room that makes use of the well-known centralized complex event processing engine Esper in order to effectively detect inter-domain malicious port scan activities. The Esper engine is deployed by the SR administrator and correlates a massive amount of network traffic data exhibiting the evidence of distributed port scans. The chapter presents two inter-domain SYN scan detection algorithms that have been designed and implemented in Esper and then deployed within the Semantic Room. The two algorithms are the Rank-based SYN (R-SYN) port scan detection algorithm and the Line Fitting port scan detection algorithm. The usefulness of the collaboration employed by the Semantic Room programming model in terms of detection accuracy of the inter-domain port scan attacks is shown. In addition, the chapter shows how Line Fitting is able both to achieve a higher detection accuracy with a smaller number of SR members compared to R-SYN, and to exhibit better detection latencies than R-SYN in the presence of low link bandwidths (i.e., less than 3 Mbit/s) connecting the SR members to the Esper engine deployed by the SR administrator.

L. Aniello · G.A. Di Luna · R. Baldoni
Dipartimento di Ingegneria Informatica, Automatica e Gestionale Antonio Ruberti, Università degli Studi di Roma "La Sapienza", Roma, Italy

L. Aniello
e-mail: aniello@dis.uniroma1.it

G.A. Di Luna
e-mail: diluna@dis.uniroma1.it

R. Baldoni
e-mail: baldoni@dis.uniroma1.it

G. Lodi (✉)
Consorzio Interuniversitario Nazionale Informatica (CINI), via Ariosto 25, Roma, Italy
e-mail: lodi@dis.uniroma1.it

R. Baldoni, G. Chockler (eds.), *Collaborative Financial Infrastructure Protection*,
DOI 10.1007/978-3-642-20420-3_7, © Springer-Verlag Berlin Heidelberg 2012

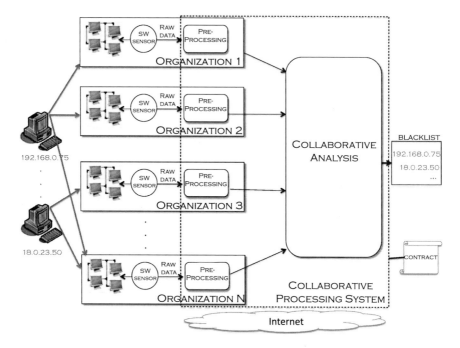

Fig. 7.1 Semantic Room for inter-domain stealthy port scan detection. Attackers execute malicious port scans against some SR members participating in the Semantic Room

7.1 Introduction

We describe a specific instance of a Semantic Room that detects inter-domain port scanning activities, as depicted in Fig. 7.1. The Semantic Room consists of two principal components: a *Complex Event Processing engine* which realizes the collaborative analysis of Fig. 7.1 and the *SR Gateway*, co-located at each Semantic Room (SR) member network, that carries out pre-processing activities. The SR Gateway captures network packets (raw data in Fig. 7.1) and executes a pre-processing on those packets; that is, it filters out the packets that are not relevant with respect to the processing of the specific port scan detection algorithm (it might also aggregate the packets in order to reduce the overall computation to be performed at the event engine side). The pre-processed packets coming from different SR Gateways (i.e., different SR member networks) are sent to the Complex Event Processing engine. The engine correlates the data in order to discover spatial and/or temporal relationships among apparently uncorrelated data that would have been undetected by in-house intrusion detection systems (IDSs).

Complex event processing (CEP) and stream processing (SP) systems play an important role in the IT technologies. IBM System S [8] has been used by market makers in processing high-volume market data and obtaining low latency results, as reported in [17]. System S (like other CEP/SP systems, e.g., [12, 15]) is based on event detection across distributed event sources. However, all these systems exhibit high cost of ownership.

To this end, we use the open source CEP system Esper, which exhibits low cost of ownership compared to other similar systems [8] and has the ability of dynamically adapting the detection logic by integrating/removing SQL queries for facing new threats that may arise.

We designed two novel port scan detection algorithms; namely, the *Rank-based SYN (R-SYN)* port scan and *Line Fitting* which are both implemented on top of the Semantic Room through a set of SQL-like queries of the Esper's Event Processing Language (EPL) that can be configured at run time.

We carried out an experimental evaluation in order to compare the two algorithms and assess their detection and false positive rates. We used for such a purpose real network traces that include malicious port scans. The assessment aims to evaluate the impact of the collaborative approach employed by the Semantic Room programming model on those metrics. Additionally, we computed the latency of the detection in both algorithms when 3, 6, and 9 SR members participate in the Semantic Room. Results show that an increased number of SR members leads to a more accurate detection. At the same time, collaboration has a reasonable impact on the detection latency. In this latter case, in the presence of link bandwidths connecting the SR members to the Complex Event Processing engine in the range of [6.5 Mbit/s, 3 Mbit/s], the Semantic Room exhibits detection latencies which are acceptable for the inter-domain port scan detection application. In general, we observe that Line Fitting is able to achieve high levels of accuracy with a smaller number of SR members than R-SYN; with low link bandwidths (less than 3 Mbit/s) it also shows better detection latencies compared to R-SYN.

Related Work   Many free IDSs exist that are deployed in enterprise settings. Snort [6] is an open source network intrusion prevention/detection system. It performs real-time traffic analysis and packet logging on IP networks to detect probes or attacks. Bro [5] is an open source network IDS that passively monitors network traffic and searches for suspicious activity. Its analysis includes detection of specific attacks using both defined signatures and events patterns, and unusual activities. Recently, collaborative approaches to implementing IDSs have been proposed in a variety of works [7, 13, 14, 18]. In contrast to standalone IDSs, collaborative IDSs significantly reduce time and improve efficiency of misuse detections by sharing information on attacks among the IDSs distributed at multiple organizations [19]. The main principle underlying these approaches, namely large-scale information sharing and collaborative detection, is similar to the one employed by the architecture proposed in this paper. These systems, however, are highly optimized for specific types of attacks, whereas our Esper-based architecture is a general-purpose system which can be effective against diverse attack scenarios.

The issue of using massive CEP among heterogeneous organizations forming a critical infrastructure for detecting network anomalies and failures has been suggested and evaluated in [21]. Also, the usefulness of collaboration and sharing information for telco operators with respect to discovering specific network attacks has been pointed out in [16], and in [20] the problem of event dissemination and processing to face cyber attacks has been raised in the context of inter-utility large power systems. In these works, it has been clearly highlighted that the main limitation of the collaboration approach concerns the confidentiality requirements. These requirements may be specified by the organizations that share data and can make the collaboration itself hardly possible as the organizations are typically not willing to disclose any private and sensitive information. In our collaborative system this is also a critical issue; however, as described in the previous chapters of this book, we have deeply investigated how our architecture can be adapted to handle such issues.

The rest of this chapter is organized as follows. Section 7.2 introduces the Rank-based SYN (R-SYN) port scan detection and Line Fitting algorithms for inter-domain stealthy port scan detection. Section 7.3 describes the architecture we designed and implemented for the Semantic Room for port scan detection based on Esper. Section 7.4 discusses the principal experimental results we have obtained from an evaluation of the two algorithms. Finally, Sect. 7.5 provides the chapter conclusions.

7.2 Inter-domain Stealthy Port Scan Detection Algorithms

We show the benefits of the collaborative approach employed by the Semantic Room programming model in the case of inter-domain stealthy port scan detection (see Chap. 3 for a detailed analysis of this type of cyber attack). We consider a Transmission Control Protocol (TCP) SYN (half-open) port scan; in particular, recall that in a TCP SYN port scan, a scanner S sends a SYN packet to a target T on a specific port P and waits for a response. If a SYN-ACK packet is received, S can conclude that P is open and optionally reply with an RST packet to reset the connection. We call these kinds of connections *incomplete connections*. In contrast, if an RST-ACK packet is received, S can consider P as closed. If no packet is received at all and S has some knowledge that T is reachable, then S can conclude that P is filtered. Otherwise, if S does not have any clue on the reachability status of T, it cannot assume anything about the state of P.

Not all the port scans can be considered malicious. For instance, there exist search engines that carry out port scanning activities in order to discover web servers to index [10]. It thus becomes crucial to distinguish accurately between actual malicious port scanning activities and benign ones. To this end, we have devised two different port scan detection algorithms: the R-SYN port scan detection and the Line Fitting port scan detection algorithms. Each algorithm is described in detail in the following sections.

7.2.1 Rank-Based SYN (R-SYN) Port Scan Detection Algorithm

Rank-based SYN (R-SYN) port scan detection combines in a novel fashion two principal port scan detection techniques: *half-open connections detection* (HOC) and *failed connections detection* (FC) [22].

To this end, R-SYN works as follows: (i) it recognizes half-open connections; (ii) it recognizes failed connections; (iii) for each source IP address x, it maintains the pairs (IP address, TCP port) probed by x; and, finally, (iv) using a proper ranking mechanism, it assigns a mark r to each source IP address x: if r is higher than a predefined threshold, x is considered a scanner and included in a blacklist.

Half-Open Connections Detection (HOC)

This technique analyzes the sequence of SYN, ACK, RST packets in the three-way TCP handshake. In normal activities the sequence (i) SYN, (ii) SYN-ACK, (iii) ACK occurs. To detect a SYN port scan, the algorithm searches for connections in the form of: (i) SYN, (ii) SYN-ACK, (iii) RST (or nothing). We refer to those connections as *incomplete connections*. In essence, the purpose of this technique is the production of a list of IP addresses that have carried out incomplete connections. For each IP address x included in this list, we define $HOC(x)$ as the profile produced by this technique related to the incomplete connections issued by x.

Failed Connections Detection (FC)

In order to detect failed connections, we identify connections to both unreachable hosts and closed ports. Hosts are considered unreachable if a sender, after a time interval from the sending of a SYN packet, does not receive either SYN-ACK or RST-ACK packets, or if it receives an ICMP packet of type 3 that indicates that the host is unreachable. In addition, we identify connections to closed ports looking for RST-ACK reply packets. In essence, the purpose of this metric is to produce a list of IP addresses that attempted to perform connections to unreachable hosts or closed ports. For each IP address x included in this list, we define $FC(x)$ as the profile produced by this technique related to the failed connections issued by x.

Visited (IP Address, TCP Port)

The previous two techniques are also in charge of tracing the pairs (IP address, TCP port) that identify the ports probed by any source IP address that has been listed by either the HOC or FC technique. The need to maintain these pairs originates from the observation that a scanner does not repeatedly perform the same operation toward a single (IP address, TCP port): once any status information is obtained, a scanner likely carries out other probes toward different targets. Therefore, monitoring all the pairs (IP address, TCP port) visited by each source IP address allows us to sharpen the accuracy of our detection, since this helps in distinguishing malicious access behaviors from normal ones. For each monitored IP address x, we define $V(x)$ as the data structure representing which pairs (IP address, TCP port) have been probed by x.

Ranking

The results of the previous steps are used for implementing a ranking mechanism that we have designed with the aim of capturing different aspects of the behavior of a generic scanner carrying out a SYN port scan. For a given IP address x, we define $rank(x)$ as follows: $rank(x) = f(HOC(x), FC(x), V(x))$. This ranking is compared ($\geq$) to a fixed threshold (see below) in order to decide whether to mark an IP address as a scanner.

7.2.2 Line Fitting Port Scan Detection Algorithm

The underlying principle of the Line Fitting SYN port scan detection algorithm concerns the observation that a scanner does not repeatedly perform the same operation toward specific hosts or ports: if the attempt fails on a $T:P$ a scanner likely carries out a malicious port scan toward different targets [23].

The rational behind the Line Fitting algorithm can be summarized as follows. Let $(ip, port)$ be the pair that identifies a destination host and a TCP port. Given a set of pairs $C : IP \times Port$, where IP is the set of IP addresses and $Port$ is the set of TCP ports, the purpose of an inter-domain stealthy SYN port scan is to find out the subset $A \subseteq C$ representing active TCP ports. A pair $(ip_j, port_i)$ is active if and only if a service on port $port_i$ is available at the destination IP ip_j. The standard behavior for a scanner is to issue a few requests for each element in C in order to obtain the status of the pair $(ip_j, port_i)$.

From these observations we define $I = C \setminus A$ as the set of *inactive* pairs: every request issued to an element in I may lead to a failure. As failures are common during port scan activities, we can assume that $I \neq \emptyset$ and that $|I| \geq |A|$.

The Line Fitting algorithm takes into account the set F_h which is a multiset of failures generated by the source host h (an element of I generated by h becomes an element of the set F_h).

We use the multiset since the multiplicity of any failure is crucial: we observe that in the case of a normal failure (e.g., DNS crashes, service unavailability) the set F_h contains few elements with high multiplicity. In contrast, in the case of a port scan the set includes many elements with low multiplicity. An ideal scanner issues few connections toward different (IP, port) pairs exhibiting a "fitting curve" behavior; i.e., a horizontal line $y = bx + q$ where $b = 0$, considering the pairs on the x-axis and the multiplicities on the y-axis. In contrast, a non-ideal malicious port scan behavior can emerge when b is close to 0.

Therefore, the Line Fitting algorithm correlates data of the TCP three-way handshake, looking for patterns that are similar to a horizontal line representing few requests toward different (IP, port) pairs distributed over time. The patterns can be found by applying a linear fitting algorithm with the elements in F_h, and then checking the similarity between the obtained fitting line and the ideal one. The algorithm we have designed and implemented (Algorithm 1) can be described as follows.

Algorithm 1: Line Fitting algorithm

---

1. $\forall x \in F_h$ if (x is inlier) List_h.add(x)
2. (b, q) = LinearFitting(List_h);
3. if (Match(b, q)) {
4. portscanner(h); }

For all the elements x of type [*destIP*, *port*, *multiplicity*], the check at line 1 of the algorithm "if x is inlier" is done using the mean and standard deviation of the series $m(F_h)$, which is the list of multiplicities of all elements in F_h. If the multiplicity of x is in the interval $[m - kd, m + kd]$ where m is the mean, d the standard deviation, and k a constant value, x is considered an inlier and is counted for the linear fitting (line 2 of the algorithm). The linear fitting is realized through the least squares method, and it produces two values of the fitting curve, namely, b and q. These values are then analyzed: if b and q are $<=$ than specific thresholds (the Match method in line 3 of the algorithm; we set these thresholds to 1 and 6 respectively in our implementation), then the source host h is considered a scanner and included in a blacklist (line 4 of the algorithm).

7.3 Esper-Based Semantic Room for Inter-domain Stealthy Port Scan Detection

Figure 7.2 illustrates the architecture of the Esper-based Semantic Room. The architecture consists of the SR Gateway components installed at each SR member and a single Esper [4] CEP engine instance deployed at any of the available organizations (in our design we assumed that the SR administrator deploys the Esper engine for processing purposes). These two components are described in detail below.

SR Gateway

Traffic data are captured from the monitored networks of SR members. The data are to be normalized and transformed to Plain Old Java Objects (POJOs) in order to be analyzed by the Esper engine. To this end, the Gateway component has been designed and implemented so as to (i) take as input the flows of network data (*TCP data* in Fig. 7.2), (ii) filter them to maintain packets related to TCP three-way handshaking only, and, finally (iii) wrap each packet in a proper POJO to be sent to Esper.

We implemented TCPPojo for TCP packets. The POJO maps every field in the header of the protocol. POJOs are serialized and sent through Java sockets to Esper. When sending the POJOs our implementation maintains the order of the packets captured within the single SR member, which is crucial when evaluating sequence operators in the Esper engine.

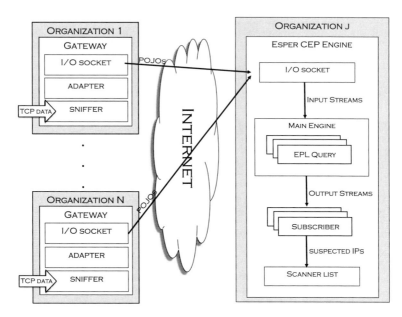

Fig. 7.2 Collaborative Esper-based Semantic Room architecture

Complex Event Processing (CEP)

The Esper CEP engine [4] receives POJOs that represent the events it has to analyze
(input streams). The processing logic is specified in a high-level SQL-like language
named the Event Processing Language (EPL). In order to detect malicious port scanning activities, a number of EPL queries are defined and executed by the engine, as
shown in Fig. 7.2. EPL queries run over a continuous stream of POJOs and produce
output streams. When an EPL query finds a match against its clauses in its input
stream, it generates a new tuple that is added to its output stream. A *Subscriber* is a
Java object that can be subscribed to a particular output stream so that whenever the
query outputs a new tuple, the *update()* method of the Subscriber is invoked using
the tuple as argument.

We have implemented both the R-SYN and Line Fitting algorithms for port scan
detection as a set of EPL queries in Esper.

7.3.1 R-SYN Implementation in Esper

Each detection technique of the R-SYN port scan detection algorithm is implemented using a combination of EPL queries and subscribers. The EPL queries are in
charge of recognizing any packet patterns which reveal an anomalous behavior according to the detection metric. Subscribers are invoked whenever such matches are
verified; they update global data structures we have created to maintain the status

about the behavioral profile of each IP address that has a chance of being suspected in the future. All the detection techniques use general queries that filter specific packets of interest. For instance, the following query filters SYN packets:

```
insert into syn_stream
select sourceIP, destIP, ...
from TCPPojo where SYNFlag=true and ACKFlag=false
```

We use further filtering queries that act on the TCPPojo input stream: one for SYN-ACK packets, one for RST packets, one for ACK packets, and a final one for RST-ACK packets.

Half-Open Connections Detection

Incomplete connections are identified using the following query:

```
insert into halfopen_connection
  select ...
  from pattern [
    every a = syn_stream -> (
      ( b = syn_ack_stream(...) -> (
        <c> and not <d>
      ) where timer:within(10 sec) ) ) ]
```

In the case of half-open connections we have developed an EPL query that exploits the peculiar *pattern* construct of Esper so as to detect patterns of incomplete connections. In particular, a is the stream of SYN packets, b is the stream of SYN + ACK packets, $\langle c \rangle$ is a filter for RST packets, and $\langle d \rangle$ is the stream of ACK packets that would correctly complete the three-way handshaking. The entire pattern matches if involved packets are within a time window of 10 seconds.

Further queries are then used and bound to Subscribers for filtering IP addresses that made more than T_{HO} (equal to 2) incomplete connections. A list of such IPs named $list_{HO}$ is updated for this purpose.

Failed Connections Detection

In failed connections detection, connection attempts to both unreachable hosts and closed ports are recognized. For brevity, we include below an example of an EPL query we have developed with the aim of discovering attempts to connect to unreachable hosts. A similar query can be specified for detecting closed ports.

```
insert into host_unreach
select ..., 1 as value
from pattern [
```

```
every a = syn_stream ->
  timer:interval(10 sec) and
  not ( (<b> or <c>) and not <d> ) ]
```

In this query, we search an event pattern in which a SYN packet is not followed by any packet matching the expression $((\langle b \rangle$ or $\langle c \rangle)$ and not $\langle d \rangle)$ within a time interval of 10 seconds. b is the stream of SYN + ACK packets, c is the stream of RST + ACK packets, and d the stream related to ICMP packets. A list of IP addresses $(list_{FC})$ that satisfy this query is updated.

Visited (IP Address, TCP Port)

Based on the previous detection metrics we trace and update the *failures* stream having *sourceIP*, *sourcePort*, *destIP*, and *destPort* fields. The following query creates a stream containing the information required for computing the failures (i.e., in the query the so-called *stat* values):

```
insert into visited_destIP_destPort_stream
select sourceIP, destIP,
       destPort, count(*) as stat
from failures
group by sourceIP, destIP, destPort
```

The Subscriber registered for this stream updates the data structure named *stat* representing the map of pairs [IP address, TCP port] that have been visited.

We then need further queries in order to (i) create a multiset with elements representing the pair (IP address, Destination address), (ii) add new elements to that multiset, and (iii) update the multiplicity of the elements in the multiset. We use the Esper construct *win:keepall()* which is a window indexed by source IP address that maintains the multiplicity of the failure. Another Subscriber is used in this case that installs dynamically a new filter query whose output stream is used in the ranking phase (see below). To this end, we implemented the Esper On-Demand Snapshot Query that allows us to free the engine to maintain a persistent query in memory; this query is called only when required, and it allows us to find in the quickest way all the failures generated by a given source IP address.

Ranking

We implemented a ranking mechanism that associates a rank to suspicious hosts evaluated in the previous phase. Given an IP address x, $HOC(x)$ $(FC(x))$ is equal to 1 if and only if x belongs to $list_{HOC}$ $(list_{FC})$, 0 otherwise. $V(x)$ is computed considering the *stat* values earlier described.

With $HOC(x)$, $FC(x)$, and $V(x)$ we can then compute $rank(x)$: when it exceeds a certain threshold, x is marked as a scanner. In the tests of our experimental evaluation (see next section) the threshold for ranking is set to 0.52. In doing so, we have implemented the following Esper queries:

```
insert into rank
select id, type, rank from RankEvent

//Total rank
insert into rank_final
select id, sum(rank) as ag_rank
from rank.std:unique(id,type)
group by id
```

The first query projects id, type (i.e., *HO*, *FC*, *V*), and rank fields from the input stream *RankEvent* generated by the subscribers of the previous metrics, and the second query returns the total rank associated with a single IP address (i.e., a single id). The generated *rank* stream is used by a final query Esper that outputs an event representing the scanner IP address.

7.3.2 Line Fitting Implementation in Esper

For the implementation of the Line Fitting algorithm we first use the general queries introduced in Sect. 7.3.1 that filter specific packets of interest. We then keep track, in the *halfopen_connection* output stream, of incomplete connections using the same Esper query as the one used by the R-SYN algorithm (see Sect. 7.3.1)

In addition, we need to maintain the connections to unreachable hosts and closed ports. To this end, we use the same query introduced for the R-SYN algorithm that detects connection attempts to unreachable hosts, and we use the query below that recognizes connection attempts to closed ports. In this case we search patterns of SYN packets followed by RST-ACK packets within a time interval of 5 seconds.

```
//Connections to Closed Ports (CP)
insert into closed_port
select ....
from pattern[every a=syn_stream --> <c>
where timer:within(5 sec)]
```

Finally, Line Fitting needs to create the stream of events representing failed connections (*failures*); for this purpose, we use the following queries:

```
//Create failures stream from CP
insert into failures
```

```
select id,dst,1 as card
from closed_port
where closed=1

//Create failures stream from HU
insert into failures
select id,dst,1 as card
from host_unreach
where down=1

//Create failures stream from HO
insert into failures
select id,dst,1 as card
from halfopen_connection
```

and for each pair (IP, port) it returns the multiplicity of the multiset using the following query:

```
insert into multiset
select sourceIP,destIP,destPort,count(*) as N
from failures
group by sourceIP,destIP,destPort
```

Only one Subscriber is associated with Line Fitting: it generates the list of scanner IP addresses waiting for 5 distinct events of type *failures* from the HO, HU, and CP streams and applies the least square method for the final computation.

7.4 Experimental Evaluation

We have carried out an experimental evaluation of the two algorithms. Such evaluation aims at assessing two metrics; namely, the *detection accuracy* in recognizing distributed stealthy port scans and the *detection latency*.

Testbed

For our evaluation we used a testbed consisting of a cluster of 10 Linux virtual machines (VMs), each of which is equipped with 2GB of RAM and 40GB of disk space. The 10 VMs were hosted in a cluster of 4 quad core 2.8 GHz dual processor physical machines equipped with 24GB of RAM. The physical machines are connected to a LAN of 10Gbit.

The layout of the components on the cluster consisted of one VM dedicated to host the Esper CEP engine. Each of the remaining 9 VMs represented the resources made available by 9 simulated financial institutions participating in the Esper-based Semantic Room. Each resource hosted the SR Gateway component. We emulated a large-scale deployment environment so that all the VMs were connected with each

Table 7.1 Content of the traces

	trace 1	trace 2	trace 3	trace 4	trace 5
Size (MB)	3	5	85	156	287
Number of source IPs	10	15	36	39	23
Number of connections	1429	487	9749	413962	1126949
Number of scanners	7	8	7	10	8
Number of packets	18108	849816	394496	1128729	3462827
3-way-handshake packets	5060	13484	136086	883500	3393087
Length of the trace (s)	5302	601	11760	81577	600
3-way-handshake pckt rate (p/s)	0.95	22.44	11.57	10.83	5655

other through an open source WAN emulator we have used for such a purpose. The emulator is called WANem [9], and it allowed us to set specific physical link bandwidths in the communications among the VMs.

Traces

We used five intrusion traces. The first four were used in order to test the effectiveness of our algorithms in detecting malicious port scan activities, whereas the latter was used for computing the detection latency (see next paragraph). All traces include real network traffic of a network that has been monitored. The traces are obtained from the ITOC research web site [2], the LBNL/ICSI Enterprise Tracing Project [3], and the MIT DARPA Intrusion Detection project [1]. The content of the traces is described in Table 7.1. In each trace, the first TCP packet of a scanner always corresponded to the first TCP packet of a real port scan activity.

Detection Accuracy

In order to assess the accuracy of R-SYN and Line Fitting, we partitioned the traces simulating the presence of 9 financial institutions participating in the Esper-based Semantic Room; the resulting sub-traces were injected to the available Gateways of each SR member in order to observe what the two algorithms were able to detect. To this end, we ran a number of tests considering four accuracy metrics (following the assessment described in [11]): (i) *TP* (*True Positive*) which represents the number of suspicious hosts that are detected as scanners and are true scanners; (ii) *FP* (*False Positive*) which represents an error of the detection, that is, the number of honest source IP addresses considered as scanners; (iii) *TN* (*True Negative*) which represents the number of honest hosts that are not indeed detected as scanners; (iv) *FN* (*False Negative*) which represents a number of hosts that are real scanners that the

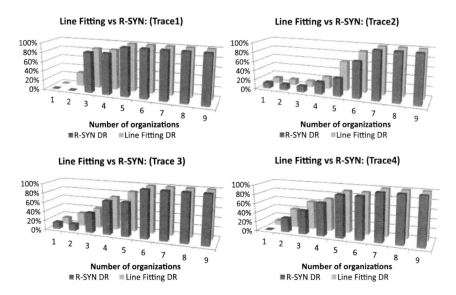

Fig. 7.3 Port scan detection rate vs. number of SR members for R-SYN and Line Fitting algorithms. Each SR member contributes to the processing with a number of network packets that is on average 1/9 of the size of the trace

systems do not detect. With these values we computed the *Detection Rate*, *DR*, and the *False Positive Rate*, *FPR*, as follows:

$$DR = \frac{TP}{TP + FN}$$

$$FPR = \frac{FP}{FP + TN}$$

(7.1)

In all traces, with the exception of trace 4, we observed that none of the two algorithms introduced errors in the detection of port scanners; that is, in those cases the FPR was always 0% in our tests. In trace 4 of size 156MB, R-SYN exhibited an FPR equal to 3.4% against an FPR equal to 0% of Line Fitting; that is, R-SYN introduces 1 False Positive scanner.

Figure 7.3 shows the obtained results for the detection rate (DR). In this figure, it emerges that the collaboration can be beneficial for sharpening the detection of port scanners. In both algorithms, augmenting the number of participants in the collaborative processing system (i.e., augmenting the volume of data to be correlated) leads to an increase of the detection rate as computed above. However, the behavior of the two algorithms is different: Line Fitting (light gray bars in Fig. 7.3) converges more quickly to the highest detection rate compared to R-SYN (black bars in Fig. 7.3); that is, in Line Fitting a smaller number of participants to the collaborative processing system and then a lower volume of data are required in order to achieve 100% of the detection rate. This is principally due to the higher number of processing steps R-SYN executes and to the fact that R-SYN's subscribers have to accumulate packets in order to carry out their Threshold Random Walk (TRW) computation. In addition, R-SYN examines both good and malicious behaviors, assigning a positive score to good ones. This implies that in some traces R-SYN has to wait for more packets in order to effectively mark IP addresses as scanners.

Detection Latency

In the port scan attack scenario, the detection latency should be computed as the time elapsed between when the first TCP packet of the port scan activity is sent by a certain IP address and when the Semantic Room marks that IP address as a scanner (i.e., when it includes the address in the blacklist). Note that we cannot know precisely which TCP packet should be considered the first of a port scan, since that depends on the true aims of who sends the packet. As already stated, in our traces the first TCP packet of a scanner corresponds to the first TCP packet of a real port scan activity, so that we can compute the detection latency for a certain IP address x as the time elapsed between the sending of the first TCP packet by x and the detection of x as a scanner.

In doing so, we need the timestamps of the packets. For this purpose we developed a simple Java application named `TimerDumping` which (i) takes a trace as input; (ii) sends the packets contained in the trace (according to the original packet rate) to the Gateway using a simple pipe; and (iii) maintains the timestamp of the first packet sent by each source IP address in the trace.

We deployed an instance of `TimerDumping` on each VM hosting the SR Gateway component. Each `TimerDumping` produces a list of pairs $\langle ip\_address, ts \rangle$, where ts is the timestamp of the first TCP packet sent by $ip\_address$. The timestamps are then used as beginning events for detection latency computation. Since there are more `TimerDumping` instances, pairs with the same IP address but different timestamps may exist. In those cases, we consider the oldest timestamp.

Timestamps are generated using local clocks of the hosts of the cluster. In order to ensure an acceptable degree of synchronization, we configured all the clustered machines to use the same Network Time Protocol (NTP) server which has been installed in a host located at the same local area network (LAN). The offset between local clocks is in the order of 10 milliseconds, which is accurate for our tests as latency measures are in the order of seconds.

For detection latency tests we used a trace of 287MB and changed the physical link bandwidths to the Esper engine in order to show in which setting one of the two algorithms can be preferable. Link bandwidth is controlled by the WANem emulator. We varied the physical link bandwidth using the WANem emulator with values ranging from 1 Mbit/s up to 6.5 Mbit/s. Figure 7.4 shows the average detection latency in seconds we have obtained in different runs of the two algorithms.

As illustrated in this figure, for reasonable link bandwidths of a large-scale deployment scenario (between 3 Mbit/s up to 6.5 Mbit/s) both algorithms show a similar behavior with acceptable detection latencies for the inter-domain port scan application (latencies vary between 0.6 to 35 seconds). However, Line Fitting outperforms R-SYN in the presence of relatively low link bandwidths (looking at the left-hand side of the curves, Line Fitting exhibits a detection latency of approximately

Fig. 7.4 R-SYN and Line
Fitting detection latencies in
the presence of 3, 6, and 9 SR
members in the Semantic
Room. We varied the
bandwidth between 1 Mbit/s
up to 6.5 Mbit/s

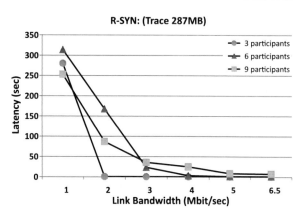

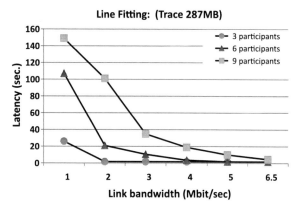

150 seconds when 9 participants are available against 250 seconds for R-SYN). In addition, in the case of R-SYN only, results show that when the collaborative system is formed by a higher number of participants (e.g., 9), detection latencies are better than those obtained with smaller collaborative systems. This is principally caused by the larger amount of data available when the number of participants increases: more data allow us to detect the scanners more quickly. In contrast, when 3 or 6 participants are available, we need to wait more in order to achieve the final result of the computation. This behavior is not shown for Line Fitting, for which an increased amount of information is not sufficient to overcome the drawback related to the congestion on low link bandwidths (e.g., 1 Mbit/s).

7.5 Conclusions

In this chapter we presented a Semantic Room based on the Esper Complex Event Processing engine. The Semantic Room is able to protect financial institutions willing to share specific data and thus detect malicious inter-domain port scanning attacks. Two port scan detection algorithms have been designed and implemented: the

Line Fitting and R-SYN algorithms. Results show the effectiveness of the collaboration, as when the number of SR members is enlarged, the percentage of detection of scanners increases. As for detection latencies, the collaboration has a reasonable impact: in the presence of link bandwidths in the range of [3 Mbit/s, 6.5 Mbit/s] the two algorithms exhibit detection latencies that are acceptable for our application. However, we note that Line Fitting outperforms R-SYN in terms of both detection accuracy and latency.

We are investigating how to distribute the processing over a network of Esper sites in order to scale in terms of participating SR members. As shown in the performance results, the link bandwidth of Esper becomes a bottleneck when the number of members sending data increases. Thus, we are planning as future works to create a network of Esper sites able to distribute the load of the members' data and execute a first line of data aggregation and correlation.

References

1. 2000 DARPA intrusion detection scenario specific data sets. http://www.ll.mit.edu/mission/communications/ist/corpora/ideval/data/2000data.html
2. ITOC research: CDX datasets. http://www.itoc.usma.edu/research/dataset/index.html
3. LBNL/ICSI enterprise tracing project. http://www.icir.org/enterprise-tracing/
4. Where complex event processing meets open source: Esper and NEsper. http://esper.codehaus.org/ (2009)
5. Bro: an open source Unix based Network intrusion detection system (NIDS). http://www.bro-ids.org/ (2010)
6. Snort: an open source network intrusion prevention and detection system (IDS/IPS). http://www.snort.org/ (2010)
7. DShield: cooperative network security community—internet security. http://www.dshield.org/indexd.html/ (2011)
8. System S. http://domino.research.ibm.com/comm/research_projects.nsf/pages/esps.index.html (2010)
9. WANem the wide area network emulator. http://wanem.sourceforge.net/ (2011)
10. Jung, J., Paxson, V., Berger, A.W., Balakrishnan, H.: Fast portscan detection using sequential hypothesis testing. In: Proceedings of the IEEE Symposium on Security and Privacy (2004)
11. Zhou, C.V., Karunasekera, S., Leckie, C.: Evaluation of a decentralized architecture for large scale collaborative intrusion detection. In: Proc. of the 10th IFIP/IEEE International Symposium on Integrated Network Management (2007)
12. Akdere, M., Çetintemel, U., Tatbul, N.: Plan-based complex event detection across distributed sources. PVLDB 1(1), 66–77 (2008)
13. Locasto, M.E., Parekh, J.J., Keromytis, A.D., Stolfo, S.J.: Towards collaborative security and P2P intrusion detection. In: IEEE Workshop on Information Assurance and Security, United States Military Academy, West Point, NY, 15–17 June (2005)
14. Poncelet, P., Verma, N., Trousset, F., Masseglia, F.: Intrusion detection in collaborative organizations by preserving privacy. In: Advances in Knowledge Discovery and Management, December (2009)
15. Tang, C., Steinder, M., Spreitzer, M., Pacifici, G.: A scalable application placement controller for enterprise data centers. In: 16th International Conference on World Wide Web (2007)
16. Xie, Y., Sekar, V., Reiter, M.K., Zhang, H.: Forensic analysis for epidemic attacks in federated networks. In: ICNP, pp. 43–53 (2006)

17. Zhang, X.J., Andrade, H., Gedik, B., King, R., Morar, J., Nathan, S., Park, Y., Pavuluri, R., Pring, E., Schnier, R., Selo, P., Spicer, M., Uhlig, V., Venkatramani, C.: Implementing a high-volume, low-latency market data processing system on commodity hardware using IBM middleware. In: Proc. of the 2nd ACM Workshop on High Performance Computational Finance, New York, USA, pp. 1–8 (2009)

18. Zhou, C.V., Karunasekera, S., Leckie, C.: A peer-to-peer collaborative intrusion detection system. In: 13th IEEE International Conference on Networks, Kuala Lumpur, Malaysia, November (2005)

19. Zhou, C.V., Leckie, C., Karunasekera, S.: A survey of coordinated attacks and collaborative intrusion detection. Comput. Secur. **29**(2010), 124–140 (2009)

20. Hauser, C.H., Bakken, D.E., Dionysiou, I., Gjermundrød, K.H., Irava, V.S., Helkey, J., Bose, A.: Security, trust, and QoS in next-generation control and communication for large power systems. Int. J. Comput. Inf. Sci. **4**(1/2), 3–16 (2008)

21. Huang, Y., Feamster, N., Lakhina, A., Xu, J.(Jun): Diagnosing network disruptions with network-wide analysis. In: Proc. of the 2007 ACM SIGMETRICS International Conference on Measurement and Modeling of Computer Systems, pp. 61–72. ACM, New York (2007)

22. Aniello, L., Lodi, G., Baldoni, R.: Inter-domain stealthy port scan detection through complex event processing. In: Proc. of 13th European Workshop on Dependable Computing, Pisa, 11–12 May (2011)

23. Aniello, L., Lodi, G., Di Luna, G.A., Baldoni, R.: A collaborative event processing system for protection of critical infrastructures from cyber attacks. In: Proceedings of the 30th Conference on System Safety, Reliability and Security (SAFECOMP), Napoli, September (2011)

Chapter 8
Distributed Attack Detection Using Agilis

Leonardo Aniello, Roberto Baldoni, Gregory Chockler, Gennady Laventman,
Giorgia Lodi, and Ymir Vigfusson

Abstract We introduce Agilis—a lightweight collaborative event processing platform that can be deployed in a Semantic Room to facilitate sharing and correlating event data generated in real time by multiple widely distributed sources. Agilis
aims to balance simplicity of use and robustness on the one hand, and scalable performance in large-scale settings on the other. To this end, Agilis is built upon the
open source Hadoop's MapReduce infrastructure augmented with a RAM-based
data store and several locality-oriented optimizations to improve responsiveness and
reduce overhead. The processing logic is specified in a flexible high-level language,
called Jaql, which supports data flows and SQL-like query constructs. We demonstrate the versatility of the Agilis framework as well as its utility for collaborative
attack detection by showing how it can be leveraged in the following two attack
scenarios: stealthy inter-domain port scanning, and a botnet-driven HTTP session
hijacking attack. We evaluate the performance of Agilis in both these scenarios and,

G. Chockler (✉) · G. Laventman
IBM, Research Division, Haifa University Campus, Mount Carmel, Haifa 31905, Israel
e-mail: chockler@il.ibm.com

G. Laventman
e-mail: laventman@il.ibm.com

Y. Vigfusson
School of Computer Science, Reykjavík University, Menntavegur 1, 101 Reykjavík, Iceland
e-mail: ymir@ru.is

L. Aniello · R. Baldoni
Dipartimento di Ingegneria Informatica, Automatica e Gestionale Antonio Ruberti, Università
degli Studi di Roma "La Sapienza", Via Ariosto 25, 00185 Roma, Italy

L. Aniello
e-mail: aniello@dis.uniroma1.it

R. Baldoni
e-mail: baldoni@dis.uniroma1.it

G. Lodi
Consorzio Interuniversitario Nazionale Informatica (CINI), via Ariosto 25, Roma, Italy
e-mail: lodi@dis.uniroma1.it

R. Baldoni, G. Chockler (eds.), *Collaborative Financial Infrastructure Protection*,
DOI 10.1007/978-3-642-20420-3_8, © Springer-Verlag Berlin Heidelberg 2012

in the case of inter-domain port scanning, compare it to Semantic Room, which deploys the centralized high-end event processing system called Esper. Our results show that while Agilis is slower than Esper in a local area network, its relative performance improves substantially as we move toward larger scale distributed deployments.

8.1 Introduction

In this chapter we introduce *Agilis*—a lightweight collaborative event processing platform that can be deployed in a Semantic Room to facilitate sharing and correlating event data generated in real time by multiple widely distributed organizations (e.g., banks, utility companies, and government institutions) in real time, and at a longer time scale. Agilis is built upon the open source Hadoop's MapReduce infrastructure augmented with a RAM-based data store and several locality-oriented optimizations to improve responsiveness and reduce overhead. The primary innovative aspects of Agilis include (1) the ability to incorporate multiple styles of data analysis (such as online processing calibrated by models extracted from historical data) within a single processing framework; (2) the ability to specify the event processing logic in a high-level SQL-like language, called Jaql [4]; (3) scalable performance due to data partitioning, parallelized data processing via MapReduce [16], locality awareness, and a RAM-based storage system that avoids disk I/O bottlenecks; (4) fault tolerance through replication; and (5) leveraging of open source components, which streamlines the code verification and certification, improves portability and interoperability, and reduces the complexity and management costs compared to the existing distributed event processing systems (e.g., [11]).

To demonstrate the effectiveness of the Agilis collaborative detection capabilities, we conducted extensive experimentation on the live system using the following two attack scenarios: stealthy inter-domain port scanning, which is typically employed by hackers for reconnaissance, and a botnet-driven HTTP session hijacking.

In the case of inter-domain port scanning, we implemented the R-SYN algorithm introduced in Chap. 7 in Jaql, and experimentally evaluated it on Agilis deployed at a collection of virtual machines connected through a WAN simulator called WANem [10] and hosted on a cluster of Intel servers. To assess the implications of the Agilis distributed architecture, we compared the performance of R-SYN on Agilis with its implementation on the centralized complex event processing engine Esper [9]. The results show that Agilis requires a slightly higher number of data sources in order to achieve 100% detection accuracy, which is due to a wider spread of the information being submitted for global correlation. On the other hand, in terms of attack detection latency, while Agilis is slower than Esper in a local area network (LAN), its relative performance improves substantially as we move toward larger numbers of data sources deployed on a large scale, which is an evidence of superior scalability.

To further demonstrate the versatility and flexibility of Agilis, we configured the platform to detect the botnet-driven HTTP session hijacking attack that we introduced in Sect. 3.5. The idea is that with hundreds of thousands and sometimes millions of bots controlled by the same operator [19, 20], brute-force attacks on protocols protected by hard-to-guess identifiers become feasible. We consider the hypothetical attack against the session identifiers of the current version of the PHP web server from Sect. 3.5.1 (Chap. 3), but our techniques are intended to demonstrate the value of collaboration. Agilis not only can detect that low-rate attacks are taking place, but it can also identify and block individual bots that are conducting attacks. If attacks are being conducted against multiple sites, even at different points in time, Agilis is able to leverage the information about suspicious behavior and provide better protection against malicious hosts.

The rest of this chapter is organized as follows. Section 8.2 describes the Agilis platform. Sections 8.3 and 8.4 introduce the distributed port scanning and botnet-driven HTTP session hijacking attacks, discuss the detection techniques along with their Agilis-based implementations, and present the results of the experimental performance study. Section 8.5 concludes the chapter and proposes directions for future work.

8.2 Agilis Event Processing Middleware

Agilis is a distributed event processing platform for sharing and correlating event data generated at real time by multiple sources which may be geographically distributed. To simplify programming, the processing logic is specified in a high-level language, called *Jaql* [4], and expressed as a collection of *Jaql queries*. Each query consists of SQL-like constructs combined into flows using the "→" operator (a few examples of the Jaql queries can be found in the following sections).

The queries are processed by the Jaql front-end, which breaks them into a series of MapReduce jobs [16], which are then executed on the Hadoop [2] infrastructure (see Fig. 8.1). The MapReduce framework lends itself naturally to supporting collaborative processing due to the mutual independence of the Map tasks, which as a result, can be placed close to the respective sources of their input data (see Sect. 8.2.1).

Each MapReduce job submitted by the Jaql front-end consists of portions of the original query wrapped into the interpreting code in Java. The data is communicated through the platform-independent JavaScript Object Notation (JSON) [5] format, which streamlines integration of the data stored in a variety of formats. In the context of collaborative processing, this feature is useful for combining data of different natures into a single cohesive flow. For example, in addition to real-time data, which can be supplied through a RAM-based data store or a message queue, some of the participants may choose to also provide long-lived historical data which can be loaded from stable storage, such as a distributed file system (e.g., the Hadoop Distributed File System (HDFS) [7]) or a database.

8.2.1 Collaboration and Scalability

Agilis is deployed on a collection of physical (or virtual) machines, henceforth referred to as *Agilis nodes (ANs)*, spread over a number of (possibly widely) dis-

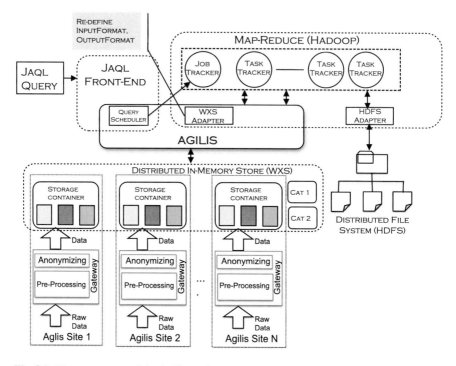

Fig. 8.1 The components of the Agilis runtime

tributed *Agilis sites (ASs)*. Each AS corresponds to a single organization partici-pating in the Agilis-mediated collaborative event processing and is responsible for hosting at least one AN. The specific components contained within the boundaries of each AS are *Gateway* (see Sect. 8.2.2), *Data Storage*, and Hadoop's *Task Tracker (TT)*. The TT instance hosted at each AN is in charge of managing the lifecycle of locally executed Map and Reduce tasks as well as monitoring their progress. The TT instances are coordinated by a single instance of the *Job Tracker (JT)* component, which is deployed at one of the ANs. The JT is also responsible for handling the incoming MapReduce jobs submitted by the Jaql front-end.

To reduce the latency and overhead associated with the disk I/O, Agilis imple-ments support for a RAM-based data store, which can be used for feeding the real-time input data as well as storing the intermediate and output data generated by MapReduce. We chose the Java-based *IBM WebSphere eXtreme Scale (WXS)* sys-tem [8] as an implementation of the RAM-based store due to its scalability, robust-ness, and interoperability with other components of our design. WXS exposes an abstraction of a *map* consisting of relational data records. For scalability, a WXS map can be split into a number of *partitions,* each of which is assigned to a separate WXS *container*. The information about the available WXS containers as well as the mapping of the hosted maps to the live containers is maintained internally by the WXS *Catalog* service, which is replicated for high availability.

In Agilis, the entire input data is treated as a *single* logical WXS map, which is partitioned so that each AN hosted within a particular AS is responsible for storing a portion of the local event data produced at that site. Subsequently, each partition is mapped to a single Hadoop input split (which is the minimum unit of data that can be assigned to a single Map task), and processed by an instance of the Map task scheduled by the JT through one of the local TTs. To ensure co-location of the input splits with their assigned Map tasks, Agilis provides a custom implementation of Hadoop's *InputFormat* API, which is packaged along with every MapReduce job submitted to JT by the Jaql front-end (see Fig. 8.1). In particular, the information about the physical locations of the input splits is coded into the InputFormat's *getSplits* implementation, which queries the WXS Catalog to extract the endpoints (IP and port) of the WXS containers hosting the corresponding WXS partitions. In addition, the implementation of *createRecordReader* is used to create an instance of *RecordReader*, which codes the logic to convert the input data to a form that can be consumed by an instance of the Map task.

To further improve locality of processing, we utilize the WXS embedded SQL engine to execute simple SQL queries directly on the data stored within the container. Specifically, our implementation of *RecordReader* recognizes the SQL *select*, *project*, and *aggregate* constructs (all of which are understood by the embedded SQL engine) by interacting with the Jaql interpreter wrapper, and delegates their execution to the SQL engine embedded into the WXS container.

As we demonstrate below, these locality optimizations are effective in substantially reducing the amount of intermediate data reaching the reduce stage, thus contributing to the system's scalability.

8.2.2 Data Pre-processing

The Gateway is a component co-located with the organization supporting the collaborative processing that feeds WXS partitions. Raw data are given as input to the gateway which pre-processes the data (e.g., they could be aggregated and filtered) before storing them in WXS containers. The gateway could also include the logic to anonymize to sanitize the data before injecting into Agilis. To reduce data transfer overhead, the WXS containers and Gateway are typically hosted on the same AN.

8.2.3 Overview of Agilis Operation

The execution of the Jaql queries is mediated through a scheduler co-located with the Job Tracker (JT). In the current implementation, the scheduler accepts the MapReduce jobs (along with some configuration parameters) associated with each submitted query, and resubmits them to JT for execution on a configured periodic cycle.

The pre-processed data are fed into Agilis by the Gateway component and stored in the WXS containers located on the local ANs. The data stored in the WXS containers are processed by the locally spawned Map tasks as explained above. The intermediate results are then stored in temporary buffers in RAM created through WXS, from where they are picked up by the Reduce tasks for global correlation. The final results are then stored in either WXS or HDFS (as prescribed by the configuration data submitted with each Jaql query).

One limitation of the above approach is that each repeated submission of the same collection of MapReduce jobs incurs the overhead of processing initialization and re-spawning of the Map and Reduce tasks, which negatively affects the overall completion time (see Section "*Detection Latency*" page 166). Another deficiency stems from the lack of dynamic adjustment to the incoming data rates, as a result of which the processing can be initiated on an incomplete input window, or cause it to overflow. We are currently working on implementing improvements to the scheduler as well as modifications to the Hadoop scheduling infrastructure to support one-time instantiation of the MapReduce jobs, and better coordination between the input data feeds and the execution scheduling.

8.3 Distributed Port Scan Attack

We have implemented the R-SYN algorithm introduced in Chap. 7 in Agilis. The principal processing steps are described below in isolation.

8.3.1 Pre-processing: Agilis's Gateway

The Gateway component is deployed locally at each Agilis site (AS) and is responsible for: (i) sniffing Transmission Control Protocol (TCP) packets flowing through the monitored network of an organization; (ii) recognizing incomplete and failed connections; (iii) maintaining the pairs (IP address, TCP port) probed by suspected source IP addresses; and (iv) storing all the produced detection information into the co-located Data Storage.

Specifically, the raw data captured from the organization's network are properly filtered in order to use only the TCP three-way handshake packets. Then, once a SYN packet is recognized, an instance of a finite state machine (FSM) is allocated by the Gateway and updated when other packets concerning the same TCP connection are captured. The Gateway uses the FSM in order to detect correct, incomplete, and failed connections.

Incomplete and Failed Connections

The FSM models patterns of packets related to the three-way handshake phase of the TCP as they are seen from the point of view of a source host S which begins a

Fig. 8.2 The FSM of Agilis's
Gateway

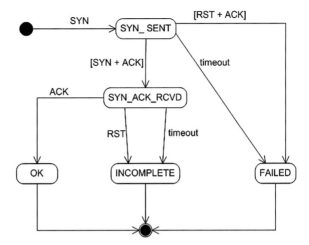

connection to a destination host D. The transitions in the FSM represent the sending
of a packet (e.g., *SYN* sent by S), the receipt of a packet (e.g., the transition marked
as [*SYN* + *ACK*] in Fig. 8.2 received by S; we use square brackets to indicate this
kind of packet), and the expiration of a timeout (e.g.: the edge marked as *timeout* in
Fig. 8.2).

Due to the presence of the two timeout transitions shown in Fig. 8.2, it is certain
that the FSM reaches the final state eventually, thus classifying the connection as
correct (i.e., OK in Fig. 8.2), incomplete, or failed. The FSM instance can then be
deleted.

Visited (IP Address, TCP Port)

The Gateway maintains all the pairs (IP address, TCP port) probed by suspected
source IP addresses. Once an incomplete or failed connection is identified, the Gateway considers it only if its destination (IP address, TCP port) pair has not been
visited yet by its source IP.

The final output of the Gateway is a set of suspected IP addresses, each one
associated with the number of both incomplete and failed connections that have
been considered. Such a set is continuously updated and stored in the Agilis WXS
partition local to the AS hosting the Gateway.

8.3.2 Agilis Query Execution

The processing specified by the Jaql query consists in grouping by IP address the
outputs of all available Gateways. The sets of suspected IP addresses stored in different WXS partitions are merged so that a single set of suspected IPs is produced
with which to associate the number of both incomplete and failed connections issued
by each of these IPs over the networks of ASs.

Ranking

The pair [(incomplete connections count), (failed connections count)] is the mark produced by the R-SYN implementation in Agilis for each suspected IP. This mark is compared to a fixed pair of thresholds, one for incomplete connections and another threshold for failed connections. If at least one of these thresholds is exceeded, the IP is considered a scanner.

The final output of Agilis (i.e., the set of scanner IP addresses detected by the system) is stored into WXS partitions for use by the ASs.

The Jaql query which implements the ranking computation is the following:

```
read($ogPojoInput(
    "SuspectedIP",
    "agilis.portscan.data.SuspectedIP"))
-> group by $ip = {$.ip} into {
        ip: $ip.ip,
        incompleteConnections: sum($[*].incompleteConnections),
        failedConnections: sum($[*].failedConnections)}
-> filter
    $.incompleteConnections > 4 or
    $.failedConnections > 12
-> transform {$.ip}
-> write($ogPojoOutput(
    "ScannerIP",
    "agilis.portscan.data.ScannerIP",
    "ip"));
```

The objects representing IP addresses suspected by any ASs are first read from the *SuspectedIP* WXS map (i.e., the *read* statement) and grouped by IP address, summing up their counters related to incomplete and failed connections (i.e., the *group by* and *sum* statements).

The resulting merged set is then filtered using two fixed thresholds (i.e., the *filter* statement), projected to the *ip* field (i.e., the *transform* statement) and stored into the *ScannerIP* WXS map (i.e., the *write* statement).

8.3.3 Agilis vs. Esper: Evaluation

We have carried out an experimental evaluation of Agilis and Esper prototypes. The evaluation aims at assessing two metrics: the *detection accuracy* in recognizing distributed stealthy port scans and the *detection latency*.

Testbed   For our evaluation we used a testbed consisting of a cluster of seven Linux virtual machines (VMs), each of which was equipped with a minimum 2GB of RAM and 40GB of disk space. The seven VMs were hosted in a cluster of 4 quad core 2.8 GHz dual processor physical machines equipped with 24GB of RAM. The physical machines were connected to a LAN of 10 Gbit.

Table 8.1 Content of the traces

	trace 1	trace 2	trace 3
Size (MB)	85	156	287
Source IPs	36	39	23
Connections	9749	413962	1126949
Scanners	7	10	8
Packets	394496	1128729	3462827
3wh packets	136086	883500	3393087
Length (s)	11760	81577	600
3wh packet rate (p/s)	11.57	10.83	5655

The layout of the components on the cluster in the case of Esper consisted of one VM dedicated to host the Esper Complex Event Processing (CEP) engine. Each of the remaining six VMs represented the resources made available by six simulated organizations participating in the collaborative processing system. Each resource hosted the Gateway component.

In contrast, the layout of the Agilis components on the cluster consisted of one VM dedicated to host all of the Agilis management components; that is, Job Tracker and WXS Catalog Server. Each of the remaining six VMs represented a single AS and hosted Task Tracker, WXS container, and Gateway.

In order to emulate a large-scale deployment environment, all the VMs were connected through an open source WAN emulator we have used for such a purpose. The emulator, called WANem [10], allowed us to set specific physical link bandwidths in the communications among the VMs.

Detection Accuracy

Traces   We used three intrusion traces in order to test the effectiveness of our prototypes in detecting malicious port scan activities. All traces include real network traffic of a network that has been monitored. The sizes of the traces were 85MB, 156MB, and 287MB, respectively, and they were downloaded from the MIT DARPA Intrusion detection project [1] and the ITOC research web site [3]. The content of the traces is described in Table 8.1. Let us also add that in each trace the first TCP packet of a scanner always corresponded to the first TCP packet of a real port scan activity.

Results   In order to assess the accuracy of Agilis and Esper, we partitioned the traces simulating the presence of six organizations participating in the collaborative processing systems; the resulting sub-traces were injected to the available Gateways of each participant in order to observe what Agilis and Esper were able to detect. We used Eq. (7.1) in Chap. 7 in order to compute the detection accuracy of the two systems.

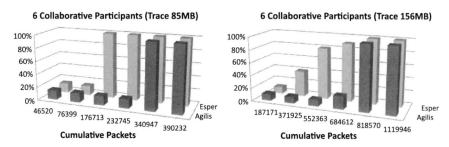

Fig. 8.3 Port scan detection rate in a collaborative environment with six organizations. We use the traces of 85MB and 156MB, respectively. Bars show the number of packets required to achieve 100% detection rate in Agilis and Esper

We observed that neither of the two systems introduced errors in the detection of port scanners. In other words, the False Positive Rate was always 0% in our tests. The results are shown in Fig. 8.3.

The collaboration can be beneficial for sharpening the detection of port scanners. In both systems, augmenting the volume of data to be analyzed (i.e., augmenting the number of participants in the collaborative processing system) leads to an increase of the detection rate as computed above.

However, the behavior of the two systems is different: in general, Esper achieves a higher detection rate with a smaller amount of data compared to Agilis. This is mainly caused by the two different approaches employed by the systems. In Esper the detection decision can be more accurate, as the central CEP engine owns the entire view of what is happening among the available participants. In the Agilis fully distributed approach the alert information is more dispersed among the participants; thus, to obtain a high detection rate, it is required to have a certain critical number of participants.

Detection Latency

In the port scan attack scenario, the detection latency should be computed as the time elapsed between when the first TCP packet of the port scan activity is sent by a certain IP address and when the collaborative processing system marks that IP address as scanner (i.e., when it includes the address in the blacklist). Note that we cannot know precisely which TCP packet should be considered the first of a port scan, since that depends on the true aims of who sends the packet. As already stated, in our traces the first TCP packet of a scanner corresponds to the first TCP packet of a real port scan activity; thus, we can compute the detection latency for a certain IP address x as the time elapsed between the sending of the first TCP packet by x and the detection of x as a scanner.

Latency Computation Implementation   In order to obtain the timestamps of the sending of TCP packets, we developed a simple Java application named Timer-Dumping which (i) takes a trace as input; (ii) sends the packets contained in the trace (according to the original packet rate) to the Gateways using a simple pipe; and (iii) maintains the timestamp of the first packet sent by each source IP address in the trace.

We deployed an instance of `TimerDumping` on each VM hosting a Gateway (in both the Agilis and Esper systems). Each `TimerDumping` produces a list of pairs $\langle ip\_address, ts \rangle$, where ts is the timestamp of the first TCP packet sent by $ip\_address$. The timestamps are then used as beginning events for the detection latency computation. Since there are more `TimerDumping` instances, pairs with the same IP address but different timestamps may exist. In those cases, we consider the oldest timestamp.

Timestamps are generated using local clocks of the hosts of the cluster. In order to ensure an acceptable degree of synchronization, we configured all the clustered machines to use the same Network Time Protocol (NTP) server which was installed in a host located at the same LAN. The offset between local clocks is on the order of 10 milliseconds, which is accurate for our tests (latency measures are on the order of seconds).

Agilis Latency Computation   In the current Agilis implementation, the Jaql queries cannot be made *persistent* yet; that is, at the end of each time interval of the query evaluation (i.e., batch window), a repeated submission of the same collection of MapReduce jobs incurs. This issue notably impacts the detection latency evaluation (see results below). To this end, we are planning to extend Agilis in order to allow it to compile Jaql queries once, keeping the queries running continuously without the need to initialize them at every batch window. However, since this implementation is still not available at the time of this writing, we estimate the detection latencies we could obtain in the case of persistent Jaql queries. This estimation is based on the following observations. Let us consider the detection of a certain scanner x: we can identify which iteration of the query execution has generated such a detection. Let i be this iteration. Since x has not been detected at iteration $i - 1$, we know that the data required for the detection were not in the system at that time (otherwise the detection would have taken place), so there was no way for the system to detect x before iteration i started. This means that, even if we had the optimal Agilis implementation with no query initialization at each batch window, we could not detect x before iteration i starts; however, we can expect to detect it before iteration i ends, due to the improvement in Agilis that could be obtained using persistent queries. From these observations, we estimate the latency as the average between the time at which the detection iteration begins and the time at which it ends.

Results   For these tests we have used the trace of 287MB and different physical link bandwidths in order to show in which setting one of the two systems could be preferable. The link bandwidth is controlled by the WANem emulator. We varied the physical link bandwidth using the WANem emulator with values ranging from 6.5 Mbit/s up to 500 kbit/s where we kept constant the aggregate data rate sniffed from the organizations' networks. This value in our experiment is equal to 3828 Mbit/s and is the sum of the data rates sniffed within each single organization. Figure 8.4 illustrates the results we have obtained.

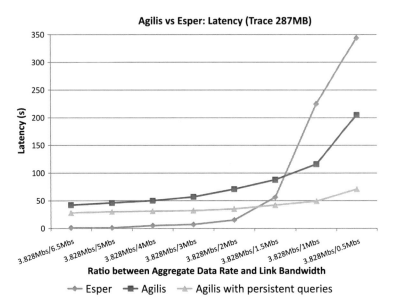

Fig. 8.4 Scanner detection latency. It considers the ratio between the aggregate data rata coming from all organizations (3828 Mbit/s) and the link bandwidth available at each organization site for the collaborative system. Collaboration is carried out by six organizations

The assessment results show that Esper itself is never a bottleneck. However, its centralized approach can become an issue when the ratio between the aggregate data rate and link bandwidth increases (i.e., the link bandwidth available at each site decreases). In the tests, we first observed the behavior of Agilis and Esper in a LAN environment characterized by a high available link bandwidth: Esper exhibits an average latency of 1 second, whereas Agilis shows an average latency of 30 seconds using its current implementation, and 20 seconds of estimated latency in the case of persistent queries. Hence, Esper in a LAN environment notably outperforms Agilis.

This scenario changes for large-scale deployments. Figure 8.4 shows the average detection latency in seconds we have obtained in different runs of two systems. As illustrated in this figure, when the link bandwidth starts decreasing, the latency of Esper rapidly increases. This is mainly caused by the large amount of data that is sent to Esper and must be correlated by the engine. In contrast, the distributed approach of Agilis is advantageous: the locality-awareness mechanisms employed by Agilis (i.e., processing is carried out at the edges locally to each Gateway) lead to an exchange on the network of a smaller amount of data. Therefore, when the link bandwidth decreases, the detection latency exhibited by Agilis is significantly lower than the one experienced by Esper (right side of Fig. 8.4). This is particularly evident in the case of Agilis's estimated latency (i.e., the latency that could be obtained in the case of persistent queries). Therefore, Agilis scales better in terms of large-scale deployments and number of participants. The latter leads to an increase of the aggregate data rate, and the system exhibits detection latencies like the ones on the right side of Fig. 8.4. The former decreases the ratio shown in Fig. 8.4, thus creating the same effect of having the latencies shown on the right side of the figure.

8.4 Botnet-Driven HTTP Session Hijacking Attack

As we have hinted at earlier in the book, bigger botnets produce more profit for their operators. The sources of revenue for these botnet operators include high-volume spamming campaigns—the Storm botnet generated between $7000–$9500 of revenue per day in 2008 from spam operations [17], click fraud—Clickbot.A could have cost Google $50,000 in advertising revenue had an attack gone unnoticed [12], theft—the crew behind the Zeus botnet managed to move $70 million offshore from the U.S. using stolen bank credentials and credit card numbers [15], extortion by threatening to launch distributed denial-of-service (DDoS) attacks [21], as well as various other scams.

We discussed several targeted botnet attacks in Sect. 3.5 (Chap. 3), including their ability to perform brute-force attack protocols whose security relies on elements that are *hard to guess*, such as passwords, temporary keys, or cookies. Here are some examples.

- Modern TCP implementations use a 32-bit random initial sequence number in the SYNACK packet to prevent blind spoofing attacks. Guessing this value enables an attacker to pose as a legitimate entity and compromise fundamentally insecure protocols such as Domain Name System (DNS).
- Many web sites deal with password reset requests by e-mailing a URL with a random identifier to the account owner. If these identifiers are sufficiently short, a botnet can be used to scan for valid numbers (and even to issue the "forgot password" requests) and then set the password of an unsuspecting account.
- Users tend to use minimally complex passwords on web sites [13]. This can make distributed scans for common user names and passwords alluring to hackers, as witnessed by the onslaught of failed log-in attempts on Secure Shell (SSH) servers [14].

In this section, we will describe a botnet attack against the session identifiers in the latest version of the PHP web server from Sect. 3.5.1 (Chap. 3) and show how the Agilis framework can be used to detect such an attack.

Recall that the attacker performs an offline, distributed computation to determine the internal state of the pseudo-random number generator (PRNG). The attacker then waits for a victim client to log in to the PHP server. We can assume that the attacker knows the time of the log-in within a second accuracy (if the site displays "users online", for instance) and the IP address range of the victim (suggesting a targeted attack). However, even with this much knowledge of the victim, she will have to guess the microsecond of the log-in time (of which there are 2^{20} possibilities) which lends itself to an active distributed attack against the target PHP server. Each request will try a different session ID cookie corresponding to the guess of the microsecond. The web server will see only a series of invalid cookies (MD5 sums) without any visible pattern, but the information that they are invalid is sufficient to detect and avert the attack.

8.4.1 Evaluation of Agilis

Attackers may conduct low-rate attacks to avoid detection and blacklisting of their bots, and instead mount them against different targets. It is also likely that attackers would attempt to compromise multiple accounts on the target site, and thus one would expect to see the same bots being used for different attacks. A cooperative network between defenders, such as the one we propose, leverages the collective information about suspicious behavior to ensure that (a) large-scale botnet attacks against web servers are detected, and (b) individual bots can be blocked. We will show how Agilis can achieve these two goals.

Traces   Because we are not aware of brute-force attacks having taken place against web session IDs, we augmented a real-world HTTP trace of mutually cooperating sites with synthetic attacks. In particular, we used the trace from the cluster of 30 web servers hosting the web site for the World Cup 1998 match in France [18], focusing on the period between 6/2/98–6/16/98. Even though the trace is dated and may not be representative of current browsing behavior, it provides high request load, diurnal variations in the request patterns, and intense flash crowds during the actual soccer games. Each of these characteristics puts additional stress on our detection algorithms.

The trace has no explicit user sessions, so we emulated them as follows. Each user provided her current session ID with each request for an HTML content page. The session is considered to have expired 6 hours after it was started, so the first subsequent request after this interval triggers an "invalid cookie" error, and the user then receives a new session ID. This means that invalid session IDs are submitted not only by attackers—regular web users may sometimes submit cookies that have been expired or invalidated on the server—which makes detection more difficult.

Attack Detection   In the first experiment we asked: *"How effective is Agilis in detecting large-scale attacks at different rates?"* The adversary launched four low-rate brute-force attacks at 50K, 10K, 5K, and 3.6K requests per hour, respectively, on June 6, 8, 10, and 12 against all 30 web servers. Each attack lasted for several hours and used bots at random from a 100,000 node botnet. The web servers shared all of their request logs with Agilis.

As a detection strategy, we expect the percentage of requests with invalid cookies to remain similar modulo flash crowds. Thus we constructed an hour-by-hour baseline model of this fraction over a 24-hour cycle using the average of the first three days of the trace (before any games are played). We set the alarm threshold to be double the baseline percentage, in anticipation of later flash crowds. We used the following Jaql query for detection.

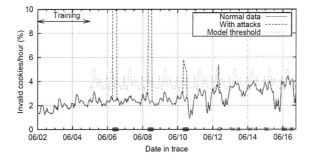

Fig. 8.5 *Botnet attack detection*: Four web session brute-force attacks taking place during a busy period for the web site and all detected by Agilis with a threshold model on fraction of requests with invalid cookies (*green*). *Circles* indicate detection of true attacks, and *crosses* are false positives incurred during flash crowds

```
$res = join $log, $model
where $log.Hour == $model.Hour
into {logDate: $log.Date, $log.Hour, logRatio:
    $log.Ratio, modelRatio: $model.Ratio}
-> transform {$.logDate, time: now(),
    result: ($.logRatio > $.modelRatio*2)};
```

As seen in Fig. 8.5, all four attacks were successfully detected by Agilis (denoted by red circles). The detection occurred within 10 minutes from the start of each attack, and this delay is an Agilis parameter. The simple threshold model produced a 6.1% rate of false positives (blue crosses in the figure) due to flash crowds that took place in the latter half of the trace.

A more sophisticated model, such as an adaptive threshold, special considerations for flash crowds, or one that exploits a richer feature set would likely reduce the rate of false positives. We believe that Agilis and Jaql offer a simple and compelling interface and environment to implement such a model.

Individual Bots   The next problem we tackled was to discover and blacklist individual bots that send multiple requests. We focused on the attack on June 6, during which the botnet collectively sent 50,000 requests per hour for 5 hours in a row. Even though bots can exist in large numbers, the attacks we have described still depend on each bot issuing a number of requests on average. If a client repeatedly misbehaves, such as trying many invalid session identifiers in a short amount of time, potentially during different attacks on different sites, we can blacklist the IP. To prevent damage incurred by false positives, a client on the blacklist may not be quarantined from all service, but rather must solve a CAPTCHA or fully reauthenticate to successfully log on.

We created a simple model to discover and list misbehaving nodes, i.e., a client who has tried more than 5 invalid session IDs in the past 24 hours, or one whose rate of triggering invalid requests is too high. The Jaql query we used inside the individual bot detection is:

Fig. 8.6 *Performance*: We
vary the rate of available
bandwidth between Agilis
nodes and measure the time it
takes to process the bot
detection query for the 1.08
million requests on June 6 in
the trace

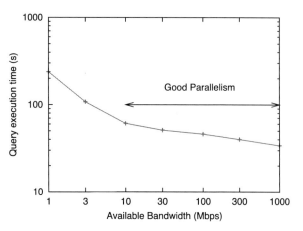

```
$logRes = $logResTmp -> filter $.Bad > 5 or
($.Ratio > 0.5 and $.TimeDiff > 0
    and ($.TimeDiff/$.Bad) < 2)
-> transform {$.ClientId, $.minDate};
```

`Ratio` is the fraction of bad requests, and `TimeDiff` the number of hours since
the first request from this client.

Using the combined data from all the web servers, this query allowed Agilis to
identify and stop 58,319 bots out of the 91,573 bots that issued invalid queries during this time, or 64%. The conditions in the filter can be further relaxed to improve
detection rate at the cost of increasing false positives. If the web sites had not cooperated and instead were segmented into two coalitions with each group receiving
half of the requests, the detection algorithm would only have discovered about 35%
of the bots each, and 48% if they combined their blacklists. Three independent sites
do even worse; about 25% of bots are discovered at each site, and collectively only
39% of the bot army is known and blocked. This experiment thus shows the benefits
of cooperation—*information never hurts*.

Performance   Finally, we explored the effect of different bandwidth speeds on
the detection latency. In this setup, we imagined that the requests for June 6 are
arriving at a fixed rate r to Agilis, and then we varied r. Note that the output on
each node is written only on the local partition instead of a different HDFS server,
which would hamper the performance. In Fig. 8.6 we see the scalability of query
processing time as we vary the amount of bandwidth available between each pair of
Agilis nodes. When little bandwidth (1 Mbps or 3 Mbps) is available, the latency
depends primarily on the time spent by Reducers waiting for the incoming intermediate data produced by the Mappers. When higher bandwidth is available, this
bottleneck is eliminated, and the query processing can be seen to parallelize very
well. We deduce that Agilis scales well as we grow the bandwidth rates.

8.5 Conclusions

In this chapter we described Agilis, an Internet-scale distributed event processing platform well suited to instrument collaborative security environments. We demonstrated the potential of Agilis on a large scale and its flexibility in accommodating different complex attack scenarios. To this end, we first considered a distributed stealthy port scan attack and compared an Agilis-based Semantic Room with a centralized event processing approach implemented in Esper. The results of the comparison show that the Esper-based Semantic Room reaches 100% of detection accuracy with less available input data (i.e., with less independent sources) than the Agilis-based Semantic Room. This is due to Esper's centralized view on input data, which cannot be available with Agilis's distributed and parallel processing.

When either the link bandwidth reduces at each participating site or the number of participants increases or both, the detection latency of Agilis outperforms that of the Esper-based approach. This is possible because of the locality awareness and scalability optimizations implemented in Agilis. Finally, we demonstrated the versatility of Agilis in detecting botnets attempting to determine web session IDs of users.

Despite the benefits of Agilis, a number of improvements to the platform are under analysis and implementation. These improvements include modifying the Hadoop scheduling infrastructure to support one-time instantiation of the MapReduce jobs and better coordination between the input data feeds and the execution scheduling.

References

1. 2000 DARPA intrusion detection scenario specific data sets. http://www.ll.mit.edu/mission/communications/ist/corpora/ideval/data/2000data.html
2. Hadoop. http://hadoop.apache.org/
3. ITOC Research CDX Datasets. http://www.itoc.usma.edu/research/dataset/index.html
4. Jaql. http://www.jaql.org/
5. JavaScript Object Notation (JSON). http://www.json.org/
6. DShield: Cooperative Network Security Community—Internet Security. http://www.dshield.org/indexd.html/ (2009)
7. Hadoop-HDFS architecture. http://hadoop.apache.org/common/docs/current/hdfs_design.html (2009)
8. IBM WebSphere eXtreme scale. http://www-01.ibm.com/software/webservers/appserv/extremescale/ (2009)
9. Where complex event processing meets open source: Esper and NEsper. http://esper.codehaus.org/ (2011)
10. WANem the wide area network emulator. http://wanem.sourceforge.net/ (2011)
11. Amini, L., Jain, N., Sehgal, A., Silber, J., Verscheure, O.: Adaptive control of extreme-scale stream processing systems. In: ICDCS'06: Proceedings of the 26th IEEE International Conference on Distributed Computing Systems, p. 71. IEEE Computer Society, Washington (2006)
12. Daswani, N., Stoppelman, M.: The anatomy of Clickbot.A. In: Proc. of Workshop on Hot Topics in Understanding Botnets, Berkeley, CA, USA (2007). USENIX Association

13. Florêncio, D.A.F., Herley, C.: A large-scale study of web password habits. In: Proceedings of the 16th International Conference on World Wide Web, WWW'07, Banff, Alberta, Canada, pp. 657–666. ACM, New York (2007)
14. Goodin, D.: Server-based botnet floods net with brutish SSH attacks. http://www.theregister.co.uk/2010/08/12/server_based_botnet/ (accessed on 01/24/11) (2010)
15. Gross, G., McMillian, R.: Five Arrested in Scam Involving Theft via Botnet, vol. 10 (2010)
16. Jeffrey, D., Ghemawat, S.: MapReduce: simplified data processing on large clusters. Commun. ACM 51(1), 107–113 (2008)
17. Kanich, C., Kreibich, C., Levchenko, K., Enright, B., Voelker, G.M., Paxson, V., Savage, S.: Spamalytics: an empirical analysis of spam marketing conversion. In: Proc. of ACM CCS'08, pp. 3–14. ACM, New York (2008)
18. Jin, T., Arlitt, M.: 1998 World Cup Web Site Access Logs, August (1998)
19. DefenseIntelligence Matt Thompson. Mariposa Botnet Analysis, October 2009. Updated February (2010)
20. Microsoft. Battling Botnets for Control of Computers. Microsoft: Security Intelligence Report 9 (2010)
21. Weber, J.E., Paulson, R.A.: Cyberextortion: an overview of distributed denial of service attacks against online gaming companies. Issues Inf. Syst. 7, 52–56 (2006)

Chapter 9
Collaborative Attack Detection Using Distributed Hash Tables

Enrico Angori, Michele Colajanni, Mirco Marchetti, and Michele Messori

Abstract This chapter describes a distributed architecture for collaborative detection of cyber attacks and network intrusions based on distributed hash tables (DHTs). We present a high-level description of the distributed architecture for collaborative attack detection. In particular, we highlight the two main functional blocks: the collaboration layer, realized through a DHT, and the engine for complex event processing. We then describe the implementation of a working prototype of the proposed architecture that represents one of the Semantic Rooms of the Co-MiFin project. Our reference implementation is implemented through well-known open source software. In particular, the DHT leverages Scribe and PAST, while we use Esper as the CEP engine. We demonstrate how the proposed implementation can be used to realize a collaborative architecture for the early detection of real-world attacks carried out against financial institutions. We focus on the detection of Man-in-the-Middle attacks to demonstrate the effectiveness of our proposal. Finally, we highlight the main advantages of the proposed architecture with respect to traditional (centralized and hierarchical) solutions for intrusion detection. In particular, we address the issues of fault tolerance, scalability, and load balancing.

E. Angori
Elsag Datamat, via Laurentina 760, Rome, Italy
e-mail: enrico.angori@selexelsag.com

M. Colajanni · M. Marchetti · M. Messori
University of Modena and Reggio Emilia, via Vignolese 905, Modena, Italy

M. Colajanni
e-mail: michele.colajanni@unimore.it

M. Marchetti (✉)
e-mail: mirco.marchetti@unimore.it

M. Messori
e-mail: michele.messori@unimore.it

R. Baldoni, G. Chockler (eds.), *Collaborative Financial Infrastructure Protection*,
DOI 10.1007/978-3-642-20420-3_9, © Springer-Verlag Berlin Heidelberg 2012

9.1 Introduction

This chapter describes a new architecture for distributed and collaborative event processing that has been designed and developed within the scope of the CoMiFin project. This architecture relies on multiple distributed Complex Event Processing (CEP) engines that perform cooperative analysis of high volumes of events. Cooperation among the different CEP engines is realized through message exchange. In particular, all the CEP engines are connected to a completely decentralized communication overlay, implemented through distributed hash tables (DHTs). This peer-to-peer overlay is used to receive events to process, to distribute those events among cooperative CEP engines, to forward intermediate results produced by a CEP engine to one or more other CEP engines for further processing, and to disseminate the final processing results.

The proposed architecture does not depend on the technology used to implement the cooperative CEP engines. It can be (and has been) used with both custom CEP engines and with well-known, open source CEP engines such as Esper [1]. Moreover, it is not tied to a specific event processing logic that is implemented by the collaborative CEP engines. Hence, it can be used to support different event processing algorithms. Within CoMiFin, the architecture presented in this chapter has been used for the implementation of a distributed attack detection algorithm devoted to the early detection of Man-in-the-Middle attacks. Due to the inherent properties of the underlying DHT, the distributed architecture for event processing described in this chapter inherits high scalability, fault tolerance (due to the lack of single points of failure), and load balancing capabilities.

The high-level design of the proposed architecture for collaborative attack detection is presented in Sect. 9.2. An implementation of the proposed architectures, realized using well-known and open source software, is described in Sect. 9.3. This prototype is the base over which we implemented one of the CoMiFin Semantic Rooms devoted to detect Man-in-the-Middle attacks. Details about this Semantic Room, such as the implementation of attack-specific CEP rules, are given in Sect. 9.4. Finally, Sect. 9.5 highlights the benefits inherited from the use of DHT with respect to centralized and hierarchical architectures for attack detection already proposed in the security literature.

9.2 Architecture Design

A high-level design of the proposed architecture is shown in Fig. 9.1.

The *Processing Container* is the logical block that implements a given event processing algorithm. The events to be analyzed are produced by several, possibly distributed, event sources. Without loss of generality, we assume that an event is a finite set of fields, in which each field has a name and a value. We also assume that events are typed, meaning that each event has a specific type, and that all the elements of the same type have the same fields.

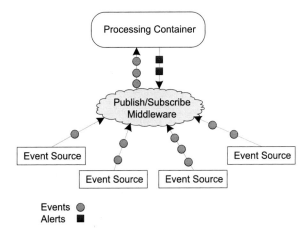

Fig. 9.1 High-level overview of the collaborative architecture for distributed event processing

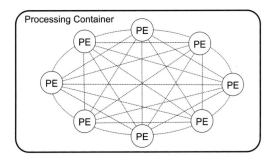

Fig. 9.2 Architecture of the Processing Container

Event sources publish events to a publish/subscribe middleware, through which events become available to the Processing Container. The Processing Container gathers all the events that are relevant with respect to the implemented analysis algorithm and publishes the analysis results to the same communication middleware, thus making them available to all the interested parties. Within the scope of the Co-MiFin project, the Processing Container presented in this chapter has been used to implement a Semantic Room for the detection of Man-in-the-Middle attacks (see Sect. 9.4).

The main requirements that drove the design of the Processing Container proposed in this chapter are high scalability and the lack of a single point of failure. To accomplish these goals a Processing Container comprises several independent *Processing Elements*, that cooperate by exchanging messages over a peer-to-peer overlay realized through a *distributed hash table* (DHT). The logical architecture of a Processing Container is shown in Fig. 9.2.

The DHT overlay network is completely decentralized and implements the abstraction of a fully connected mesh network among all the collaborative Processing Elements. This communication scheme is resilient to failures in the underlying network links and can autonomously adapt to changes in the number of Processing Elements that belong to the same Processing Container.

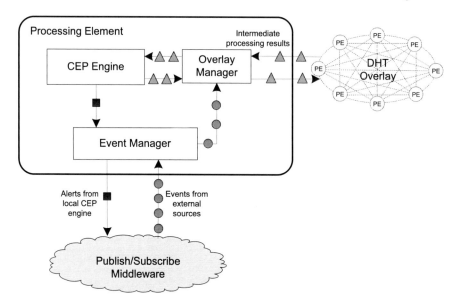

Fig. 9.3 Architecture of a Processing Element (PE)

All the Processing Elements included in a Processing Container are functionally equivalent. Each Processing Element performs the following tasks:

- it retrieves events generated by external event sources through the publish/subscribe middleware shown in Fig. 9.1;
- it forwards events to the Processing Element that needs them to perform analysis over the DHT overlay network;
- it receives and analyzes events from the DHT overlay network;
- it publishes alerts generated by the event analysis algorithm to the publish/subscribe middleware shown in Fig. 9.1.

The architecture of a single Processing Element is shown in Fig. 9.3. It comprises three main components: the *Event Manager*, the *Overlay Manager*, and the *CEP Engine*, described in Sects. 9.2.1, 9.2.2, and 9.2.3, respectively.

9.2.1 Event Manager

The Event Manager is the only interface between a Processing Element and elements that do not belong to its Processing Container. It has two main purposes: to receive events produced by external sources and to make alerts available to external consumers. These activities are performed by communicating over the publish/subscribe middleware shown in Fig. 9.3.

Let L be a finite list of event types that are of interest with respect to the event processing algorithms implemented by a Processing Container. Hence, all the Processing Elements belonging to the Processing Container will retrieve events by subscribing to the publish/subscribe middleware.

In particular, we require the publish/subscribe middleware to implement the semantics of a *queue* [29]. When an external event source publishes an event, the publish/subscribe middleware appends the event to the queue of all the events of the same type, even if they have been generated by different external sources. The publish/subscribe middleware then hands over the queued messages to all the Processing Elements that registered themselves as consumers for the queue. In particular, event retrieval is performed in a round-robin fashion, thus sharing the load related to event gathering equally among all the Processing Elements that belong to the same Processing Container (each message is received by only one Processing Element, which removes the message from the queue). After having retrieved an event from the publish/subscribe middleware, the Event Manager sends it to the local Overlay Manager (i.e., the Overlay Manager that belongs to the same Processing Element).

The Event Manager is also responsible for publishing the results generated by the local CEP Engine to the publish/subscribe middleware, thus making them available to all the interested parties. In this case, we require the publish/subscribe middleware to implement the semantics of a *topic* [29]. As soon as the CEP Engine produces an alert, the alert is forwarded to the Event Manager. The Event Manager then publishes the alert to the topic (defined in the publish/subscribe middleware) that corresponds to the type of the alert. The publish/subscribe middleware then makes the alert available to all the parties that subscribed to this topic, thus allowing all the subscribers to receive it.

9.2.2 Overlay Manager

The Overlay Manager is the only component of a Processing Element that is connected to all the other Processing Elements belonging to the same Processing Container. All the Overlay Managers are members of the same peer-to-peer overlay network that is based on a DHT. This overlay network implements the abstraction of a fully connected mesh (as shown in Fig. 9.2). Each Overlay Manager can receive messages generated by any other Overlay Managers and can send messages to other Overlay Managers through the DHT overlay. Moreover, within each Processing Element, the Overlay Manager is connected to the Event Manager and to the CEP Engine.

An Overlay Manager performs three tasks:

- it receives events from the Event Manager of the local Processing Element;
- it forwards intermediate processing results generated by the local CEP Engine to other Processing Elements connected to the same DHT overlay;
- it receives intermediate processing results generated by other Processing Elements connected to the same DHT overlay.

Each Overlay Manager is assigned an identifier, called *nodeID*, that is unique within the Processing Container. The value of nodeID is used to determine which

Overlay Manager will be the one responsible for handling a message sent over the DHT overlay.

When an Overlay Manager receives an event from the local Event Manager or from the local CEP Engine, the event is transformed into one or more messages that are transmitted over the DHT overlay. The number of messages triggered by an event depends on the type of event, and on the specific event analysis algorithms implemented by the CEP Engines of the Processing Container. After receiving an event, the Overlay Manager prepares a different message for all the fields (or group of fields) that are of interest to the event processing algorithm. Each message is labeled with a *messageID* whose value is computed by hashing the field (or group of fields) of interest.

As an example, let us consider a very simple event processing algorithm whose goal is to identify the IP addresses of machines that generate a large number of events. A simple and scalable solution to this problem would be to partition the IP address space among all the Processing Elements that belong to the Processing Container. Each Processing Element then has to maintain a counter for each IP address that belongs to its share of address space and that generated at least one event. For this algorithm to work, we must guarantee that each Processing Element receives all the events generated by an IP address for which the Processing Element is responsible. This constraint can be easily satisfied using the proposed architecture for collaborative event processing. In this context, each event has only one field of interest, that is, the IP address of the machine that generated it. Hence, when an Overlay Manager receives the event from the Event Manager, it prepares only one message whose messageID is the hash of the IP address. The original event, which contains the source IP address, is enclosed in the message as its payload.

The messageID is used to identify which Processing Element is responsible for receiving and analyzing a message. Each Processing Element is responsible for a portion of the hash space, depending on the nodeID of its Overlay Manager and on the implementation details of the DHT overlay. In the proposed implementation, for any given message the recipient Overlay Manager is the one having the minimum distance between the nodeID and the messageID.

After having created a message, the sender Overlay Manager inserts the message into the DHT and notifies the recipient Overlay Manager that a new message is present.

The recipient Overlay Manager is then responsible for retrieving the event from the DHT and passing it to its local CEP Engine for event analysis. On the other hand, if a message with the same messageID has already been sent over the DHT, the Overlay Manager can just signal the recipient that a new copy of the same message has been issued, without sending the same message another time.

After being notified of the presence of a new message whose messageID falls within its portion of the hash space, the Overlay Manager retrieves the message from the DHT, extracts the event from the message, and forwards the event to the local CEP Engine for actual analysis.

This collaboration approach enables an effective network-based and distributed event processing scheme. In particular, the reliance on DHT overlays makes the proposed scheme robust to failures and able to autonomously adapt to changes in the number of Processing Elements that belong to the same Processing Container. Moreover, it guarantees that all the Overlay Managers receive all the messages that are relevant with respect to the event processing algorithm implemented by the CEP Engine, while minimizing network overhead.

9.2.3 CEP Engine

The Complex Event Processing Engine (CEP Engine) is the component of a Processing Element that analyzes the events received from the Overlay Manager. Our architecture is not dependent on a specific CEP Engine implementation; hence it is possible to implement a Processing Element based on any CEP technology. Moreover, it is also possible to implement hybrid Processing Containers in which different Processing Elements rely on heterogeneous CEP Engines.

A CEP Engine interacts directly with the Event Manager and with the Overlay Manager of the same Processing Element. Each CEP Engine has to analyze an event stream that is generated by the local Overlay Manager. After it has analyzed each event, a CEP Engine can generate an alert or can issue a new event.

Events generated by the CEP Engine may represent intermediate processing results and require further analysis by a (possibly different) CEP Engine. These intermediate events are forwarded to the local Overlay Manager, and are handled exactly as events generated by external event sources.

If the CEP Engine generates an alert, it is immediately forwarded to the Event Manager, which will make the alert available to all the external parties that subscribed to the appropriate topic of the publish/subscribe middleware shown in Fig. 9.3.

The processing rules that are used by the CEP Engine for event analysis depend on the specific algorithm implemented by the Processing Container. A discussion of the event processing rules that have been used for the detection of Man-in-the-Middle attacks, together with an experimental evaluation of their effectiveness, is provided in Sect. 9.4.

9.3 Prototype Implementation

The architecture for distributed event processing proposed in this chapter and described in Sect. 9.2 has been developed within the scope of the CoMiFin project. In particular, it is possible to deploy a CoMiFin Semantic Room that leverages a Processing Container as event processing technology. This choice allows CoMiFin to inherit all the benefits of the proposed architecture, thus achieving high scalability, fault tolerance, load distribution, and the ability to autonomously adapt to changes in the number of Processing Elements that belong to the Processing Container.

This section describes how the main components of the proposed architecture for collaborative event processing have been implemented. In particular, the implementation of the main components of a Processing Element (Overlay Manager, Event Manager, and CEP Engine), are described in Sects. 9.3.1, 9.3.2, and 9.3.3, respectively.

Moreover, the implementation of a Semantic Room requires tight integration with other CoMiFin components. The proposed implementation provides all the required interfaces with the CoMiFin Gateway, the Information Manager and Metrics Monitoring components, as described in Sects. 9.3.4, 9.3.5, and 9.3.6.

The CoMiFin Semantic Room based on the distributed event processing architecture presented in this chapter also supports intra-Semantic Room (intra-SR) connectivity. Hence, it is able to leverage alerts generated by other (possibly heterogeneous) Semantic Rooms to improve event processing by autonomously adapting event processing rules to an ever-changing threat landscape at runtime. Intra-SR connectivity is described in Sect. 9.3.7.

Software packages, technical documentation, and Unified Modeling Language (UML) diagrams for all the components of CoMiFin are available as CoMiFin project deliverables.

9.3.1 Implementation of the Overlay Manager

As described in Sect. 9.2.2, the Overlay Manager is the component that enables cooperation among different Processing Elements. It does this by exchanging events and messages through the DHT overlay network that connects all the Processing Elements that belong to the same Processing Container (see Fig. 9.2).

To guarantee interoperability among different hardware platforms, the Overlay Manager has been implemented in Java. It relies heavily on the FreePastry [8] libraries, a Java implementation of the Pastry [3] DHT overlay network. In particular, the Overlay Manager uses two different applications that are built on Pastry: PAST [4, 5] and Scribe [6, 7].

Several methods require network communications, and this may cause delay or message loss. To correctly manage these events, the software utilizes continuations; these are a well-known and widely used abstraction, like that in Java Listeners. Compared to RMI/RPC-style calls, they are not blocking, so when the Overlay Manager, or another class, invokes a method supported by a continuation, it can continue its work without (directly) taking care of the result of the invocation.

PAST is a distributed file system built on top of Pastry. It provides a persistent peer-to-peer storage utility that the Processing Elements use to implement distributed, replicated, and fault-tolerant storage of CoMiFin Events and Alerts. Each PAST node, identified by an ID of 128 bits (nodeID), acts both as a storage repository and as a client access point. Any file inserted into PAST is identified by a 160-bit key, namely fileId (messageId in our case). When a new file is inserted into PAST, Pastry directs the file to the nodes whose nodeID is numerically closer to the

128 most significant bits of messageId, each of which stores a copy of the file. The number of involved nodes depends on the replication factor chosen for availability and persistence requirements.

Scribe is a completely decentralized middleware for publish/subscribe communication. It was specifically designed to implement a distributed and robust event notification infrastructure, with support for both unicast and multicast communication among peers.

After receiving a CoMiFin Event (generated by an external source) from the Event Manager, the Overlay Manager analyzes it and generates a variable number of messages to be sent over the DHT overlay. The number of messages depends on the configuration of the Overlay Manager, and by the type of CoMiFin Event. A rule of thumb is to generate a different message for every field of the CoMiFin Event that is of interest with respect to the event processing algorithm implemented by the Processing Container. A detailed example related to the identification of Man-in-the-Middle attacks is described in Sect. 9.4.

Each message has a messageID that is computed by hashing the relevant field of the CoMiFin Event. All the other information that is contained in the original Co-MiFin Event can be included in the body of the message. The Overlay Manager then uses PAST to store the message within the distributed file system, thus making the message accessible to all the Processing Elements that participate in the Processing Container. The PAST overlay uses the messageID field as a key for message routing, thus storing each message on the Processing Element whose nodeID is most similar to the message ID.

All messages are stored in multiple copies, according to a configurable replication factor. This solution ensures that if a Processing Element fails, an exact replica of the messages stored in the failed node is stored in one or more of its neighbors on the DHT overlay (i.e., the Processing Elements having nodeID nearer to the nodeID of the failed Processing Element). To achieve best performance we rely on the built-in content replication functionality of PAST to implement the message replication on the nodes of the Processing Container.

Among all the Processing Elements that receive a copy of the message, only one is responsible for event analysis. In our implementation, the Processing Element having the highest nodeID is elected as the responsible Processing Element by the Overlay Manager that writes the message on the distributed storage. Since PAST supports only a silent write in its storage, the Overlay Manager has to notify the responsible Processing Element explicitly after having submitted a new message that requires analysis. These notifications are implemented as unicast messages sent through Scribe to the same Processing Element that is responsible for the analysis of the message. The nodeID of the responsible Processing Element can be retrieved through the PAST APIs. The notification contains the messageID of the message that must be analyzed.

After receiving a notification of a new message through Scribe, the Overlay Manager of the responsible Processing Element retrieves the message whose messageID is included in the notification from its local share of the distributed storage implemented through PAST. The message (both its messageID and its content) is then forwarded to the CEP Engine for actual analysis.

Depending on the analysis algorithm, the nature of the message, and the history of messages analyzed previously, the CEP Engine may generate an intermediate processing result that requires further analysis by other Processing Elements belonging to the same Processing Container. If this is the case, the intermediate processing result is encapsulated in a well-formed CoMiFin Event and forwarded to the Overlay Manager. The Overlay Manager then processes the intermediate processing result exactly as if it were generated by an external source and received through the Event Manager.

9.3.2 Implementation of the Event Manager

The Event Manager is a software component that is included in all the Processing Elements (see Fig. 9.3). It accomplishes two tasks. The first one is to receive Co-MiFin Events from external event sources and to forward these events to the local Overlay Manager. The second one is to receive CoMiFin Alerts from the local CEP Engine and to forward these alerts to all the interested parties. Additional details can be found in Sect. 9.2.1.

Communication between Processing Elements and other components of CoMi-Fin is mediated by a publish/subscribe middleware that provides the abstractions of queues and of topics. In the CoMiFin prototype, this middleware implementation is based on Java Message Service (JMS). JMS provides a Java message-oriented middleware (MOM) API that can be used for the implementation of a message-based interface between networked Java applications and is a standard component of the Java 2 Enterprise Edition platform. In particular, it has been specifically designed for the implementation of reliable, loosely coupled, and asynchronous interfaces between different components of distributed applications.

CoMiFin Events that are generated from external event sources are gathered by listening to a JMS queue. All the external event sources that want to participate in a Semantic Room by contributing events need to know to which queue on the JMS the Processing Elements of the Semantic Room are listening to. Events are then submitted by publishing well-formed CoMiFin Events on this queue. It is also possible for a Semantic Room to process different types of events by listening to multiple queues, possibly provided by different JMS servers.

When a Processing Element is started, the Event Manager reads the name of the JMS server to connect to from its configuration files. The configuration also contains the name of the queues and of the topics to which the Event Manager has to register itself. All the Processing Elements that belong to the same Processing Container are always listening to the same JMS queue, waiting for incoming CoMiFin Events. The implementation of queues in JMS ensures that each CoMiFin Event is received by exactly one Processing Element, and that the distribution of CoMiFin Events among Processing Elements is performed according to a fair round-robin policy.

After receiving a CoMiFin Event from the JMS server, the Event Manager analyzes it. CoMiFin Gateways are able to optimize the efficiency of network communications by coalescing multiple CoMiFin Events into a single composite event. The Event Manager then unpacks the composite event and forwards each CoMiFin Event to the Overlay Manager.

Eventually, event processing carried out by the local CEP Engine will cause the generation of an alert. The CEP Engine forwards the alert to the Event Manager, which encapsulates the alert in a well-formed CoMiFin Alert message. The Event Manager then publishes the CoMiFin Alert on one or more topics in the JMS server, depending on the type of alert and on the configuration of the Event Manager. Participating financial institutions and other interested parties can access CoMiFin Alert by subscribing to the relevant topics on the JMS server.

9.3.3 Implementation of the CEP Engine

Each Processing Element has a local CEP Engine that performs (soft) real-time analysis of the stream of messages that the local Overlay Manager gathers from the DHT overlay based on PAST. The CEP Engine implementation is based on Esper [1], which is an open source engine for event processing. Esper is a widely used CEP engine implemented in Java and is able to apply event processing rules written in Event Processing Language (EPL).

By leveraging Esper and EPL, the CEP Engine included in the Processing Element, which is part of our prototype, is able to apply complex event processing rules that make use of several useful abstractions and functions. In particular, our CEP Engines provide support for time-based and row-based batched windows, time-based and row-based sliding windows, event rates, absence of events, and transactions composed of multiple low-level events. Moreover, the syntax of EPL rules is very similar to the syntax of standard SQL queries. Hence human operators who are already familiar with SQL can understand and write rules for event processing with reduced effort.

A realistic use-case scenario, in which the CEP Engines of the Processing Elements have been configured with EPL rules for the detection of Man-in-the-Middle attacks against financial institutions, is described in Sect. 9.4.

9.3.4 Integration with the CoMiFin Gateway

Within the scope of CoMiFin, the external entities that produce events to be analyzed are financial institutions that participate in a Semantic Room. To participate, each financial institution has (at least) one CoMiFin Gateway that is used as the interface between the local network of the financial institution (where local events are produced and gathered) and the CoMiFin Semantic Room. CoMiFin Gateways can be configured by the participating financial institution to actively collect events from multiple local event sources. Local events are then preprocessed (filtered, anonymized, and aggregated), and encapsulated in well-formed CoMiFin Events.

Communications between CoMiFin Gateways and Semantic Rooms are mediated by the publish/subscribe middleware described in Sect. 9.3.2, implemented through a JMS server. CoMiFin Gateways forward events to the Semantic Room by sending them to the queue on which the Processing Elements of the Semantic Room are listening. On the other hand, alerts generated by the Semantic Room can be received by the Gateways (as well as by any other party that is interested in receiving them and authorized to do so) by subscribing to the topics that correspond to the alert types generated by the Semantic Room.

9.3.5 Integration with the Information Manager

The Information Manager (see Chap. 6) is a fundamental component for upholding high standards of quality for the data exchanged by all the partners that participate in CoMiFin. Its purpose is to dynamically adjust the level of trust assigned to each partner on the basis of a continuous assessment of a partner's past behavior, direct experience, recommendation, referral, and roles.

Trust information is then used by the Semantic Room to produce a quantitative evaluation of the quality of the alerts that have been produced, based on the level of trust that is assigned to the partners who contributed the events that caused the emission of the alert. Moreover, the Information Manager is also interested in receiving all the alerts produced by a Semantic Room, as well as metrics that express the level of participation of Semantic Room members (number, rate, and trustworthiness of CoMiFin Events contributed by each Semantic Room participant). Indeed, all this information is taken into account for the dynamic update of the level of trust of all the financial institutions that participate in CoMiFin. Hence, the flow of information between the Semantic Room and the Information Manager is bidirectional.

As for other CoMiFin components, communication between a Semantic Room and the Information Manager are mediated by a publish/subscribe middleware based on JMS. In particular, all the Processing Elements of the Semantic Room receive updates of the trust metric associated to the Semantic Room participants by subscribing to the relevant topic on a JMS server. Trust updates are then consumed by the local CEP Engine of each Processing Element and are used to compute the level of trust that is associated to all the CoMiFin Alerts produced by the same CEP Engine.

Several different algorithms can be used for trust computation, depending on the specific event processing algorithm implemented by the Semantic Room. In the current prototype, trust computation is implemented through rules in EPL format, as are the rules for event processing.

On the other hand, CoMiFin Alerts can be received by the Information Manager component by subscribing to the same topics of the JMS server where the Semantic Room publishes its alerts.

9.3.6 Integration with the CoMiFin MeMo

Since a Semantic Room is a complex and distributed system in itself, the ability to monitor the performance of its components is of paramount importance. In CoMiFin, this requirement is fulfilled through the integration of all the components of the proposed Processing Container with the CoMiFin Metric Monitoring (MeMo) component, already described in Chap. 5.

Among all the active Processing Elements, one is elected as *Monitoring Station*. The Monitoring Station collects all the relevant metrics from the Processing Elements that belong to the same Processing Container and performs local aggregations of performance data. Aggregated data are then forwarded to the CoMiFin MeMo for further analysis and to allow their graphical representation through the CoMiFin Dashboard.

This solution decouples the activities of the CoMiFin MeMo from the topology and from the internals and details of a CoMiFin Semantic Room implemented through the Processing Container proposed in this chapter. Hence it is possible to dynamically reconfigure the Semantic Room (e.g., by modifying the number of Processing Elements on the fly) without having to reconfigure the entire monitoring infrastructure.

9.3.7 Intra-SR Connectivity

One of the most advanced features of CoMiFin, that builds upon the powerful abstraction of Semantic Room for information sharing and collaborative event processing, is the ability to exchange information among different Semantic Rooms. This feature is called *intra-SR connectivity*, and it allows a CoMiFin Semantic Room to leverage useful information and security alerts that have been generated by a different Semantic Room in order to improve the effectiveness of its collaborative event processing algorithm.

We remark that the two communicating Semantic Rooms can be completely different. They can implement heterogeneous event processing algorithms, they can be deployed to fulfill different purposes, their membership can be different, the analyzed events can be syntactically and semantically different. However, if the security alerts generated by a Semantic Room (Source SR) can provide useful information for another Semantic Room (Destination SR), and if the contract that regulates the Source SR allows security alerts to be forwarded to other Semantic Rooms, the Destination SR can receive the security alerts generated by the Source SR by subscribing to the intra-SR communication channel. In the current prototype, intra-SR connectivity is implemented as a publish/subscribe MOM, realized through JMS.

Depending on the event processing algorithm implemented by the Destination SR, alerts generated by the Source SR can take part in event processing (exactly like other events produced by the CoMiFin Gateway of the Semantic Room participants) or can be managed as special kinds of events. An example of how a Semantic Room can leverage intra-SR connectivity to dynamically adapt its collaborative event processing algorithm according to an ever-changing threat landscape is described in Sect. 9.4.

9.4 A Use Case: Collaborative Detection of Man-in-the-Middle Attacks

This section describes a use case of the solution for collaborative and distributed event processing described in Sects. 9.2 and 9.3. This use case focuses on the early detection of Man-in-the-Middle (MitM) attacks and is one of the prototypes that were used to demonstrate the capabilities of CoMiFin.

9.4.1 Attack Scenario

A MitM attack is performed by hijacking and intercepting the communication between a legitimate user of a service (e.g., a customer of a bank) and the server that is delivering the service (a server of the bank that hosts the home-banking web application). After they have been hijacked, the customers authenticate against a server that is controlled by the attacker. The attacker can then relay the authentication credentials to the legitimate server, and behave as a middleman in all the subsequent transactions. A detailed description of MitM attacks, their consequences, and several strategies that have been used in the recent past by attackers to fraud financial institutions is included in Chap. 3.

The system prototype has been deployed in a controlled laboratory environment. We have simulated a realistic deployment of CoMiFin that includes two different Semantic Rooms. The former one is implemented through the collaborative event processing architecture presented in this chapter, and is devoted to the detection of MitM attacks targeting the Semantic Room participants. The latter is implemented through Agilis (described in Chap. 8) and aims to detect distributed portscan activities.

The scenario for MitM detection includes three different financial institutions. Each financial institution contributes CoMiFin Events to the MitM Semantic Room through a CoMiFin Gateway. In particular, a CoMiFin Event is created whenever a customer logs into the home-banking web site of one of the participating financial institutions. The event contains the following information:

- the IP address from which the customer logged into the home-banking web site
- an identifier of the service to which the customer logged in. The identifier must be unique within the same financial institution (i.e., no two services of the same financial institution can have the same identifier, whereas it is possible for services belonging to different financial institutions to have the same identifier)

- an identifier of the customer that logged in. The identifier must be unique within the same financial institution (i.e., no two customers of the same financial institution can have the same identifier, whereas it is possible for customers of different financial institutions to have the same identifier)
- an identifier of the financial institution that is generating the CoMiFin Event. This identifier has to be unique within the Semantic Room
- the time at which the customer logged in.

We remark that there is no need for a financial institution to include in the CoMiFin Event real values for sensitive fields such as the identifier of the customer and the identifier of the service. The only constraint is for the same customer (service) to be always labeled with the same identifier. Hence the identifiers of customers and of services are pseudonyms that have no meaning for anyone outside the financial institution that generated the CoMiFin Event.

The considered scenario also includes trust updates, generated by the CoMiFin Information Manager, and intra-SR connectivity with the Semantic Room based on Agilis. The MitM Semantic Room constantly receives updates on the level of trust that is assigned to the financial institutions that contribute CoMiFin Events. Moreover, security alerts generated by the Agilis Semantic Room, which identifies the IP address of computers in the Internet that are involved in portscan activities against other financial institutions, are received by the MitM Semantic Room in (soft) real time.

9.4.2 Event Preprocessing

The stream of CoMiFin Events generated by the participating financial institution is handled cooperatively by all the Processing Elements that belong to the MitM Semantic Room. CoMiFin Events are dispatched in a round-robin fashion, and each event is received by the Event Manager (see Sect. 9.2.1) of a single Processing Element. Event processing starts when the Event Manager analyzes each CoMiFin Event and builds the messages that will then be inserted in the DHT overlay.

A good indicator of a likely MitM attack is represented by several successful accesses of different customers to the same service from the same IP address in a short time frame. Hence, it is possible for the Event Manager to generate a message whose messageID is computed as the result of a cryptographic hash function of the concatenation of the identifier of the source IP address and of the identifier of the service.

$$messageID = hash(source\_IP \oplus serviceID)$$

Since message routing on the DHT overlay is determined by the messageID, all the log-in events generated from the same IP address to the same service will be received by the same Processing Element. Hence, each Processing Element can detect a likely MitM attack by analyzing the subset of messages for which it is responsible, and checking whether the number of accesses from the same IP address to the

```
@Name: EnhanceWithTrust
@Statement:
insert into
    FullComifinEvent
select
    raw.id,
    raw.source_ip,
    raw.userid,
    raw.log_time,
    raw.OriginFI,
    raw.service,
    trust.Trust,
    trust.Confidence,
    raw.received_tmstp,
    trust.timestamp
from
    MitMSRComifinEvent as raw unidirectional left outer join
        trust on raw.OriginFI=trust.OriginFI
order by
    raw.received_tmstp-trust.timestamp asc
limit 1
```

Fig. 9.4 EPL statement for merging CoMiFin Events and trust updates

same service within a bounded time window exceeds a certain (static or dynamic) threshold.

9.4.3 CEP Rules

Event analysis is performed independently by each Processing Element, according to an event processing algorithm expressed through a set of EPL rules (see Sect. 9.2.3) written for the Esper CEP engine.

While a comprehensive explanation of all the processing rules used to detect MitM attacks is out of the scope of this book, in the following we provide a short description of the most important EPL statements. Our goal is to give the reader an idea of both the expressiveness of EPL rules and the capabilities of the proposed architecture for collaborative event processing.

Since the proposed event processing algorithm leverages trust information generated by the CoMiFin Information Manager, it is necessary to fuse data coming from two different event streams: the messages received through the DHT overlay and the trust updates generated by the Information Manager. This activity is performed by the EPL statement *EnhanceWithTrust*, represented in Fig. 9.4.

Note that the statement is similar to an SQL query. The aim of this statement is to merge the information included in messages coming from the DHT overlay (the *MitMSRComivinEvent* event stream) with trust and confidence data included in the

```
@Name: EnhanceWithSuspectedIP
@Statement:
insert into
    UltimateComifinEvent
select
    FullComifinEvent.raw.id as id,
    FullComifinEvent.raw.source_ip as source_ip,
    FullComifinEvent.raw.userid as userid,
    FullComifinEvent.raw.log_time as log_time,
    FullComifinEvent.raw.OriginFI as OriginFI,
    FullComifinEvent.raw.service as service,
    FullComifinEvent.trust.Trust as Trust,
    FullComifinEvent.trust.Confidence as Confidence,
    SuspectedIpEvent.count as
        count from FullComifinEvent unidirectional left outer join
        SuspectedIpEvent.std:unique(source_ip) on
        FullComifinEvent.raw.source_ip = SuspectedIpEvent.source_ip
```

Fig. 9.5 EPL statement for handling intra-SR connectivity with the Agilis Semantic Room

trust updates (the *trust* event stream). This operation generates a new data stream, called *FullComifinEvent*.

If intra-SR connectivity is implemented, the Destination SR needs to take care of the alerts generated by the Source SR. This activity is performed by the EPL statement represented in Fig. 9.5.

This statements merges the *FullComifinEvent* data stream with the *SuspectedIpEvent* data stream. SuspectedIPEvent is a data stream that includes the IP addresses which have been identified by the Agilis Semantic Room as sources of portscan activities against financial institutions. Since these IP addresses are already known to misbehave, they will undergo a stricter scrutiny with respect to other IP addresses. This EPL statement augments the *FullComifinEvent* data stream by adding a *count* property to all the events that have been generated by a suspected IP address. The resulting event stream is named *UltimateComifinEvent*.

Finally, the *UltimateComifinEvent* data stream is analyzed to detect likely MitM attacks. This activity is performed by the EPL statement shown in Fig. 9.6.

This EPL statement defines a pattern of events that correspond to a MitM attack, and raises an alert whenever this pattern is detected within the *UltimateComifinEvent* event stream. This pattern is verified if there are at least *threshold* (a configurable number) of different events having the same identifier and contained within a specified time frame. If none of the IP addresses associated to the events being considered has been suspected by the Agilis Semantic Room, then the length of the time frame is given by the parameter *temporal_window*. On the other hand, if the considered IP addresses have already been suspected by the Agilis Semantic Room, then the length of the time frame is automatically increased by adding *add_to_window* to the base *temporal_window*.

```
@Name: RaiseAlert
@Statement:
    select *
from
    pattern [
        ( every e1=UltimateComifinEvent) ->
          [threshold] e2=UltimateComifinEvent(e2.id=e1.id )
            while (
            e2.log_time-e1.log_time <
            ((coalesce(e1.count,0)/coalesce(e1.count,1))*add_to_window)
            +temporal_window
          )
    ]
```

Fig. 9.6 EPL statement for analyzing the enhanced event stream and raising MitM alerts

9.4.4 Experimental Validation

Experimental validation of the prototype described in Sect. 9.3 was carried out by using the testbed that was prepared for the CoMiFin project. This testbed is composed of several (both physical and virtual) networked machines, geographically distributed among Italy, Hungary, and Israel. A complete description of the CoMiFin testbed is out of the scope of this chapter, and can be found in the CoMiFin deliverables.

The three cooperating financial institutions were simulated by deploying three distinct instances of the CoMiFin Gateway. Each Gateway sent a stream of CoMiFin Events to the Semantic Room devoted to MitM detection, at a rate of about 1000 events per minute. In our tests, this Semantic Room comprised eight Processing Elements.

To verify the ability of the proposed CEP algorithm to detect MitM attacks without triggering false positives, we built a custom data set of customer activities that was used by the Gateways to generate their event streams. Our data set is composed of a baseline of normal activities involving legitimate users whose events do not match the pattern described by the EPL statement presented in Fig. 9.6. Hence, any alert raised by the MitM Semantic Room and related to one of these events is to be considered a false positive, and to be avoided.

On top of this baseline, we artificially introduced events related to three different instances of MitM attacks. Two of these instances were examples of "high-volume" MitM activities, in which customers' log-in activities to the same service and IP address from distinct users were above the detection threshold (i.e., more than *threshold* events in a *temporal_window*; see Fig. 9.6).

The third instance of MitM attack that we injected on top of our baseline data set was harder to detect, since it represented a "low-volume" MitM attack. In particular, events related to this attack were below the normal detection threshold, but above the extended detection threshold used for the analysis of events generated by IP for which an alert had already been generated by the Agilis Semantic Room (i.e., more than *threshold* events in a time frame of *temporal_window* + *add_to_window*; see Fig. 9.6).

Experiments carried out on the CoMiFin testbed allowed us to confirm that the MitM Semantic Room based on the proposed collaborative architecture for event processing behaved as expected. No false positives were raised during the experiment, and both "high-volume" instances of MitM attacks were detected as soon as a sufficient number of events had been received by the Semantic Room.

The "low-volume" MitM attack allowed us to verify the effectiveness of the intra-SR communication mechanism. At the beginning of the experiment, the MitM Semantic Room was not able to detect this attack. However, as soon as the MitM Semantic Room received a Portscan Alert from the Agilis Semantic Room that identified the same IP address from which the "low-volume" attack originated as a misbehaving traffic source, the Processing Elements of the MitM Semantic Room adapted to this new threat landscape by increasing the length of the time window used for the analysis of the events originated by the suspected IP address. This autonomous reaction (carried out without the need for human intervention) led to the detection of the "low-volume" MitM attack.

The performance of the proposed architecture for collaborative event processing, expressed in terms of the number of events that it is able to process in the unit of time, is difficult to quantify exactly, since it depends on the deployment of the collaborative Processing Element. In our testbed, the eight Processing Elements were deployed in eight different virtual machines deployed on two physical hosts, and were able to sustain an aggregated event throughput of about 3000 events per minute (1000 events per minute for each of the three financial institutions that participated to the Semantic Room). By monitoring the resource usage of each Processing Element, as well as the number of events that they processed, we were able to confirm that the load was evenly balanced among all the Processing Elements.

9.5 Related Work

This section highlights the benefits of a distributed approach over traditional solutions for intrusion detection. In particular, we compare the proposed architecture for distributed event processing with two other architectures that have already been proposed in the security literature. A popular application in this field is the processing, aggregation, and correlation of security events generated by distributed intrusion detection systems. The first architecture, described in Sect. 9.5.1, is based on a centralized CEP engine that receives and analyzes all the events produced by multiple sources. The second architecture, described in Sect. 9.5.2, is based on a hierarchical design, in which multiple CEP engines are arranged as a tree.

Fig. 9.7 Centralized solution
for event processing

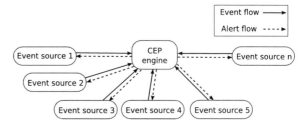

9.5.1 Centralized Architecture

The simplest and most widely adopted approach for the implementation of an event processing architecture is based on a centralized solution, as depicted in Fig. 9.7.

All the events produced by the distributed event sources are relayed to a centralized CEP engine that aggregates and processes all the alert streams.

In the context of information security, a similar architecture was first envisioned in [9], published in 1991. In this seminal work, all the high-level functions of the centralized modules depicted in Fig. 9.7 (alert aggregator, alert database, and management interface) are implemented in a single logical node, called *central manager*. The central manager receives security events generated by two classes of distributed sensors, called *host manager* (HIDS) and *LAN managers* (NIDS). Using modern intrusion detection terminology, it is possible to say that this paper described a centralized architecture for distributed and hybrid intrusion detection. A prototype implementation of the architecture proposed in [9] has been described in [10].

Another early prototype of a centralized architecture for the detection of security breaches, called NSTAT, was proposed in [11]. This architecture, based on the STAT framework for intrusion detection [12], is composed of a single STAT process that acts as a centralized aggregator by fusing the security events coming from multiple, distributed USTAT sensors (acting as distributed sources of security events) in a single audit trail.

Similar architectures have also been proposed in several other papers, focusing more on the definition of novel strategies and algorithms for security event processing than on the underlying architecture that enables cooperation among distributed sources of security events. Notable examples are [13, 17], and [14], in which event fusion strategies are applied in the IDS context. Data clustering schemes for security events classification in centralized architectures for intrusion detection have also been studied in [15].

Another architecture based on a centralized design for the processing of security-related events generated by multiple and distributed sources is proposed in [16]. It focuses on securing event forwarding between the distributed event sources (called *elementary detectors*) and the centralized event processing element (the *manager*). In [16] all the elementary detectors have a private key, used to sign messages. All the communications are mediated by a novel architectural element, called *message queue*, that wraps each message in a logical envelope. The main elements of the envelope are a per-sender and monotonically increasing message counter and an SHA1

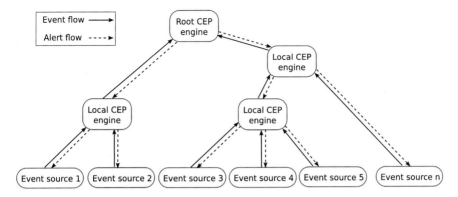

Fig. 9.8 Hierarchical architecture for event processing

digest computed over the elementary detector's private key, the message counter, and the message itself. This scheme prevents attackers from abusing the architecture by inserting fake messages or by replaying the same event several times.

Besides research efforts and prototypes, centralized solutions for the processing of security-related events generated by distributed sources represent a commonly deployed solution in many enterprise network scenarios. In the context of network security, almost all the major vendors in the field of intrusion detection and prevention sell hardware appliances that implement the high-level functions of alert aggregator, alert database, and management interface, and that can be used to monitor and gather alerts from multiple distributed IDSs and IPSs. Some examples are the *Sourcefire defense center*™ [18], TopLayer's *SecureCommand*™ [19], Datamation® *Dragon IDS/IPS* [20], and Qbik's *NetPatrol* [21]. Similar architectures can also be built upon open source software, such as the *Prelude IDS* framework [22].

Centralized solutions can be easily adopted in many realistic application scenarios. However, since all the events have to be analyzed by a centralized CEP engine, the scalability of this solution is inherently limited by the computational capacity of the hardware and software stack used to implement the CEP engine.

9.5.2 Hierarchical Architecture

To overcome the scalability issues that are inherent in centralized CEP engines, hierarchical architectures for event processing have been proposed. The main idea is to reduce the workload of the centralized CEP engine by building a hierarchy of intermediate CEP engines. Each intermediate CEP engine analyzes a subset of the events and relays its partial processing results to CEP engines that belong to the higher tier.

A typical example of hierarchical architecture event processing is shown in Fig. 9.8.

Like any other distributed CEP architectures, a hierarchical architecture is composed of several distributed and possibly heterogeneous event sources. In order to achieve a higher scalability than a centralized architecture (see Fig. 9.7), all the events generated by the distributed sources are not forwarded to a single CEP engine. Instead, the hierarchical architecture leverages a multitude of *local CEP engines*, organized in layers. Each local CEP engine belonging to the lowest layer (leaf CEP engine) receives alerts directly from a subset of the distributed event sources. These alerts are aggregated and correlated locally, and the partial results generated by the local analysis are relayed to a CEP engine belonging to a higher layer. As a result of the local aggregation and correlation, the number of events relayed by a local CEP engine is much smaller than the number of received events. However, using proper event processing algorithms, all the information that is relevant to a particular analysis algorithm is maintained and forwarded to the higher levels of the architecture. The *root CEP engine* is the highest CEP engine of the whole hierarchy, and receives and correlates partial processing results that are representative of all the activities performed in the monitored environment.

As shown by the comparison between Figs. 9.7 and 9.8, a centralized architecture is logically and functionally equivalent to a hierarchical architecture in which the CEP hierarchy (bounded by the gray box in Fig. 9.8) is collapsed into a single centralized alert CEP engine, whose computational capacity is enough to handle the event streams generated by all the distributed event sources.

Note also that it is not necessary for the aggregation hierarchy to be shaped as an *n*-ary tree, or to be perfectly balanced. The in-degree of each element in the hierarchy, modeled as a directed graph, can be adapted to reflect the characteristic of each deployment scenario. The height of the subtrees connecting the event sources to the root CEP engine can also vary.

Several examples of hierarchical architectures for event processing have been proposed in the literature. In the field of information security and intrusion detection, the first example is GrIDS [23], a graph-based IDS specifically tailored for the detection of Internet worms. In GrIDS, each component is composed by two software modules: an *engine* and a *software manager*. Engines belonging to the lowest level are responsible for collecting security events generated by event sources (both network and host IDSs). These events are used to build a sub-graph representing the traffic flows among the monitored hosts. Each engine then forwards its sub-graph to the higher level engine, which fuses all the received graphs and relays its aggregated results to a higher engine in the hierarchy. This fusion and relaying procedure is repeated until the root engine is reached. Each engine is coupled with a software manager, whose purpose is to build and manage the architecture hierarchy.

Other hierarchical architectures that follow the design shown in Fig. 9.8 are [25–27]. These papers do not introduce any architectural innovation; they focus on developing new strategies for event aggregation and fusion. The works proposed in [26] and [27] explore new alert aggregation schemes based on neural networks and statistical classification, on top of a standard hierarchical architecture. Another hierarchical architecture that complies with the design of Fig. 9.8 is presented in [2]. The event sources employed by this architecture are Operational IDSs (also called honeypots), and the local CEP engines (called *managers*) cooperate, implementing a distributed event filtering algorithm. This cooperation strategy ensures that only relevant events reach the root CEP engine, thus reducing its computational load.

While hierarchical architectures can scale much better than centralized architectures, both approaches suffer from the presence of a single point of failure. A centralized architecture becomes useless if the centralized CEP engine fails or becomes unreachable. The same happens to a hierarchical architecture in case of a failure of the root CEP engine. Moreover, a failure of any local CEP engine within the hierarchy cause the complete isolation of all the CEP engines that are connected to the root CEP engine through the failed local CEP engine.

This issue is acknowledged and mitigated in [28] and [24] by introducing some redundancy in their hierarchical architecture. In [28] each local CEP engine (called a *monitor*) can relay its partial aggregation results to more than one higher level CEP engine, thus creating multiple redundant paths toward the root CEP engine. This design choice allows the architecture to tolerate faults of some of the intermediate monitors, at the expense of an increased complexity in the architecture design and management.

In [24], each local CEP engine (called a *director*) is associated with a *surrogate agent*, whose aim is to take over the director's duties in case of a fault. In this case, the price for high availability of directors is paid in terms of additional hardware components needed to provide redundancy.

Another problem of hierarchical architectures is represented by the lack of load balancing among the intermediate nodes in the hierarchy. If only one of the event sources of Fig. 9.8 starts producing a high-throughput event stream, then the load of the local CEP engines that are in the path between the event source and the root CEP engine will increase. Eventually, one of these CEP engines will become a bottleneck, dropping events or partial processing results, while the load experienced by local CEP engines in other branches of the hierarchy can be negligible. Hence, a hierarchical architecture can be overloaded by relatively small workloads, compared to the aggregated computational capacity of all the CEP engines that compose the hierarchy.

Our architecture offers the following advantages compared to the hierarchical approach: fault tolerance, scalability, and load balancing.

Fault Tolerance

The completely distributed nature of the proposed architecture is inherently fault-tolerant and lacks the single points of failure that are typical of hierarchical and centralized architectures, in which alert aggregation, correlation, and analysis functions are aggregated in the root node of the architecture [2]. This node represents a single point of failure, and when it is unreachable the hierarchical architecture is unable to complete any collaborative task. The effectiveness of hierarchical architectures can be impaired even by failures of the nodes belonging to intermediate layers of the tree. As an example, a failure of one of the tier-1 nodes causes the isolation of the complete subtree having the faulty node as its root.

On the other hand, the proposed architecture leverages a completely distributed, network-driven aggregation and correlation technique. Each Processing Element is responsible for processing only a subset of events. If a Processing Element becomes unreachable, only the events that would have been handled by the faulty Processing Element are lost, while all the other Processing Elements are not influenced by the failure. Moreover, depending on the implementation of DHT routing of the overlay network, the collaborative Processing Elements can detect the failure of a peer and autonomously modify their local overlay routing tables accordingly. Hence, the proposed architecture is able to autonomously reorganize itself and restore its efficiency without human intervention.

Message replication schemes can also be used to reduce the (minimal and transitory) losses of events due to the failure of a collaborative Processing Element. In the current implementation (see Sect. 9.3), it is possible to set a replication constant k denoting that, for each event, k copies are created and maintained by the DTH overlay. One event is sent to the Processing Element whose unique identifier (nodeID) is responsible for the event key (messageId). The other $k - 1$ events are sent to the $k - 1$ nearest neighbors, thus guaranteeing full reliability for up to $k - 1$ concurrent failures. Moreover, the overlay network can be periodically inspected to ensure that the DHTs always contain k replicas of each event, and to create additional replicas if this constraint is not met. Experimental evaluation of message loss probability for a higher number of concurrent faults is presented in Sect. 9.4. Admittedly, high values of k cause an increase in the network overhead, since more messages have to be transmitted over the overlay network. However, it is possible to achieve the desired trade-off between overhead and fault tolerance by tuning the value of k.

Scalability

Hierarchical architectures are based on a multi-tier event processing infrastructure connecting the lowest layer CEP engines (the leaves of the tree) to the root CEP engine. Each node in the hierarchical architecture is able to process events generated by a finite number n of lower layer CEP engines, depending on the computational complexity of the event processing operations and on bandwidth constraints. Hence, a hierarchical architecture can be modeled as an n-ary tree, whose number of intermediate elements grows with the number of the leaves. The design and maintenance of this hierarchical architecture is a manual task that requires continuous management. Moreover, hierarchical architectures are not able to autonomously adapt to churn and dynamic membership. The hierarchy must be reconfigured whenever one or more local CEP engines leave the architecture or if new local CEP engines are added to the architecture.

On the other hand, in the proposed architecture both the event processing operations and maintenance of the DHT overlay are distributed among the Processing Elements. Hence, there is no need for a separate management infrastructure. This is a huge advantage in terms of scalability and ease of management, because it is not necessary to reconfigure the architecture hierarchy, possibly by adding or removing new layers to the management tree, whenever the number of Processing Elements changes.

Load Balancing

Another advantage of the proposed DHT-based distributed architecture is represented by its intrinsic load balancing properties compared with those of collaborative architectures based on a hierarchical design. While increasing efficiency, this design choice leads to load imbalance among the nodes of the hierarchical architecture, since the computational load on the root can be significantly higher than the load of the intermediate nodes. As a result, root services can only be hosted on hardware that is much more powerful with respect to hardware requirements of intermediate nodes.

Let us consider a scenario in which only one event source is particularly active, and generates a high volume of events. In the context of CoMiFin, this is a realistic scenario that may happen if one of the institutions that participates in the Semantic Room is undergoing an attack, while the others are not. In a similar situation, the load related to event gathering and analysis is unevenly distributed, because only the nodes related to the attacked network are involved in event management. Hence, an attacker could easily overload the path connecting the attacked networks to the hierarchy root by attacking a few selected networks connected to the same higher level nodes.

Uneven load distribution and overload risks are mitigated by the proposed distributed event processing scheme. Events generated by one event source are retrieved by all the Processing Elements in a round-robin fashion. Moreover, the Processing Element that analyzes an event is determined by the key that the Overlay Manager assigns to the event. Hence there is no single path through which all the events generated by an external event source are transmitted. Even if one event source produces a very high event volume, this scenario is well managed and the load is automatically distributed among many Processing Elements.

References

1. Esper: Event Processing for Java. Available online at http://www.espertech.com/products/esper.php
2. Colajanni, M., Gozzi, D., Marchetti, M.: Collaborative architecture for malware detection and analysis. In: Proc. of the 23rd International Information Security Conference (SEC 2008), Milan, Italy, Sep. 2008
3. Rowstron, A., Druschel, P.: Pastry: Scalable, distributed object location and routing for large-scale peer-to-peer systems. In: Proc. of the IFIP/ACM International Conference on Distributed Systems Platforms (Middleware), Heidelberg, Germany, Nov. 2001
4. Druschel, P., Rowstron, A.: PAST: A large-scale, persistent peer-to-peer storage utility. In: 8th Workshop on Hot Topics in Operating Systems (HotOS VIII), Schoss Elmau, Germany, May 2001

5. Rowstron, A., Druschel, P.: Storage management and caching in PAST, a large-scale, persistent peer-to-peer storage utility. In: Proc. of the 18th ACM Symposium on Operating Systems Principles (SOSP'01), Chateau Lake Louise, Banff, Canada, May 2001

6. Rowstron, A., Kermarrec, A.M., Castro, M., Druschel, P.: SCRIBE: The design of a large-scale event notification infrastructure. In: Proc. of the 3rd International Workshop on Networked Group Communication (NGC2001), UCL, London, UK, Nov. 2001

7. Castro, M., Jones, M.B., Kermarrec, A.M., Rowstron, A., Theimer, M., Wang, H., Wolman, A.: An evaluation of scalable application-level multicast built using peer-to-peer overlays. In: Proc. of the Infocom'03, San Francisco, CA, USA, Apr. 2003

8. FreePastry library. Available online at http://www.freepastry.org/FreePastry/

9. Snapp, S.R., Brentano, J., Dias, G.V., Goan, T.L., Grance, T., Heberlein, L.T., Ho, C.-L., Levitt, K.N., Mukherjee, B., Mansur, D.L., Pon, K.L., Smaha, S.E.: A system for distributed intrusion detection. In: Compcon Spring '91. Digest of Papers from the IEEE Computer Society Thirty-sixth International Conference, San Francisco, CA, USA, Feb. 1991

10. Snapp, S.R., Brentano, J., Dias, G.V., Gihan, V., Goan, T.L., Terrance, L., Heberlein, L.T., Ho, C.-L., Levitt, K.N., Mukherjee, B., Smaha, S.E., Grance, T., Teal, D.M., Mansur, D.: DIDS (distributed intrusion detection system)—motivation, architecture, and an early prototype. In: Internet besieged: countering cyberspace scofflaws, pp. 211–227. ACM Press/Addison-Wesley, New York (1998). ISBN:0-201-30820-7

11. Kemmerer, R.A.: NSTAT: a model-based real-time network intrusion detection system. Tech. report, University of California at Santa Barbara, Santa Barbara, CA, USA (1998)

12. Ilgun, K., Kemmerer, R.A., Porras, P.A.: State transition analysis: a rule-based intrusion detection approach. In: IEEE Transactions on Software Engineering, IEEE Press, Piscataway (1995)

13. Bass, T.: Multisensor data fusion for next generation distributed intrusion detection systems. In: Proc. of the 1999 DoD-IRIS National Symposium on Sensor and Data Fusion (NSSDF), Laurel, MD, USA, May 1999

14. Bass, T.: Intrusion detection systems and multisensor data fusion. Communication of the ACM 43(4) (2000)

15. Zhang, Y.-F., Xiong, Z.-Y., Wang, X.-Q.: Distributed intrusion detection based on clustering. In: Proc. of the 2005 International Conference on Machine Learning and Cybernetics, Guangzhou, China, Apr. 2005

16. Wu, Y.-S., Foo, B., Mei, Y., Bagchi, S.: Collaborative intrusion detection system (CIDS): a framework for accurate and efficient IDS. In: Proc. of the 19th Annual Computer Security Applications Conference, Las Vegas, NV, USA, Dec. 2003

17. Wang, Y., Yang, H., Wang, X., Zhang, R.: Distributed intrusion detection system based on data fusion method. In: Proc. of the Fifth World Congress on Intelligent Control and Automation (WCICA 2004), Hangzhou, China, Jun. 2004

18. Sourcefire®, Sourcefire Defense Center™. http://www.sourcefire.com/products/3D/defense_center

19. Top Layer Security®, SecureCommand™IPS Centralized Management Solution. http://www.toplayer.com/content/products/intrusion_detection/index.jsp

20. Datamation®, Dragon IDS/IPS: Distributed IDS/IPS Platform with Multiple Detection Methods. http://products.datamation.com/security/id/1192208840.html

21. Qbik®, NetPatrol. http://www.wingate.com/products/netpatrol/features.php?fid=68

22. Prelude IDS technologies, Prelude IDS homepage. http://www.prelude-ids.org/

23. Staniford-Chen, S., Cheung, S., Crawford, R., Dilger, M., Frank, J., Hoagland, J., Levitt, K., Wee, C., Yip, R., Zerkle, D.: GrIDS—a graph-based intrusion detection system for large networks. In: Proc. of the 19th National Information Systems Security Conference, Baltimore, MD, USA, Oct. (1996)

24. Ragsdale, D., Carver, C., Humphries, J., Pooch, U.: Adaptation techniques for intrusion detection and intrusion response systems. In: Proc. of the IEEE International Conference on Systems, Man, and Cybernetics (SMC 2000), Nashville, TN, USA, Oct. 2000

25. Debar, H., Wespi, A.: Aggregation and correlation of intrusion-detection alerts. In: Proc. of the 4th International Symposium on Recent Advances in Intrusion Detection (RAID 2001), Davis, CA, USA, Oct. 2001

26. Zhang, Z., Li, J., Manikopulos, C.N., Jorgenson, J., Ucles, J.: A hierarchical anomaly network intrusion detection system using neural network classification. In: Proc. of 2001 WSES Conference on Neural Networks and Applications (NNA '01), Tenerife, Canary Islands, Feb. 2001

27. Zhang, Z., Li, J., Manikopulos, C.N., Jorgenson, J., Ucles, J.: HIDE: a hierarchical network intrusion detection system using statistical preprocessing and neural network classification. In: Proc. of the 2001 IEEE Workshop on Information Assurance and Security, West Point, NY, USA, Jun. 2001

28. Balasubramaniyan, J.S., Garcia-Fernandez, J.O., Isacoff, D., Spafford, E.H., Zamboni, D.: An architecture for intrusion detection using autonomous agents. In: Proc. of the 14th Annual Computer Security Applications Conference (ACSAC 1998). Scottsdale, AZ, USA, Dec. 1998

29. Eugster, P.T., Felber, P.A., Guerraoui, R., Kermarrec, A.: The many faces of publish/subscribe. ACM Comput. Surv. **35**(2) (2003)

Glossary

Android Android is an operating system for mobile devices such as smartphones and tablet computers. It is developed by the Open Handset Alliance led by Google.

Anti-Phishing Working Group The Anti-Phishing Working Group (APWG) is an international consortium that brings together businesses affected by phishing attacks, security products and services companies, law enforcement agencies, government agencies, trade associations, regional international treaty organizations, and communications companies.

Antivirus Antivirus or anti-virus software is used to prevent, detect, and remove malware, including but not limited to computer viruses, computer worms, Trojan horses, spyware, and adware.

Apache Tomcat Apache Tomcat (or Jakarta Tomcat or simply Tomcat) is an open source servlet container developed by the Apache Software Foundation (ASF). Tomcat implements the Java Servlet and the JavaServer Pages (JSP) specifications from Oracle Corporation, and provides a "pure Java" HTTP web server environment for Java code to run.

Asymmetric Digital Subscriber Line Asymmetric digital subscriber line (ADSL) is a type of digital subscriber line technology, a data communications technology that enables faster data transmission over copper telephone lines than a conventional voiceband modem can provide. It does this by utilizing frequencies that are not used by a voice telephone call.

Automated Teller Machine A computerized telecommunications device that provides the clients of a financial institution with access to financial transactions in a public space without the need for a cashier, human clerk, or bank teller.

Autonomous System An autonomous system is a collection of connected Internet Protocol routing prefixes under the control of one or more network operators that presents a common, clearly defined routing policy to the Internet.

Biometrics Biometrics (or biometric authentication) consists of methods for uniquely recognizing humans based on one or more intrinsic physical or behavioral traits. In computer science, biometrics is used as a form of identity access management and access control.

Browser A web browser is a software application for retrieving, presenting, and traversing information resources on the World Wide Web. A web browser can also

R. Baldoni, G. Chockler (eds.), *Collaborative Financial Infrastructure Protection*, 203
DOI 10.1007/978-3-642-20420-3, © Springer-Verlag Berlin Heidelberg 2012

be defined as an application software or program designed to enable users to access, retrieve, and view documents and other resources on the Internet.

Bureau of the Public Debt The Bureau of the Public Debt is an agency within the Fiscal Service of the United States Treasury Department. Under authority derived from Article I, section 8 of the Constitution, Public Debt is responsible for borrowing the money needed to operate the federal government, and it is where donations to reduce the debt can be made.

Cascading Style Sheets Cascading Style Sheets (CSS) is a style sheet language used to describe the presentation semantics (the look and formatting) of a document written in a markup language. Its most common application is to style web pages written in HTML and XHTML, but the language can also be applied to any kind of XML document, including plain XML, SVG, and XUL.

Central Processing Unit The portion of a computer system that carries out the instructions of a computer program, to perform the basic arithmetical, logical, and input/output operations of the system.

Chrome Google Chrome is a web browser developed by Google that uses the WebKit layout engine.

Closed Port A TCP port which turns out to be closed.

Command and Control Center (of a Trojan) Command and control generally refers to the maintenance of authority with somewhat more distributed decision making.

Common Vulnerabilities and Exposures The Common Vulnerabilities and Exposures (CVE) system provides a reference method for publicly known information security vulnerabilities and exposures.

Completely Automated Public Turing test to tell Computers and Humans Apart A CAPTCHA is a type of challenge-response test used in computing as an attempt to ensure that the response is generated by a person. The process usually involves one computer (a server) asking a user to complete a simple test which the computer is able to generate and grade. Because other computers are assumed to be unable to solve the CAPTCHA, any user entering a correct solution is presumed to be human.

Complex Event Processing Complex event processing consists of processing many events occurring across all the layers of an organization, identifying the most meaningful events within the event cloud, analyzing their impact, and taking subsequent action in real time.

Critical Infrastructure A term used by governments to describe assets that are essential for the functioning of a society and economy. Most commonly associated with the term are facilities for electricity generation, telecommunication, water supply, security services, and financial services, etc.

Critical Infrastructure Notification System Infrastructure which permits critical alerts to be sent to multiple recipients near simultaneously, and also provides user authentication and confirmed delivery.

Critical Infrastructure Protection Critical infrastructure protection (CIP) is a concept that relates to the preparedness and response to serious incidents that involve the critical infrastructure of a region or nation.

Cross-Site Request Forgery Cross-site request forgery, also known as a one-click attack or session riding and abbreviated as CSRF (pronounced sea-surf) or XSRF, is a type of malicious exploit of a web site whereby unauthorized commands are transmitted from a user that the web site trusts. Unlike cross-site scripting (XSS), which exploits the trust a user has for a particular site, CSRF exploits the trust that a site has in a user's browser.

Cross Site Scripting Cross-site scripting (XSS) is a type of computer security vulnerability typically found in web applications that enables attackers to inject client-side script into web pages viewed by other users. A cross-site scripting vulnerability may be used by attackers to bypass access controls such as the same origin policy.

Cryptography Cryptography is the practice and study of techniques and protocols for secure communication that overcome the influence of adversaries.

Database A database is an organized collection of data for one or more purposes, usually in digital form. The data are typically organized to model relevant aspects of reality in a way that supports processes requiring this information. The term database implies that the data is managed to some level of quality, and this in turn often implies the use of a general-purpose database management system (DBMS).

Demilitarized Zone A demilitarized zone (DMZ) is a physical or logical subnetwork that contains and exposes an organization's external services to a larger untrusted network, usually the Internet. The purpose of a DMZ is to add an additional layer of security to an organization's local area network (LAN).

Deep Packet Inspection A form of computer network packet filtering that examines the data part (and possibly also the header) of a packet as it passes an inspection point, searching for protocol non-compliance, viruses, spam, intrusions, or predefined criteria to decide if the packet can pass or if it needs to be routed to a different destination, or for the purpose of collecting statistical information.

Dependability The trustworthiness of a computing system which allows reliance to be justifiably placed on the service it delivers.

Digital Crimes Consortium Digital Crime is a highly selected consortium of information technology experts, former and active law enforcement professionals, trainers, and educators, bringing decades of experience in data recovery, digital forensics, investigations, training, incident response, and computer security.

Digital Certificate A digital certificate is an electronic "credit card" that establishes your credentials when doing business or other transactions on the Web. It is issued by a certification authority.

Distributed Hash Table A distributed hash table (DHT) is a class of a decentralized distributed system that provides a lookup service similar to a hash table; (key, value) pairs are stored in a DHT, and any participating node can efficiently retrieve the value associated with a given key. Responsibility for maintaining the mapping from keys to values is distributed among the nodes in such a way that a change in the set of participants causes a minimal amount of disruption.

Domain Name System The Domain Name System (DNS) is a hierarchical distributed naming system for computers, services, or any resource connected to the Internet or a private network. It translates domain names meaningful to humans into the numerical identifiers associated with networking equipment for the purpose of locating and addressing these devices worldwide.

Dow Jones Industrial Average The Dow Jones Industrial Average, also called the Industrial Average, the Dow Jones, the Dow 30, or simply the Dow, is a stock market index, and one of several indices created by Wall Street Journal editor and Dow Jones & Company co-founder Charles Dow.

Electronic Data Processing Electronic data processing (EDP) can refer to the use of automated methods to process commercial data. Typically, it uses relatively simple, repetitive activities to process large volumes of similar information.

Entropy In information theory, entropy is a measure of the uncertainty associated with a random variable. In this context, the term usually refers to the Shannon entropy, which quantifies the expected value of the information contained in a message, usually in units such as bits. In this context, a "message" means a specific realization of the random variable.

European Payments Council The EPC is the decision-making and coordination body of the European banking industry in relation to payments. The EPC develops the payment schemes and frameworks necessary to realize SEPA. SEPA is a European Union (EU) integration initiative in the area of payments. SEPA is the logical next step in the completion of the EU internal market and monetary union.

Event Processing Language The Event Processing Language is an SQL-like language with SELECT, FROM, WHERE, GROUP BY, HAVING, and ORDER BY clauses. Streams replace tables as the source of data with events replacing rows as the basic unit of data.

Exclusive OR The logical operation exclusive disjunction, also called exclusive OR, is a type of logical disjunction on two operands that results in a value of true if exactly one of the operands has a value of true. A simple way to state this is "one or the other but not both".

Extensible Markup Language Extensible Markup Language (XML) is a set of rules for encoding documents in machine-readable form. It is a textual data format with strong support via Unicode for the languages of the world. Although the design of XML focuses on documents, it is widely used for the representation of arbitrary data structures, for example in web services.

Fast-flux techniques Fast flux is a DNS technique used by botnets to hide phishing and malware delivery sites behind an ever-changing network of compromised hosts acting as proxies. It can also refer to the combination of peer-to-peer networking, distributed command and control, web-based load balancing, and proxy redirection used to make malware networks more resistant to discovery and countermeasures.

File Transfer Protocol File Transfer Protocol (FTP) is a standard network protocol used to transfer files from one host to another host over a TCP-based network, such as the Internet. FTP is built on a client-server architecture and utilizes separate control and data connections between the client and server.

Financial Infrastructure The financial infrastructure is the set of institutions that enable effective operation of financial intermediaries. This includes such elements as payment systems, credit information bureaus, and collateral registries. More broadly, financial infrastructure encompasses the existing legal and regulatory framework for financial sector operations.

Finite State Machine A finite state machine (FSM) is a behavioral model used to design computer programs. It is composed of a finite number of states associated to transitions. A transition is a set of actions that starts from one state and ends in another (or the same) state. A transition is started by a trigger, and a trigger can be an event or a condition.

Firefox Mozilla Firefox is a free and open source web browser descended from the Mozilla Application Suite and managed by Mozilla Corporation.

Firewall A firewall is a device or set of devices designed to permit or deny network transmissions based upon a set of rules and is frequently used to protect networks from unauthorized access while permitting legitimate communications to pass.

Global System for Mobile Communications A standard set developed by the European Telecommunications Standards Institute (ETSI) to describe technologies for second generation (or "2G") digital cellular networks.

Goal Question Metric GQM, the acronym for "goal, question, metric," is an approach to software metrics. GQM defines a measurement model on three levels: conceptual level (goal), operational level (question), and quantitative level (metric). The open literature typically describes GQM in terms of a six-step process, where the first three steps are about using business goals to drive the identification of the right metrics, and the last three steps are about gathering the measurement data and making effective use of the measurement results to drive decision making and improvements.

HTTP Secure Hypertext Transfer Protocol Secure (HTTPS) is a combination of the Hypertext Transfer Protocol (HTTP) with the SSL/TLS protocol to provide encrypted communication and secure identification of a network web server. HTTPS connections are often used for payment transactions on the World Wide Web and for sensitive transactions in corporate information systems.

Hadoop Apache Hadoop is a software framework that supports data-intensive distributed applications under a free license. It enables applications to work with thousands of nodes and petabytes of data. Hadoop was inspired by Google's MapReduce and Google File System (GFS) papers.

Hash Function A hash function is any algorithm or subroutine that maps large data sets to smaller data sets, called keys. The values returned by a hash function are called hash values, hash codes, hash sums, checksums, or simply hashes.

Hive Apache Hive is a data warehouse infrastructure built on top of Hadoop for providing data summarization, query, and analysis.

Host-based Intrusion Detection System A host-based intrusion detection system (HIDS) is an intrusion detection system that monitors and analyzes the internals of a computing system as well as (in some cases) the network packets on its network interfaces (just like a network-based intrusion detection system (NIDS) would do).

Hypertext Transfer Protocol The Hypertext Transfer Protocol (HTTP) is a networking protocol for distributed, collaborative, hypermedia information systems. HTTP is the foundation of data communication for the World Wide Web.

IP Security Internet Protocol Security (IPSec) is a protocol suite for securing Internet Protocol (IP) communications by authenticating and encrypting each IP packet of a communication session. IPSec also includes protocols for establishing mutual authentication between agents at the beginning of the session and negotiation of cryptographic keys to be used during the session.

IP Address An Internet Protocol address (IP address) is a numerical label assigned to each device (e.g., computer, printer) participating in a computer network that uses the Internet Protocol for communication. An IP address serves two principal functions: host or network interface identification and location addressing. Its role has been characterized as follows: "A name indicates what we seek. An address indicates where it is. A route indicates how to get there".

IT Security Group The IT Security Group (ISG) is one of the largest academic security groups in the world. It brings together in a single institution expertise in education, research, and practice in the field of information security.

Information Security Management Information security (ISec) describes activities that relate to the protection of information and information infrastructure assets against the risks of loss, misuse, disclosure, or damage. Information security management (ISM) describes controls that an organization must implement to ensure that it is sensibly managing these risks.

Information and Communication Technologies Often used as an extended synonym for information technology (IT), ICT consists of all technical means used to handle information and aid communication, including computer and network hardware, communication middleware, and necessary software.

Internet Control Message Protocol The Internet Control Message Protocol (ICMP) is one of the core protocols of the Internet Protocol Suite. It is chiefly used by the operating systems of networked computers to send error messages indicating, for example, that a requested service is not available or that a host or router could not be reached. ICMP can also be used to relay query messages.

Internet Explorer Windows Internet Explorer (formerly Microsoft Internet Explorer, commonly abbreviated IE or MSIE) is a series of graphical web browsers developed by Microsoft and included as part of the Microsoft Windows line of operating systems.

Internet Protocol The Internet Protocol (IP) is the principal communications protocol used for relaying datagrams (packets) across an internetwork using the Internet Protocol Suite. Responsible for routing packets across network boundaries, it is the primary protocol that establishes the Internet.

Internet Relay Chat Internet Relay Chat (IRC) is a protocol for real-time Internet text messaging (chat) or synchronous conferencing. It is mainly designed for group communication in discussion forums, called channels, but also allows one-to-one communication via private message as well as chat and data transfer, including file sharing.

Internet Service Provider An Internet service provider (ISP) is a company that provides access to the Internet. Access ISPs directly connect customers to the Internet using copper wires, wireless, or fiber optic connections. Hosting ISPs lease server space for smaller businesses and host other people's servers (colocation). Transit ISPs provide large tubes for connecting hosting ISPs to access ISPs.

Internet of Things The Internet of Things refers to uniquely identifiable objects (things) and their virtual representations in an Internet-like structure. If all objects of daily life were equipped with radio tags, they could be identified and inventoried by computers. However, unique identification of things may be achieved through other means such as barcodes or 2D-codes as well.

Intrusion Detection System An intrusion detection system (IDS) is a device or software application that monitors network and/or system activities for malicious activities or policy violations and produces reports to a management station.

Intrusion Prevention System Intrusion prevention systems (IPSs), also known as intrusion detection and prevention systems (IDPSs), are network security appliances that monitor network and/or system activities for malicious activity. The main functions of intrusion prevention systems are to identify malicious activity, log information about said activity, attempt to block/stop activity, and report activity.

Italian Banking Association The Italian Banking Association (ABI) is the industry association of banking and the financial world. It represents, protects, and promotes the interests of the system.

JBoss Application Server JBoss Application Server (or JBoss AS) is a free software/open source Java EE-based application server. An important distinction for this class of software is that it not only implements a server that runs on Java, but it actually implements the Java EE part of Java. Because it is Java-based, the JBoss Application Server operates cross-platform.

Jaql Jaql is a query language designed for JavaScript Object Notation (JSON). Jaql is primarily used to analyze large-scale semi-structured data. Core features include user extensibility and parallelism. In addition to modeling semi-structured data, JSON simplifies extensibility. Hadoop's MapReduce is used for parallelism.

Java EE Java Platform, Enterprise Edition or Java EE is a widely used platform for server programming in the Java programming language. The Java platform (Enterprise Edition) differs from the Java Standard Edition Platform (Java SE) in that it adds libraries which provide functionality to deploy fault-tolerant, distributed, multi-tier Java software, based largely on modular components running on an application server.

Java Message Service The Java Message Service (JMS) API is a Java message-oriented middleware (MOM) API for sending messages between two or more clients. It is a messaging standard that allows application components based on the Java Enterprise Edition (Java EE) to create, send, receive, and read messages. It allows the communication between different components of a distributed application to be loosely coupled, reliable, and asynchronous.

JavaScript JavaScript is a prototype-based scripting language that is dynamic, weakly typed, and has first-class functions. It is a multiparadigm language, supporting object-oriented, imperative, and functional programming styles.

Key Performance Indicator A key performance indicator (KPI) is an industry jargon term for a type of measure of performance. KPIs are commonly used by an organization to evaluate its success or the success of a particular activity in which it is engaged. Sometimes success is defined in terms of making progress toward strategic goals, but often, success is simply the repeated achievement of some level of operational goal.

Law Enforcement Agency In North American English, a law enforcement agency (LEA) is a government agency responsible for the enforcement of the laws. Outside North America, such organizations are called police services.

Linear Congruential Generator A linear congruential generator (LCG) represents one of the oldest and best-known pseudo-random number generator algorithms.

Linux Linux is a computer operating system which is based on free and open source software. Although many different varieties of Linux exist, all are Unix-like and based on the Linux kernel, an operating system kernel created in 1992 by Linus Torvalds.

Local Area Network A local area network (LAN) is a computer network that interconnects computers in a limited area such as home, school, computer laboratory, or office building. The defining characteristics of LANs, in contrast to wide area networks (WANs), include their usually higher data transfer rates, smaller geographic area, and lack of a need for leased telecommunication lines.

London Stock Exchange The London Stock Exchange is a stock exchange located in the city of London, England, within the United Kingdom. As of December 2010, the Exchange had a market capitalization of US\$3.6 trillion, making it the fourth-largest stock exchange in the world by this measurement (and the largest in Europe).

MD5 The MD5 Message-Digest Algorithm is a widely used cryptographic hash function that produces a 128-bit (16-byte) hash value. Specified in RFC 1321, MD5 has been employed in a wide variety of security applications and is also commonly used to check data integrity.

Malware Malware, short for malicious software, consists of programming (code, scripts, active content, and other software) designed to disrupt or deny operation, gather information that leads to loss of privacy or exploitation, gain unauthorized access to system resources, and perform other abusive behavior.

MapReduce MapReduce is a framework for processing highly distributable problems across huge data sets using a large number of computers (nodes), collectively referred to as a cluster (if all nodes use the same hardware) or a grid (if the nodes use different hardware). Computational processing can occur on data stored either in a filesystem (unstructured) or in a database (structured).

Media Access Control Address A Media Access Control address (MAC address) is a unique identifier assigned to network interfaces for communications on the physical network segment. MAC addresses are used for numerous network technologies and most IEEE 802 network technologies including Ethernet. Logically, MAC addresses are used in the Media Access Control protocol sub-layer of the OSI reference model.

Message Digest A message digest is a number which is created algorithmically from a file and represents that file uniquely. If the file changes, the message digest will change.

Message-Oriented Middleware Message-oriented middleware (MOM) is software or hardware infrastructure that supports the sending and receiving of messages between distributed systems. MOM allows application modules to be distributed over heterogeneous platforms and reduces the complexity of developing applications that span multiple operating systems and network protocols. The middleware creates a distributed communications layer that insulates the application developer from the details of the various operating system and network interfaces.

Middleware Middleware is computer software that connects software components or people and their applications. The software consists of a set of services that allows multiple processes running on one or more machines to interact. This technology evolved to provide for interoperability in support of the move to coherent distributed architectures, which are most often used to support and simplify complex distributed applications.

Model-Driven Architecture Model-driven architecture (MDA) is a software design approach for the development of software systems. It provides a set of guidelines for the structuring of specifications, which are expressed as models. One of the main aims of the MDA is to separate design from architecture. As the concepts and technologies used to realize designs and those used to realize architectures have changed at their own pace, decoupling them allows system developers to choose from the best and most fitting in both domains.

MySQL MySQL is a relational database management system (RDBMS) that runs as a server providing multi-user access to a number of databases.

Nagios Remote Plugin Executor NRPE is a Nagios add-on that allows one to execute plugins on remote Linux/Unix hosts. This is useful if local resources/attributes like disk usage, CPU load, and memory usage on a remote host must be monitored. Similar functionality can be accomplished by using the check_by_ssh plugin, although it can impose a higher CPU load on the monitoring machine—especially if hundreds or thousands of hosts have to be monitored.

Nagios Service Check Acceptor NSCA is a Nagios add-on that allows the sending of passive check results from remote Linux/Unix hosts to the Nagios daemon running on the monitoring server. This is very useful in distributed and redundant/failover monitoring setups.

National Institute of Standards and Technology The National Institute of Standards and Technology (NIST) is a measurement standards laboratory and a non-regulatory agency of the United States Department of Commerce. The institute's official mission is to: "Promote US innovation and industrial competitiveness by advancing measurement science, standards, and technology in ways that enhance economic security and improve our quality of life".

National Security Authority The National Security Authority (NSM) is a Norwegian security agency (Direktorat) established on 1 January 2003 as the successor to Forsvarets sikkerhetsstab (FO/S). It is responsible for preventative national security, ICT security matters, including the national CERT (NorCERT), identifying national objects of special interest, and reducing their vulnerability to internal and external threats.

Network-Based Intrusion Detection System A network-based intrusion detection system (NIDS) is an intrusion detection system that uses network security monitoring (NSM) of network traffic to try to detect malicious activity such as denial of service attacks, port scans, or even attempts to crack into computers.

Network-Based Intrusion Prevention System Monitors the entire network for suspicious traffic by analyzing protocol activity.

Opera Opera is a web browser and Internet suite developed by Opera Software with over 200 million users worldwide. The browser handles common Internet-related tasks such as displaying web sites, sending and receiving e-mail messages, managing contacts, chatting on IRC, downloading files via BitTorrent, and reading web feeds. Opera is offered free of charge for personal computers and mobile phones.

Operating System An operating system (OS) is a set of programs that manages computer hardware resources and provides common services for application software. The operating system is the most important type of system software in a computer system. Without an operating system, a user cannot run an application program on their computer, unless the application program is self-booting.

PHP PHP is a general-purpose server-side scripting language originally designed for web development to produce dynamic web pages. For this purpose, PHP code is embedded into the HTML source document and interpreted by a web server with a PHP processor module, which generates the web page document. It has also evolved to include a command-line interface capability and can be used in standalone graphical applications.

Payment Card Industry Data Security Standard The Payment Card Industry Data Security Standard (PCI DSS) is an information security standard for organizations that handle cardholder information for the major debit, credit, prepaid, e-purse, ATM, and POS cards.

Perl Perl is a high-level, general-purpose, interpreted, dynamic programming language. It provides powerful text processing facilities without the arbitrary data length limits of many contemporary Unix tools, facilitating easy manipulation of text files. In addition to CGI, Perl is used for graphics programming, system administration, network programming, finance, bioinformatics, and other applications.

Personal Identification Number A personal identification number (PIN) is a secret numeric password shared between a user and a system that can be used to authenticate the user to the system.

Plain Old Java Object The term "POJO" is mainly used to denote a Java object which does not follow any of the major Java object models, conventions, or frameworks.

Point of Sale A point of sale (POS), also sometimes referred to as a point of purchase (POP), or checkout is the location where a transaction occurs. A "checkout" refers to a POS terminal or more generally to the hardware and software used for checkouts, the equivalent of an electronic cash register. A POS terminal manages the selling process by a salesperson accessible interface. The same system allows the creation and printing of the receipt.

Polizia Postale e delle Comunicazioni Polizia Postale e delle Comunicazioni is an Italian law enforcement agency that has a specific department devoted to protection from cyber attacks.

Presidential Decision Directive Presidential Directives, better known as Presidential Decision Directives or PDDs, are a form of executive order issued by the President of the United States with the advice and consent of the National Security Council.

Pretty Good Privacy Pretty Good Privacy (PGP) is a data encryption and decryption computer program that provides cryptographic privacy and authentication for data communication. PGP is often used for signing, encrypting, and decrypting texts, e-mails, files, directories, and whole disk partitions to increase the security of e-mail communications.

Privacy Information privacy, or data privacy, is the relationship between collection and dissemination of data, technology, the public expectation of privacy, and the legal and political issues surrounding them.

Pseudo-random Number Generator A pseudo-random number generator (PRNG), also known as a deterministic random bit generator (DRBG), is an algorithm for generating a sequence of numbers that approximates the properties of random numbers.

Publish/Subscribe Publish/subscribe (or pub/sub) is a messaging pattern where senders (publishers) of messages do not program the messages to be sent directly to specific receivers (subscribers). Rather, published messages are characterized into classes, without knowledge of what, if any, subscribers there may be. Subscribers express interest in one or more classes and only receive messages that are of interest, without knowledge of what, if any, publishers there are. This decoupling of publishers and subscribers can allow for greater scalability and a more dynamic network topology.

Random Access Memory Random access memory (RAM) is a form of computer data storage. RAM is often associated with volatile types of memory (such as DRAM memory modules), where its stored information is lost if the power is removed. Many other types of non-volatile memory are RAM as well, including most types of ROM and a type of flash memory called NOR-Flash.

Reliability Reliability (systemic definition) is the ability of a person or system to perform and maintain its functions in routine circumstances, as well as in hostile or unexpected circumstances.

Remote Method Invocation The Java Remote Method Invocation Application Programming Interface (API), or Java RMI, is a Java application programming interface that performs the object-oriented equivalent of remote procedure calls (RPCs).

Request for Comments In computer network engineering, a Request for Comments (RFC) is a memorandum published by the Internet Engineering Task Force (IETF) describing methods, behaviors, research, or innovations applicable to the working of the Internet and Internet-connected systems.

Return On Investment In finance, return on investment (ROI) is the ratio of money gained or lost on an investment relative to the amount of money invested. The amount of money gained or lost may be referred to as interest, profit/loss, gain/loss, or net income/loss. The money invested may be referred to as the asset, capital, principal, or the cost basis of the investment. ROI is usually expressed as a percentage.

Rivest, Shamir, and Adleman In cryptography, RSA (which stands for Rivest, Shamir, and Adleman, who first publicly described it) is an algorithm for public-key cryptography. RSA is widely used in electronic commerce protocols, and is believed to be sufficiently secure given sufficiently long keys and the use of up-to-date implementations.

Router A router is a device that forwards data packets between telecommunications networks, creating an overlay internetwork. A router is connected to two or more data lines from different networks. When data comes in on one of the lines, the router reads the address information in the packet to determine its ultimate destination. Then, using information in its routing table or routing policy, it directs the packet to the next network on its journey or drops the packet.

SHA1 The Secure Hash Algorithm (SHA) is one of a number of cryptographic hash functions published by the National Institute of Standards and Technology as a U.S. Federal Information Processing Standard. SHA1 is a 160-bit hash function which resembles the earlier MD5 algorithm.

Secure Sockets Layer Secure Sockets Layer (SSL) is a cryptographic protocol that provides communication security over the Internet. SSL encrypts the segments of network connections above the transport layer, using asymmetric cryptography for privacy and a keyed message authentication code for message reliability.

Secure Communication When two entities are communicating and do not want a third party to listen in, they need to communicate in a way not susceptible to eavesdropping or interception. This is known as communicating in a secure manner or secure communication.

Security Information and Event Management Security information and event management (SIEM) solutions are a combination of the formerly disparate product categories of SIM (security information management) and SEM (security event management). SIEM technology provides real-time analysis of security alerts generated by network hardware and applications.

Segregation of Duties Segregation of duties (SoD) is the concept of having more than one person required to complete a task. In business the separation by sharing of more than one individual in one single task prevents fraud and error.

Service Level Agreement A service level agreement is a part of a service contract where the level of service is formally defined. In practice, the term SLA is sometimes used to refer to the contracted delivery time (of the service) or performance. As an example, Internet service providers will commonly include service level agreements within the terms of their contracts with customers to define the level(s) of service being sold in plain language terms.

Service Level Specification A service level specification (SLS) is a subset of an SLA and describes the operational characteristics of the SLA. The SLS may consist of expected throughput, drop probability, latency, constraints on the ingress and egress points at which the service is provided, indicating the "scope" of the service, traffic profiles which must be adhered to for the requested service to be provided, disposition of traffic submitted in excess of the specified profile, and marking and shaping services provided.

Shared Secret Systems Secret sharing refers to a method for distributing a secret among a group of participants, each of whom is allocated a share of the secret. The secret can be reconstructed only when a sufficient number of shares are combined together; individual shares are of no use on their own.

Short Message Service Short Message Service (SMS) is a text messaging service component of phone, web, or mobile communication systems, using standardized communications protocols that allow the exchange of short text messages between fixed line or mobile phone devices.

Simple Object Access Protocol SOAP, originally defined as Simple Object Access Protocol, is a protocol specification for exchanging structured information in the implementation of web services in computer networks. It relies on Extensible Markup Language (XML) for its message format, and usually relies on other Application Layer protocols, most notably Hypertext Transfer Protocol (HTTP) and Simple Mail Transfer Protocol (SMTP), for message negotiation and transmission.

Simple Query Language Simple (Structured) Query Language (SQL) is a programming language designed for managing data in relational database management systems. Originally based upon relational algebra and tuple relational calculus, its scope includes data insert, query, update and delete, schema creation and modification, and data access control.

Single Euro Payments Area The Single Euro Payments Area (SEPA) initiative for the European financial infrastructure involves the creation of a zone for the euro or any currency whose member state wishes to notify participation and where a difference between national and intra-European cross-border payments does not exist.

Small or Medium Enterprise Small and medium enterprises (also known as SMEs, small and medium businesses (SMBs), and variations thereof) are companies whose headcount or turnover falls below certain limits.

Spam E-mails E-mail spam, also known as junk e-mail or unsolicited bulk e-mail (UBE), is a subset of spam that involves nearly identical messages sent to numerous recipients by e-mail. Definitions of spam usually include the aspects that the e-mail is unsolicited and sent in bulk.

SpyEye SpyEye is a Trojan horse that captures keystrokes and steals log-in credentials through a method known as "form grabbing". SpyEye sends captured data to a remote attacker, may download updates, and has a rootkit component to hide its malicious activity.

Stakeholder A corporate stakeholder is a party that can affect or be affected by the actions of the business as a whole.

State Treasury The State Treasury in Polish law represents the Polish state in certain legal aspects. It can be represented by various officials or institutions depending on circumstances.

Stock Exchange A stock exchange is an entity that provides services for stock brokers and traders to trade stocks, bonds, and other securities. Stock exchanges also provide facilities for issue and redemption of securities and other financial instruments, and capital events including the payment of income and dividends. Securities traded on a stock exchange include shares issued by companies, unit trusts, derivatives, pooled investment products, and bonds.

Stream Processing Stream processing (SP) deals with the task of processing multiple streams of event data with the goal of identifying the meaningful events within those streams, employing techniques such as detection of complex patterns of many events, event correlation and abstraction, event hierarchies, and relationships between events such as causality, membership, and timing, and event-driven processes.

Total Cost of Ownership Total cost of ownership (TCO) is a financial estimate whose purpose is to help consumers and enterprise managers determine direct and indirect costs of a product or system. It is a management accounting concept that can be used in full cost accounting or even ecological economics where it includes social costs.

Transmission Control Protocol The Transmission Control Protocol (TCP) is one of the core protocols of the Internet Protocol Suite. TCP provides reliable, ordered delivery of a stream of bytes from a program on one computer to another program on another computer. TCP is the protocol that major Internet applications such as the World Wide Web, e-mail, remote administration, and file transfer rely on.

Transport Layer Security Transport Layer Security (TLS) and its predecessor, Secure Sockets Layer (SSL), are cryptographic protocols that provide communication security over the Internet. TLS and SSL encrypt the segments of network connections above the Transport Layer, using asymmetric cryptography for privacy and a keyed message authentication code for message reliability.

Trivial File Transfer Protocol Trivial File Transfer Protocol (TFTP) is a file transfer protocol known for its simplicity. It is generally used for automated transfer of configuration or boot files between machines in a local environment. Compared to FTP, TFTP is extremely limited, providing no authentication, and is rarely used interactively by a user.

Trojan Horse A Trojan horse (sometimes called a Trojan) is a special computer program that pretends to do a certain thing, but in reality does something else, such as allow a stranger to access the computer and change it and read its information. In some cases the user notices; in other cases he does not. Spyware programs are current examples of programs that work in this way.

Unified Modeling Language Unified Modeling Language (UML) is a standardized general-purpose modeling language in the field of object-oriented software engineering. UML includes a set of graphic notation techniques to create visual models of object-oriented software-intensive systems.

Uniform Resource Locator A Uniform Resource Locator or Universal Resource Locator (URL) is a character string that specifies where a known resource is available on the Internet and the mechanism for retrieving it.

User Datagram Protocol User Datagram Protocol (UDP) is a communications protocol that offers a limited amount of service when messages are exchanged between computers in a network that uses the Internet Protocol (IP). Like the Transmission Control Protocol, UDP uses the Internet Protocol to actually send a data unit (called a datagram) from one computer to another.

Virtual Machine A virtual machine (VM) is a software implementation of a machine (i.e., a computer) that executes programs like a physical machine. An essential characteristic of a virtual machine is that the software running inside it is limited to the resources and abstractions provided by the virtual machine; it cannot break out of its virtual world.

Vulnerability In computer security, a vulnerability is a weakness which allows an attacker to reduce a system's information assurance.

Web Service Level Agreement A web service level agreement (WSLA) is a standard for service level agreement compliance monitoring of web services. It allows authors to specify the performance metrics associated with a web service application, desired performance targets, and actions that should be performed when performance is not met.

Wide Area Network A wide area network (WAN) is a telecommunication network that covers a broad area (i.e., any network that links across metropolitan, regional, or national boundaries). Business and government entities utilize WANs to relay data among employees, clients, buyers, and suppliers from various geographical locations. In essence this mode of telecommunication allows a business to effectively carry out its daily function regardless of location.

Worm A computer worm is a self-replicating malware computer program which uses a computer network to send copies of itself to other nodes (computers on the network), and it may do so without any user intervention. This happens due to security shortcomings on the target computer.

X.25 X.25 is an ITU-T standard protocol suite for packet switched wide area network (WAN) communication. The X.25 protocol suite was popular during the 1980s with telecommunications companies and in financial transaction systems such as automated teller machines. X.25 was originally defined by the International Telegraph and Telephone Consultative Committee (CCITT, now ITU-T) in a series of drafts and finalized in a publication known as The Orange Book in 1976.

Index